THE SHORT SEASON

THE
SHORT SEASON

A Boston Celtics Diary
1977-1978

John Powers

HARPER & ROW, PUBLISHERS
New York, Hagerstown,
San Francisco, London

1817

For Elaine and Jonathan,
who survived a long season gracefully

Photograph of Boston Garden, Courtesy of the Boston Celtics.
All others by Dick Raphael.

Portions of this work originally appeared in somewhat different form in the Boston *Globe*.

FIRST EDITION

Designed by Eve Kirch

Library of Congress Cataloging in Publication Data

Powers, John, 1948–
   The short season.
   1. Boston Celtics (Basketball team)—History.
I. Title.
GV885.52.B67P68 1979   796.32′364′0974461   78-2158
ISBN 0-06-013451-8

79 80 81 82 83 10 9 8 7 6 5 4 3 2 1

Contents

ACKNOWLEDGMENTS

To the Celtics players and front office, who were uncommonly cooperative during their roughest season.

To Mary Jane Higgins, who brought it all together with energetic enthusiasm.

To Buz Wyeth and Steve Roos at Harper & Row, whose advice and patience were most welcome.

To the people at the *Globe,* who paid for the restaurants and the air travel, and printed the grim dispatches.

To Dick Raphael, whose photographs need no comment.

And to Anne and Bill Powers, who provided sanctuary, scotch, and salvation on the Cape as this was being flung together.

I owe sincere thanks.

Celtics 1977-1978 roster

NAME	POSITION	COLLEGE	STATUS AT END OF SEASON
Zaid Abdul-Aziz	C	Dayton	Waived in February (10-day contract)
Jim ("Buzz") Ard	C	Cincinnati	Waived in November
Bob Bigelow	F	Pennsylvania	Waived in March (10-day contract)
Dave ("Disco," "Pee Wee") Bing	G	Syracuse	Retired
Tom ("Boz") Boswell	F-C	South Carolina	Played out option; signed with Denver
Don ("Duck") Chaney	F-G	Houston	Still with club
Dave Cowens	C	Florida State	Still with club
Ernie (Ernie D.) DiGregorio	G	Providence	Retired
John ("Hondo," "'Cek") Havlicek	F-G	Ohio State	Retired
Steve (Jo Bob, Bert) Kuberski	F	Bradley	Waived in December
Cedric ("Bread") Maxwell	F	Univ. of North Carolina– Charlotte	Still with club
Curtis ("Skid," C.R.) Rowe	F	UCLA	Still with club
Fred ("League") Saunders	F	Syracuse	Traded to New Orleans in February
Charlie Scott	G	North Carolina	Traded to Los Angeles in December

NAME	POSITION	COLLEGE	STATUS AT END OF SEASON
Kevin ("Bird," "Stakeman," "Snake") Stacom	G	Providence	Played out option; signed with Indiana
Kermit Washington	F	American	Traded to San Diego in July
Joseph ("Jo Jo") White	G	Kansas	Still with club
Sidney ("Wickso," "Omar") Wicks	F	UCLA	Traded to San Diego in July

Irv Levin, *Chairman of the Board*
Arnold ("Red") Auerbach, *President-General Manager*
Tom ("Hawk") Heinsohn, *Head Coach,* Dismissed in January
Tom ("Satch") Sanders, *Asst. Coach,* Replaced Heinsohn in January
K. C. Jones, *Asst. Coach*
Frank Challant, *Trainer*

"Experience don't mean shit."
                                    —Red Auerbach

PROLOGUE

Crossing Causeway Street

They were not the Original Celtics, but if you were growing up Irish around Boston in 1963, they were original enough. They wore green jerseys—didn't they?—and warmup jackets with shamrocks on them, and the owner's name was Brown. The coach was Jewish, granted, but he had red hair. We were not overly concerned with credentials.

Years later, I went out to Springfield, to the Hall of Fame, and examined an old photograph of the Original Celtics, who'd been enshrined as a team. Their names were Beckman and Holman and Dehnert and Leonard and they wore thick knee guards, and they stood shoulder to shoulder, their hair slicked back.

The sweaters were green and heavy and there were shamrocks on the front, but they were not the Celtics. The Original Celtics operated out of New York. We hated New York.

The real Celtics played down on Causeway Street, in an old brick building that doubled as a train terminal for the Boston and Maine Railroad. Driving along the expressway, you could see it looming up on the left, just where the city's North End and West End converged.

NORTH STATION, the sign read, in large blue letters. Red letters spelled out BOSTON GARDEN a few feet away. You could drive there from Dorchester, where we lived, but you rarely would. Parking was scarce and expensive and the traffic afterwards was brutal. For one 20-cent token, the MTA would drop you at the door.

"George called," my mother would say, as I returned from school, "and he's leaving two tickets for the Celtics game. If you and your brother do your homework before supper . . ."

George Sullivan was my mother's brother, and he covered the team for the afternoon *Traveler*. When I was seven he had taken me to the Fargo Building in South Boston, where the 1955 Celtics were practicing, for a formal introduction.

In the dressing room, the two finest guards ever to play on the same basketball team were lacing up sneakers, side by side. "John," my uncle said, "this is Bob Cousy and Bill Sharman." They both grinned, extending enthusiastic hands.

"Yeah, yeah," I said, unimpressed. "But where's Easy Ed Macauley?" Macauley, a fine shooting forward—Ea-a-sy Ed, the TV announcer would say, as Macauley bent his knees for a free throw—would have his jersey retired alongside Cousy's. Sharman's number would be up there, too.

In all, eleven numbers would hang from the Garden ceiling . . . so many that they decided to combine them all on one flag, divided into separate boxes, with several left empty for future use. They were running out of rafter space as it was. Each fall two new flags would go up, a green one for the Eastern Division title and a white one for the NBA championship that necessarily followed. After a while, they took down the green flags. By the time I'd left high school there were already nine white banners.

You wanted to be there for the home opener because it was a reaffirmation, a family ritual not unlike Thanksgiving dinner. "Ladeez and gentlemen, the WORLD CHAMPION BOSTON CELTICS," PA announcer Weldon Haire would boom, the voice rising, and they would come jogging out of the runway . . . Heinsohn, Russell, Sanders, Havlicek, the Jones boys, with Red Auerbach following.

The flag would go up—BOSTON CELTICS NBA WORLD CHAMPIONS—and nothing would have changed except the year.

And then the Celtics would go out and run the Pistons or the

Knicks or the Bullets into the floor, winning by 35 points, victory assured early in the second half. Auerbach, impassive, would stretch out his legs at that point and produce a fat imported cigar, lighting it ostentatiously as we all roared in approbation.

There were always tickets, George would assure us. Just let me know. Yet we went infrequently, as most Bostonians did. While the losing Bruins filled the Garden, 13,909 nearly every night, the building was rarely more than half full for the Celtics. How many times did you need to be reassured, after all?

When the alarm rang on a winter morning and I headed downstairs to begin my paper route, I would riffle through a *Globe* to check the score—Boston 143, Chicago 99, eight Celtics in double figures—and nod, satisfied, like a Brahmin millionaire glancing at the financial pages. Yes, yes, very nice indeed.

When we went to the Garden during the regular season, we took the Brahmin attitude with us. The Lakers are in town tonight, I'd muse. Better check on the investment.

So my brother, The Pork, and I would walk to the tiny subway station called Shawmut on the Harvard-Ashmont line and take the train to Washington Street, where you climbed the stairs for the elevated line and North Station . . . and 1946.

Walking along Causeway Street, you belonged to another era, one that seemed perpetually stuck at nine o'clock on some bygone Fri___ ____ _hat smelled of cigar smoke and was filled with Cad   /eed overcoats and men with flattened noses, ruined voic   ngs.

T_   all-night cafeteria, the Hayes-Bickford, on the corn   ay and Canal, filled with a rich, unrefined blend of street folk. There was a tobacco store a few hundred yards down that had cigars in tubes and fight magazines and, I liked to hope, a bookie joint in the back room. And in between, a block sprinkled with pizza places and shot-and-a-beer taverns where fuzzy TV sets were always tuned to police dramas.

As I crossed over to the Garden, with steam coming up out of the sewers, the street wet, the train wheels shrieking over my head on their way from Charlestown, I was Damon Runyon at fourteen, intrigued by the tawdriness and seduced by it. Uncle George, I thought, has the best job in the world.

The atmosphere stayed with you into the Garden, past the sidewalk newspaper vendors and the men in The Horse, drinking and arguing barside before the game. You could hear the pinball machines stuttering to your right as soon as you entered the lobby at street level, the bells keeping up a steady cacophony. There were always people playing them, kids, mostly, with no place else to go.

There were always people everywhere. On the left, the stairs to the upper level were stained with urine, and there was usually a derelict sitting on them, swilling from a bottle of Old Grand-Dad. You could smell hot dogs frying on the hole-in-the-wall grill a few feet away. Around the corner, where North Shore commuters waited on old wooden benches for their trains, you bought your tickets, looking up at the marquee overhead that told you everything Walter Brown had planned.

Bruins vs. Montreal tomorrow night. Celtics vs. Knicks Sunday afternoon. Pro wrestling. Boxing . . . Pender vs. Downes for the title. They were always fighting for the title. College hockey. The Ice Capades. You could come here every night. The Garden was yours.

The House of Magic, Brown would name it, and it was. Local columnists, thinking about dusty rafters and ancient wooden seats, would call it Grimy Garden or Ghastly Garden. King Rat lived there as chief tenant, they said. But to us, it was the sporting Louvre, a haunting smoky cockpit that said vertical the moment you walked in, balcony rising upon balcony, seats wedged in everywhere ("Only obstructed views remain," they'd say, before a big playoff game), and all of it overlooking a wooden parquet floor. Home hardwood, team publicity director Howie McHugh called it in press releases.

For two dollars you could sit in the second balcony ("nigger heaven" as white Bostonians called it, making sure no colored people could overhear) and peer down, a gallery god.

Our seats, the free ones, were on the lower level, the stadium section. You could see Auerbach talking in the huddle, circled by attentive faces. You could see the sweat pouring off Bill Russell as he came to the bench. And when the lead had reached 20 points or so, you could watch Auerbach dip into the jacket pocket—a loud plaid tonight—and extract the cigar.

You could see it on the road, too, through the eyes of Johnny

Most, the Celtics' one-man broadcast crew. "Good evening, every-one," he would say from Kiel Auditorium or Convention Hall, "this is Johnny Most, high above courtside . . . "

He had always been there, it seemed, the voice raspy and passionate, and if outsiders said he was biased, we never cared. *We* were biased. How can you listen to the guy, the New York infidel would say? What do you mean, we would reply, mystified? Johnny loves the Celts.

We would do Johnny Most imitations on street corners, our vocal cords suddenly going hoarse and urgent . . . "All right now, K. C. Jones bringin' the ball up, now quickly over to Sam, Sam back to K.C. who throws it to Havlicek in the corner . . . Jarrin' John, guarded by Meschery, looks for Russell down low, and Chamberlain is all over Russell. He's *all over* Russell, and Mendy Rudolph won't call it . . . "

We would nod, knowingly. They never *did* call it on Wilt, did they? Did he ever foul out of a game? Naww, but they'd foul Satch out, wouldn't they?

It was always Satch and Hondo and K. C. and Sam . . . it was a family, after all, with Brown as the benevolent old grandsire and Auerbach as the gruff father, and we felt we knew them all. At halftime, you could go out into the corridor at the Garden and buy the yearbook . . . a magazine, actually, stapled together and sold for 35 cents. It was crammed with box scores, gossipy notes and records and there was a full page on every Celtic, from Russell to Jack McCarthy, a chatty profile that told you what they were *really* like.

Frank Ramsey always went into the team offices as soon as the season was over, the yearbook insisted, and promptly signed a blank contract in triplicate letting Walter Brown fill in the figure. "After all," says Frank, "he knows best just how much I'm worth."

Ramsey, we were assured, would have a lifetime job within the organization, if he ever needed one. Russell, "a great fellow for entertaining acquaintants," termed his Reading home the "Russell Motel and Used Car Lot." He had invested in a Liberian rubber plantation and was thinking of retiring there.

Tom Heinsohn had developed his uncanny straight-line, no-arc shot in a CYO gym in Union City, New Jersey, where a water pipe obstructed each basket. And it *was* Satch Sanders who'd said,

"Take it easy, baby," to President Kennedy as the team was ending a White House visit. No disrespect there . . . the President was from Massachusetts. As Irish Catholics, we belonged to his family, too. No invitation needed.

Ultimately, The Pork and I decided Satch was our favorite Celtic. He was tall, skinny, and cool, sitting there swathed in towels, waiting for the call from Auerbach. "What's Satch like?" we asked George at a family gathering one Christmas. "The greatest," he said, definitively. We grinned, our instincts confirmed. "How about Sam?" "The greatest," George said, again. It might have sounded strange, he admitted, but they were all that way . . . just as we had suspected.

And when the season really started at the end of March, they would come through for you, even if you hadn't been attending regularly. The playoff semifinals might go seven games with Cincinnati or Philadelphia, but the Celtics were terrifying when the money was on the line. Ramsey always had the playoff shares figured down to the penny, they said, and he'd give his teammates a lecture on fiscal responsibility. You're playin' with *my* money now.

The Celtics never lost a seventh game. And April always brought the finals . . . and the Lakers. The Pork and I would stay up late to watch the Coast games from the Sports Arena. Drowsiness usually took us in the fourth quarter, but the game was generally in hand by then. Boston always won two of the three games in Los Angeles.

And when the series would come back to Causeway Street, we could sit in the second row courtside. John Tierney, a Boston city councillor, lived around the corner. He got free tickets, too, which he gave to his sons. We all went together and celebrated the rites of Hibernian spring . . . indoors. We had never seen the Celtics fail. Ergo, they could not fail.

Not until 1965 was there even a question. This time. Philadelphia, behind Chamberlain and Hal Greer, forced a seventh game at the Garden in the semifinals. A Chamberlain basket had cut Boston's lead to 110–109 with four seconds to play, with Bill Russell set to inbound the ball. But his pass struck a support wire connected to the basket . . . Philadelphia ball.

"Somebody bail me out," Russell said, as the Celtics huddled to discuss defense. "I blew it."

So John Havlicek had gone out to guard Chet Walker, as Greer took the ball at the baseline. And two seconds later, Johnny Most was screaming ... AND HAVLICEK STEALS IT. JOHNNY HAVLICEK STOLE THE BALL. IT'S ALL OVER. JOHNNY HAVLICEK ...

It became a byword, anywhere you went in Boston ... anywhere in the league. Havlicek, his back to Greer, had counted to five, guessed where the ball would go, and deflected it to Sam Jones, who dribbled out the clock. The Lakers would be taken down in five games in the final, and another flag, the seventh in a row, was raised in the fall.

Yet the ceremony had a twilight quality to it. Walter Brown, who'd conceived the team, named it, and believed in it when few others did, was dead. Tom Heinsohn was retiring. And so, too, was Auerbach.

He *was* the Celtics now that Brown was gone. He negotiated the lease, made the radio and TV arrangements, scouted and drafted the talent, and haggled over the contracts himself. Coaching, after all that, had begun to wear heavily upon him. How many people could you be at the same time?

He would finish out the 1965–66 season on the bench, Auerbach said, and then move on to the front office. I felt oddly hollow when I heard that, even though the man had been an intimidating figure to me up close.

At the All-Star game the year before, I'd waited outside the Garden dressing rooms, pen and paper ready. Chamberlain looked monstrous coming through the door, and Russell was supposed to scowl at autograph hunters, but I'd approached both men confidently.

I'd stepped back when Auerbach emerged, even though I'd admired him. This was *his* building, after all, and I felt barely tolerated, although Auerbach usually scrawled his name willingly, his lips pursed around the cigar. Now, the thought of him leaving made me uneasy.

What's going to happen to the tradition? I wondered. Cousy, Sharman, Ramsey, Heinsohn ... Easy Ed ... they'd all come and gone but the championships had continued because Auerbach had been the thread that connected them.

He'd been at the Fargo Building a decade ago when I was barely out of short pants. Now, I was about to graduate from high school . . . and he was still here, the brow furrowed with wrinkles, the hair turning white, but the fire still burning.

He was a civic asset, like the Old North Church, Durgin-Park Restaurant, and Arthur Fiedler . . . which was amusing, because he'd come from Brooklyn.

He was Arnold Auerbach, one of four children of a Russian Jew who'd left Minsk around the turn of the century for a three-decker on Lynch Street next to the elevated tracks. He was a high school phys ed teacher who talked his way into a head coaching job with the professional Washington Capitols at age twenty-nine and brashly won forty-nine games his first year.

And by 1950, he was in Boston with a mandate to rebuild the Celtics, who'd cost Brown half a million dollars in four years and had fallen into the Eastern Division cellar.

Auerbach was arrogant, they'd tell you. He demanded total faith in his concepts and methods, even though it was *your* money. But he had a purist's eye for talent, no matter how deeply hidden or unrefined, and he had a love and a gift for teaching fundamentals.

Auerbach could annoy you with his gamesmanship, his referee-baiting, and his absolutism. But his teams were intelligent, disciplined, and beautifully conditioned. And they won. In a hockey town where people thought of Holy Cross if they thought of basketball at all, Walter Brown could not afford a loser.

So Auerbach cleaned house in a whirlwind summer of horse-trading . . . and won immediately. And while he won, he built—with Cousy, a marvelous ballhandler and playmaker, with Sharman, a complementary shooting guard, and Macauley up front.

There were playoffs in Boston the next six years, but nothing more than that. New York or Syracuse always stood in the way, and besides, the Lakers, with George Mikan, were winning everything anyway.

Auerbach needed a big man, and he saw one in Russell, the 6–9 center for the University of San Francisco's national champions. He shot poorly—wasn't that why they doubted he could ever dominate at the professional level?—but Auerbach was intrigued with Russell's rebounding and the way he blocked shots, keeping the ball in play and deflecting it to a teammate.

Auerbach would have to give up Macauley and Cliff Hagan to St. Louis for the draft choice that would produce Russell, but it was worth it. Auerbach could use his territorial choice to get Tommy Heinsohn, Holy Cross's prolific shooting forward, and replace Macauley that way.

You built a basketball team the same way you cast for a Broadway show, Auerbach felt, looking for role players. He had his playmaking guard and his shooting guard in Cousy and Sharman. He had a shooting forward in Heinsohn (who would be the league's Rookie of the Year) and a rebounding forward in "Jungle" Jim Loscutoff. Frank Ramsey, a dependable shooter, would be his "sixth man," coming off the bench to provide an offensive spark.

And now, in Russell, Auerbach had his missing link. The Celtics won their first championship in April 1957, the following spring, defeating St. Louis in double overtime in a classic seventh game at the Garden. The dynasty had begun, and it would bear Auerbach's imprint.

He hammered into his players everything he believed about basketball. You were a professional, and you made your living at the game. So you were expected to come to training camp in shape, ready to run.

If you were overweight, Auerbach would mutter, "It's *your* fault," If you pulled a muscle, "It's *your* fault." If you threw up, "It's *your* fault."

So the Celtics invariably began each season in peak condition, winning the early games as much on stamina as superior skills. There was a psychological advantage to that. If you were Syracuse or Philadelphia, watching Boston win their first fourteen games (which they did in 1957–58), you lowered your sights early.

By February, the divisional title (and a playoff bye) virtually assured, Auerbach could shift into a lower gear, resting his veterans and developing depth, and cruise into the post season. And when it came time to play the Nats or the Warriors for money, here was Boston, drumming their collective fingers, healthy and hungry.

Auerbach trusted his instincts, above all. Statistics meant little; losing teams were loaded with 20-point averages. Could the man play defense, he wanted to know? When did he get his rebounds? Did it matter to him if he started? Because he probably wouldn't start in Boston . . . or not for a while, anyway.

So Auerbach would rummage around in the draft pile until he found what he wanted, frequently coming up with people nobody had ever heard about. Sam Jones, who would play on ten championship teams, came out of tiny North Carolina College. K. C. Jones and John Havlicek had both been overshadowed players on NCAA championship teams.

Auerbach wanted men who'd do the important, if unpleasant, little things that won games, molding them around his Cousys and Russells and Heinsohns. He wanted a defensive forward who could shut down an Elgin Baylor or a Bob Pettit. He wanted a tough defensive guard. He wanted a rebounding forward who wouldn't mind getting his nose bloodied. And he wanted a shooter, a man good enough to be a starter, who wouldn't bitch about coming off the bench and playing in spurts. The sixth man.

Yet Auerbach's genius was not so much in the assemblage of the talent as in the manipulation of it. He was a motivational master, with a dozen different approaches, tailored to the man. You did not yell at Russell, a proud, aloof black man who demanded to be dealt with as an equal. Tom Sanders and K. C. Jones were thoughtful and quiet. They did not respond well to scolding.

But Auerbach would holler at Heinsohn and Loscutoff, because they were brash, thick-skinned men who needed to have fires ignited beneath them. If you were furious with the team for a night's sloppy play (especially after a victory . . . Auerbach's best tirades came after victories), you could land on Heinsohn as Everyman. He would growl, but understood group dynamics, too. Auerbach would make him the coach one day.

It *was* a continuing exercise in group dynamics, when you looked at it, complicated by race. Heinsohn, Havlicek, and Ramsey were white. Russell, Sanders, and the Joneses were black. All of them were superb front-line players, starters for any club in the league. Auerbach was Jewish and abrasive. When you went in to talk contract, you talked to Auerbach, face to face. No agents were tolerated. "I'm not married to any of you guys," the man would remind you, year after year.

The Celtics seemed a model of racial harmony to outsiders, but Auerbach knew he was sitting on a volcano. If cliques were allowed to develop, if the team began to lose, it could all come apart in his face.

"Wait'll he has to put *four* colored guys on the floor for the tapoff," you would hear a man say, a decade before school busing divided Boston down the middle. After Heinsohn retired, Auerbach did so, with Havlicek the only white starter. There was no Götterdämmerung. The championship came as a matter of course, because the foundation had been based on mutual respect.

The Celtics traveled together, drank together, roomed together, white and black. They knew each other's moods and rhythms, and respected them. And Auerbach knew them all, and dealt with each man intuitively. In Russell, he found his greatest challenge.

Russell was intensely private, suspicious of amateur attempts at pop psychology, and Auerbach recognized that. His best motivational method, frequently, was to leave Russell alone. Before an important game, with the tension building in the Boston room, you would see Russell get up from his stall and head for the bathroom. Within moments, the sound of vomiting would float back, and the Celtics would grin. Russell was ready. Even Auerbach had no better emotional weapon in his armory.

During Auerbach's tenure, Boston never lost a championship when Russell was still standing at the end. In 1958, when St. Louis had beaten them in six games, Russell had sprained an ankle midway through the series. The following spring, with Russell healthy, the Celtics swept the Lakers in four games for the first of eight consecutive titles.

The last one, in 1966, went seven games, and after, the Lakers—again—had been left mumbling, Auerbach would shake hands all around and return to his Boston apartment to eat Chinese food, his great culinary passion. Russell would take over, as player-coach.

Yet the spell continued. The Celtics would win sixty games the next season and humble New York in the opening playoff series—and then the magic fled. Philadelphia, behind Chamberlain, quickly won the first three games in the next round, and finished off Boston in their own building by 24 points.

"Well," I thought, shooting baskets in somebody's backyard on Melville Avenue, "it's been nice." But I felt sick inside. Still, I'd hoped, as long as Auerbach's there, somewhere . . . he hated empty Aprils as much as I did. He didn't like the idea of Wilt wearing a goddamn championship ring, either. He'll build it back, and in a year, two at the absolute most . . .

Blind faith, it was, but the Church had told us that blind faith was the most rewarding, because it demanded the most of your intellect. I believed in the Virgin Birth, the Holy Trinity, and papal infallibility. It was easy to believe in Auerbach and the green jerseys. We waited one season, and watched the Celtics, dead and buried, trailing three games to one, rise from the grave and mystify Philadelphia in seven. They'd had to win two games on the 76ers' court; nobody had *ever* come back from a 3-1 deficit. And after Boston had beaten the Lakers again for the championship, you began to hear it.

Pride. The Celtics have pride. They come out onto the parquet floor and they look up at the rafters and see the white flags . . . ten of them now . . . and the jersey numbers, a new one retired almost every year. They look over and see Auerbach in his loud plaid jacket, sitting in his loge seat, and watch Russell, with his diabolic slouch, walk out for the tap . . . and everything becomes possible.

The Celtics finished fourth in the division in 1969. Nobody had ever finished fourth and won a championship. Yet, a month later, Boston was playing for the title against the Lakers, who'd traded for Chamberlain and put him alongside Elgin Baylor and Jerry West. Los Angeles won the first two games on the Coast, but it went seven. You always knew the finals would go seven; it seemed to be an immutable law of nature. Lakers owner Jack Kent Cooke (the archetypal dreaming, meddling owner, to hear a Bostonian tell it), convinced that there would finally be a championship to celebrate and rings to order, had stuffed thousands of balloons into nets along the Forum roof. When Boston had been beaten, it would be New Year's Eve and V-J Day all in one.

I would watch that game in the basement of my college club, sunk down into an old leather chair, and years later, I would remember how Don Nelson's shot had hit the rim and bounced crazily, straight up . . . and then fallen in. Boston 108, Los Angeles 106 . . . and I had looked at the ceiling and laughed. Son of a bitch.

Auerbach was laughing, too, I guessed. Later, they told me how he'd walked across the Forum floor, and glanced up at the roof, at the trapped balloons, Cooke's Folly, and smiled.

Don Nelson had been a Laker . . . and they'd given up on him. He had cleared waivers, was officially out of basketball when Auerbach had picked him up. Nelson would play eleven years in Boston alongside three generations of Celtics, and they would retire his number. Just Auerbach again, playing Rumpelstiltskin, spinning gold from straw.

The fairy tale ended that summer. After thirteen years, Russell found himself burned out mentally . . . how many times could you churn up your guts, after all? How many times could you summon up the awesome concentration and adrenaline it took to master Chamberlain, knowing that every spring it would be the same, the whole season coming down to one game, and, usually, one basket.

"How much pressure can a man stand?" TV commentator Don Gillis had said, as the camera focused in on Russell, down on one knee, a huge hand covering his face, just as they were whistling them back onto the court for overtime. That had been 1962, and Russell had just grabbed the rebound that had saved the game.

Now, seven championships later, Russell felt it was time. "I've had enough," he told Auerbach. It would take two years to rebuild this time, with Tom Heinsohn supervising the Reconstruction. The first season was a disaster—forty-eight losses, the most in the history of the franchise—and the championship passed to New York. But in professional sports, disaster produces a bonus. The worst teams choose first in the college draft. Auerbach, relishing a selection among the top five, took Dave Cowens, a fierce red-haired center out of Florida State.

"We got us a hoss," Auerbach would say, watching Cowens leap for a rebound at rookie camp, the eyes blazing, the hair wet with perspiration. It was 1956 again, and the missing link had turned up. Cowens was no Russell . . . who the hell was? . . . but he presented exciting possibilities. He could shoot from the outside, and had the quickness to go baseline. He didn't block shots the way Russell had, but he had the mobility to stalk you anywhere, bumping and grinding, the arms in your face.

And Cowens would run for 48 minutes, the legs pumping hard, sweat pouring, the red hair flopping. Like Russell, he worked on your psyche, but from the opposite perspective. You never knew when Russell would appear out of nowhere, the arm reaching up for a rebound or swatting the ball back in your face. He spooked people.

But you always knew where Cowens was, and you knew he would

be coming all night long. Watching him play, you were reminded of Butch Cassidy and Sundance, hounded by the Super Posse. "Don't they get hungry?" Butch would snarl in frustration. "Don't they get tired?"

Cowens never did, even though his face was usually distorted with anxiety and exhaustion from the second quarter onward. He won games for you in the fourth quarter, when an Abdul-Jabbar or a Lanier began to wear down from the crazy pace.

And the pace was always crazy. The Celtics had always used the fast break under Auerbach, grabbing the rebound, firing an outlet pass downcourt, bearing in on you, two-on-one for easy layups. You would work 24 seconds for your basket, setting picks, working for the good shot, and Boston would wipe it out in five seconds, the Garden shaking from the applause.

Now, with Heinsohn pacing the sidelines, the fast break had become a mania. The faces had changed . . . Jo Jo White was bringing the ball up now, looking for Nelson or Havlicek on the wing . . . but the system was the same, based around a center in constant motion.

Auerbach had never bothered with a thick playbook, stuffed with complicated set patterns. The more complex the play, the more possibilities for a breakdown. The Celtics had used seven, with an option or two on each. The execution was everything. Auerbach believed passionately in that. If you taught a man how to throw a pass, and you told a man where to be, and somebody set the pick, you could beat somebody with the same simple play all night long.

Heinsohn had kept the same philosophy—all of Auerbach's disciples did, when you looked at it. Why tamper with something that put rings on your fingers and money in your pocket, year after year? When Nelson took the coaching job at Milwaukee, the Bucks began looking like Celtics West immediately.

So as Reconstruction progressed, you saw the role players— Sanders as the defensive forward, Chaney the defensive guard, Paul Silas coming over from Phoenix as the power forward, Havlicek as the flexible swingman. The defense was an upbeat press, because that produced opponent errors that fueled your fast break. "Band on the Run," Boston writer Mike Lupica dubbed them, and like the old Celtic teams, they had multiple symbols.

White was icy poise, the face blank, the emotions under control.

Havlicek was durability in motion, the feet moving, the eyes always following the ball.

Silas was the unselfish pragmatism. The team needs the inside stuff, the rebounding and the body-to-body defense. Therefore . . .

And Cowens was the fire, self-stoked, going out to battle giants every night. The league was still in love with seven-footers, most teams building around a Chamberlain or an Abdul-Jabbar, and Cowens saw one virtually every time he went out for the tap. If David can neutralize his man, the reasoning went, we can win by dominating everywhere else.

It bore fruit, finally, in 1974, with Boston going out to Milwaukee and ripping away a seventh game from the Bucks . . . or more specifically, Abdul-Jabbar . . . and bringing back another white flag. PASS THE WORD, the bumper stickers crowed, THE CELTS ARE BACK.

There would be another championship in 1976, with the Celtics winning a bizarre triple overtime game at the Garden (the greatest ever played, some people said) and ending it at Phoenix two days later. Yet there had been a bittersweet flavor to the celebration. Nelson was retiring. Silas was unhappy with his contract. Havlicek was thirty-six years old, and had played hurt in the playoffs. And Cowens was wearing down from overwork. In Boston the center always paid the price.

They had stolen this one, Havlicek would admit. Everything had fallen the way the Celtics wanted it to. They had preferred to avoid Philadelphia, Washington, and defending champion Golden State . . . and they did. Buffalo surprised Philadelphia, Cleveland defeated Washington, and Phoenix banished Golden State in seven games. And the Celtics conquered them all in six games, each time concluding the series on the road.

I saw that championship in bits and pieces, catching televised glimpses in bars and motel rooms. After two years in the navy and one with the Harvard athletic department, I had gone to the Boston *Globe* writing about hockey, which had become my passion. They did not play basketball at Harvard . . . not in any valid sense. I had spent my college nights at Watson Rink, howling at Boston University forwards and Boston College goalies. When they hired me at the newspaper, it was with hockey in mind. They were going to need a Bruins writer in a year or two for the afternoon edition.

Instead, the opening developed elsewhere. Peter Gammons was leaving the baseball beat for *Sports Illustrated*. Bob Ryan, who had covered the Celtics for the entire Heinsohn era, would shift to the Red Sox.

Returning from the Montreal Olympics, I went in to see Dave Smith, the sports editor.

"What do you have in mind for me now?" I asked. He'd shrugged . . . he was open to suggestions. "How about the Celtics?" I wondered. Smith's eyes showed surprise. "Didn't know you were interested."

I didn't, either. I had seen more than a hundred hockey games the previous winter, everything from South Boston-Charlestown school-boy shootouts to the Bruins and Montreal. I played three times a week with various rink rats, rising at 5:00 A.M. to lace on battered skates. Most of the NBA teams looked the same to me, and when I wanted to watch a game, I tuned in for the final five minutes. Wasn't that when everything happened, anyway?

But the Celtics . . . that would be like covering the Symphony. I was fascinated by the personalities and the tradition, knowing that I could walk across Causeway Street again, just as I had in 1964, and find everything the same. Auerbach would still be there, wreathed in cigar smoke. Heinsohn still raged and paced, larger than life. Havlicek, Cowens, White . . . all of them were coming back.

Following Ryan was the only thing that bothered me. I had trouble telling a pick-and-roll from a back-door play, but Ryan had been the guardian of the game's purity, keeper of the Celtic virtues. Sloppy play and careless officiating infuriated him.

He had seen the game played well here by unselfish, intelligent men, and he came to accept nothing less. His writing was opinionated, direct and emotional; he was a favorite topic on Boston sports talk shows. "Did you hear what Ryan said about Heinsohn?" a caller would begin, and it would touch off a barrage of responses, split down the middle.

Ryan and Heinsohn had been at odds all through the champion-ship season, two emotional, outspoken men who, oddly, wanted the same thing. Like Johnny Most, they loved the Celts. The thought of criticizing Auerbach in print terrified me, but Ryan would call him a liar in a column defending Silas and his contract dispute. Auerbach said he'd punch Ryan if he saw him, but Ryan had turned up at training camp the next day, unbowed. He always showed up, defending what he'd written. I had my say, he felt. Now, here's your chance.

"Did you go to Boston College?" Auerbach wanted to know, as soon as we were introduced. Ryan had been Class of '68.

"No," I said, vastly relieved. "Harvard."

Auerbach looked at me, scowling. "That's worse."

Jesus, I thought. Second day on the beat and the relationship is shot to hell already. For months I approached him only when I had to, to check a story, and even then, asked only what I needed to. I always felt I was treading on his patience. Auerbach, after all, had begun to lose hair over this ballclub when I was in the third grade.

It was a challenge getting anything out of him, although Auerbach would never lie to a newspaperman. You asked a question, you got an answer. You just had to ask the right question. That had been Macbeth's problem with the witches.

It was the aura that scared me, I decided. It was the cigar and the growl, the hunched shoulders and the wave of the hand. I'd seen them for twenty years, and I'd kept my distance. Maybe if I'd grown up in Cleveland . . .

Actually, he was Uncle Red more often than not, and I discovered that after a while. All he wanted from a writer was fairness, and I had tried to be fair.

"Does Red have a minute or two?" I'd ask Mary Faherty, his kindly secretary. She would check.

"Go right in," she'd say, and Auerbach would be sitting behind the desk, surrounded by plaques, framed pictures, letter openers, cigar boxes, and his old Washington Capitols jacket.

"Sit down," he'd say. "You make me nervous standing up. Want half a corned beef sandwich? How about some chocolate?"

He would wave the cigar, and take off on a rambling discussion about . . . anything. He was a tennis player, still, at sixty, and he'd get you on a clay court (for the slower pace) and drive you crazy with dinks and slices. Once, he'd busted a few ribs running into the net post chasing a drop shot, and would laugh about it. Some kid, he'd say, using my own stuff against me.

You could spend an hour in Auerbach's office without realizing it, as he rolled out anecdote after anecdote. Finally, you would ask the two or three questions you'd come for. That's how Auerbach's five-minute meeting with a player became two hours, when you asked the player about it. If Auerbach had spent only five minutes talking business, it was a five-minute meeting. I learned that after about eighteen months.

And you could pass an entire afternoon hanging around the Celtics offices, because everybody there was like that, from the secretaries to Howie McHugh, the PR man who'd been there with Walter Brown three decades before. I'd walk up the urine-stained steps—some things never changed around the Garden—and push open the old metal-and-glass door with the ancient green drapes. "They washed the drapes once," McHugh would tell me, but I didn't believe him. Only the painted team logo above the door handle . . . the cocky little leprechaun, leaning on a shillelagh with one hand and spinning a ball with the other . . . told you this was the headquarters of the greatest dynasty in the history of the sport. Inside, it was a social club of sorts, a friendly face inside each cubicle. "Hey, babe," vice president Jeff Cohen would call out. He issued the statements when Auerbach wasn't around.

If I had a legal point to clear up—and given the relentless informality of the NBA, there were *always* legal points—I'd drop in on Jan Volk, another vice president, and wind up kibitzing for half an hour. The NBA was the best gossip institution since the Ladies' Sodality—twenty-two teams filled with characters who loved to talk.

And Tom Heinsohn loved to talk more than anybody. They called him Hawk—I never did figure out why—and he came out of a different age. Elizabethan, possibly, with his wit and vitality bubbling up close to the surface.

You imagined Heinsohn as belonging in an old English tavern, surrounded by tankards of ale, baying hounds, great joints of beef, wenches, minstrels, and muddy boots. He was not a delicate man, except around a painting easel—and he had little use for the passive voice, the subjunctive mood, or dusty adjectives.

He was an Anglo-Saxon type in the best sense—direct, colorful, blunt—and he believed in working where there was no obstructed view. In a day when public figures were often equal parts plastic, ice, and blue smoke, Heinsohn was sweating, lusty, and alive. He was capable of Promethean rage . . . and boisterous laughter. And he had a fine sense of where he belonged in his world. The nickname suited him. Doctor Hawkenstein, you thought, as he would lurch, glaze-eyed and stiff-legged, along the sidelines, yelling at a Tommy Nunez or a Lee Jones (there were *no* competent referees, he told me once; not really). And he didn't seem to mind the image at all.

He had a memo board in his recreation room at home with one section reserved for hate mail. CRANK CORNER, the heading said, and the letters all began similarly. Heinsohn, you animal . . . Heinsohn, you jerk. A national beer company had used retired athletes for humorous television commercials, and the most popular one had featured Heinsohn being thumbed out of a bar by referee Mendy Rudolph, an old nemesis. "Siddown, Heinsohn," you'd hear, in every arena in the league. And Heinsohn would grin . . . and shrug. I am what you see, baby.

And to a writer on deadline, he was a rich lode of one-liners and analysis. The *Globe* wanted nearly 2,500 words a day on the night of a road game . . . a running story for the early edition, another for the city run, plus a fresh angle for the afternoon paper and a notebook. Heinsohn was always available, calling you in your hotel room if he had to take an early flight or do some college scouting. "Need anything?" he'd ask. He'd be glad to have a cup of coffee before he left.

You never lacked for material around the Celtics. You could come into the locker room two hours before a game and there would be somebody to talk to. All you had to do was nod to the cop at the door. He knew you . . . which I found wondrous. In 1964, they'd hustled me down the corridor. They'll all be out in a while, fellas. Wait outside.

Now, I was Damon Runyon at twenty-eight, lugging a portable Olivetti. It was a job . . . but it was a fantasy, too. For fourteen years, I had been Hondo Havlicek, the Bouncin' Buckeye, shooting 15-foot jumpers in my backyard. Now, I found, nobody on the team called him Hondo.

"They call me a lot of things," he would explain. "Cappy [because he was the captain]. 'Cek. Sidney [Wicks] has begun calling me Alexander Chekhov." Mostly, he was 'Cek, but even after I knew him, and had shared a few dozen restaurant meals on the road, I didn't think I could be that informal. Cap'n, I decided.

That was halfway between intimacy and respect, and Havlicek would grin when I addressed him so.

It was a friendly team, although I discovered later that it was not as tightly bonded as it had been in past years. Blacks and whites (there were only four in 1976—Havlicek, Cowens, Kevin Stacom, and Steve Kuberski) tended to go their separate ways off the court. It wasn't that they didn't like each other . . . most of them simply didn't know each other, and since the Celtics no longer put two men in a room on road trips, the opportunities for that were fewer. There had been a metamorphosis since 1974 . . . by the time I arrived only Havlicek, Kuberski, Cowens, and Jo Jo White still remained from that championship team. Silas, who had been deeply respected by the old veterans, would be traded the day before the season began in a deal that brought Curtis Rowe to Boston. Rowe's best friend and former UCLA teammate, Sidney Wicks, had already been bought from Portland as insurance. The team was in transition even as we flew to Indianapolis for the opener.

The Celtics would win their first two games in 1976, including one at Milwaukee, coming from far behind to salvage each in overtime. "Don't worry," Ryan would say, laughing, when I returned. "They aren't all going to be like this."

Nothing had ever been quite like this . . . after eight games, Cowens would drop by the office and tell Auerbach he was taking a leave of absence. Personal reasons.

No Celtic—no basketball player—had ever done that before. But few basketball players had ever been like Cowens. He had no nickname . . . all you had to say was David, and everybody around the team knew whom you meant. He was his own man, and he went his own way, experimenting with whatever fascinated him, from natural foods to taxicabs. Cowens seemed moody and withdrawn if you didn't know him, and most writers approached his dressing stall hesitantly. He was totally honest . . . and sometimes that could be intimidating if you were used to postgame pablum.

But Cowens loved the game . . . he would play for lunch and carfare, you guessed . . . and he wasn't playing it well now. A championship season and a summerful of travel and his basketball camps had left him drained, possibly without his realizing it. His game was based on intensity . . . wasn't that the word Heinsohn would use, over and over? . . . and if the emotions went stale, and the fire left the eyes, you weren't watching Dave Cowens. He knew that.

So he headed south in his truck, and you heard periodic reports. Cowens was seen playing a pickup game with the Florida State junior varsity. Cowens was seen back home in Newport, Kentucky. Cowens was heading for California. He became the sporting Howard Hughes, although he couldn't quite figure out why anybody cared. He was only a basketball player.

You heard the rumors, too, each one crazier. Cowens had a terminal disease and was going home to die. Cowens and Silas were best friends, and the trade has broken his heart. Cowens hates Heinsohn. Always has. And then, on an afternoon in January, Cowens was back, just as abruptly as he'd gone. Sometimes, it was simply easier to play.

The celebration was brief. Less than a minute into that night's game with Indiana at the Garden, Charlie Scott drove the baseline and soared up along the backboard . . . he was always soaring, it was a combination of his hyperactive nature and springy legs. Somebody cut the legs out from under him, and Scott fell heavily, fracturing a forearm. Heinsohn went into shock. Scott would be gone until April. So the load fell to Havlicek and White and Cowens and Wicks, and they carried Boston to forty-four victories and second place behind Philadelphia in the division.

The opening playoff series against San Antonio was over quickly . . . a thumping victory on Causeway Street, and a turbulent one at the HemisFair. THAT OLD CELTIC MAGIC, read the cover of *Sports Illustrated,* showing a rampaging Wicks driving to the hoop.

We had taken a plane directly to Philadelphia and the second round, and White had won the first game with a splay-legged jump shot from the corner, the ball dropping just as the buzzer was sounding. This is how it used to be, I thought. Always. But the 76ers won three of the next four games, and the Celtics had to scramble wildly back on Causeway Street to stay alive. The seventh game would be at the Spectrum . . . but Boston had never lost a seventh game to any Philadelphia team. Pride, tradition, the green jerseys . . . all of them would come into play, I wrote. Philadelphia coach Gene Shue was annoyed. "There *is* no mystique," he said, before the squad left Boston for home.

The finale was close for three quarters, but the Celtics had run their veterans into the ground in Game 6. The 76ers seized the lead with one offensive burst, and the last 12 minutes were a study in exhaustion.

"AND BOSTON CALLS T-I-I-I-ME..." PA announcer Dave Zinkoff would snarl, again and again, as Heinsohn brought his people to the sidelines, hoping for a miracle.

There was none, and the last few seconds ran out amid a frantic waterfall of noise from 18,000 people, as 76er guard Lloyd Free dribbled the ball lazily in the backcourt, doing a disco shimmy, an index finger raised high. Boston had danced here after Game 1, he said, after White's shot had fallen. I'm gonna dance.

It was 83–77 today, and when it ended, a teen-ager in a white 76ers T-shirt ran onto the court and began to prance in front of Most, blowing smoke from a huge cigar. "Hey, Johnny," he yelled, his voice a mocking rasp. "Hey, Johnny. How do you like it, Johnny? Huh? How do you like it?"

I took a deep breath, gathered up the running statistics, and looked up at the scoreboard to make sure. Where the hell, I thought, is Easy Ed?

Weeks later, I checked my clip folder out of the *Globe* library, and thumbed through a season's worth of stories ... it was an old habit. Nothing ever seemed real to me until I'd written about it. Later, if I wanted to recapture a mood, I could dig up the clip and the taste and fragrance of the moment would return, as if I'd added water to freeze-dried coffee.

"Damn," I thought now. "You should have kept a diary of *this* year. All the craziness, the last-minute trades, Cowens's sabbatical, losing to Philly."

Next season, I decided. Everything from the salt air at training camp to the raising of the flag. You always assumed there would be a flag. Good percentages there. So when the Celtics win it, just scrawl the name at the top and mail it off.

I never thought about a losing season. So I found a publisher and took a fistful of reporter's notebooks with me to training camp.

SEPTEMBER

Sea Gulls and Missing Persons

Wednesday the 21st
BUZZARDS BAY, MASS.

If you want to time it, with one eye cocked for the State Police in the Plymouth underbrush, the drive consumes one hour from Boston Garden, from expressway on-ramp to Sagamore Bridge. Turning off Route 3 at the rotary, you sweep along an undulating roller coaster of a stretch along the Cape Cod Canal, past the bait shops and the clam shacks to the Massachusetts Maritime Academy, where the Celtics set up their odd blend of boot camp and seashore hideaway.

They try to make the atmosphere as pleasant as possible, given the Camp LeJeune restrictions they lay on you for ten days, and Buzzards Bay is nice for that. The locals will tell you that late September and October is the best time here, when the New York license plates have disappeared and the winter rains haven't arrived. Light traffic, lazy breakfasts in town, late nights at the Dolphin Inn over beer, pizza and cigars.

There wasn't much in the area but the Dolphin Inn, actually. Buzzards Bay shut down at suppertime during the off-season, and you had to drive to New Bedford, half an hour west, if you wanted any evening amusement.

Some of the black players would drive there for a drink and a disco. Otherwise, you could walk across the academy athletic fields to the Dolphin, a pleasant Cape-style restaurant that featured the typical fish-and-scallops fare.

At night, the bartender would prepare mini-pizzas on English muffins and serve them up with beer, and you could sit around a table until midnight, swapping basketball gossip.

Last year, when I was staying at the camp overnight, I'd gone over and found Cowens hanging out with a few trainers he knew. He was drinking glasses of beer and puffing on a cigar, and laughing heartily. I quickly discarded every preconception I'd formed about his ascetic discipline. A Spartan could be a Bacchanalian on the side, I guessed, and I was happy to find that Cowens was.

I stayed at the academy one night, then decided to commute from Boston. This year, I'll be living at my family's summer home in Harwichport, near the elbow of Cape Cod, with my wife and infant son. The academy reminds me too much of the navy, with its stark (but functional) design and reveille calls. The maritime cadet had his rituals, as I had had for two years on an aircraft carrier. And so did the Celtics.

Like the cadets, they slept in the same cinder-block barracks in strictly functional rooms—a bed, a dresser, a closet, a desk, a sink. They ate in the same mess hall . . . a lighter breakfast, maybe, since you didn't want to leave it on the floor two hours later. And they wore uniforms, too, green shorts with a reversible jersey, in case Tom Heinsohn decided to play mix 'n match, concocting combinations of veterans and rookies.

You could walk to the gym from the mess hall . . . it was pleasant, several hundred yards with the breeze coming off the canal and the gulls shrieking overhead. But most of the players would wait until 9:45 or so, then tear down the road in their cars, cramming into the training room all at once and hollering for Frankie Challant and his rolls of tape.

Heinsohn might have determined your fate, ultimately, but it was Challant you depended on for day-to-day survival. You *had* to be taped, from foot to Achilles . . . sprain a bare ankle and it brought a fine. But if you were late for practice, that was a fine, too. So the veterans would straddle the table and glance at the clock . . . 9:52

now, with four players still waiting . . . and Challant's hands would fly. Skin lube, lace and heel pads, underwrap, adhesive tape, with Challant ripping off swatches and molding them on. "Eighteen seconds if you put the clock on me," he would say, proudly.

Officially, he was the trainer, but on the road, he was a blend of traveling secretary and tour guide. Frankie had the tickets, stuffed into envelopes with the itinerary. Frankie had the per diem money—$25 a day, league rule. Frankie made sure the luggage made it from bus to plane to bus, and carried extra jerseys with him if you'd happened to leave yours in Kansas City.

And if a foot of snow had fallen overnight, and O'Hare Airport was closing down, Challant had to figure out a way to get you to New York. Five minutes ago. "Frank-ayy," Heinsohn would bellow. "Where's the bus? Where's Boswell? Didn't you wake him up? How many first-class seats on this plane?"

Here, at Buzzards Bay, Challant is always on call, as hamstrings give way and knees swell up with fluid. Opening day was never a problem . . . it was on the weekend, when players had pounded back and forth for several days on an unyielding Tartan floor, that they started coming up lame. Yet you wanted to play, especially if you were a rookie or a free agent, fighting veterans for a job. If Heinsohn never saw you, you might as well not be here.

So Challant would go to work with ultrasound treatments, deep-heat salves, and exotic taping methods, and then he would stand against the wall upstairs, waiting for bodies to come apart.

"Frank-ayy," Heinsohn would yell, every ten minutes or so, and Challant would run out to examine a finger or a foot, then come back to describe it clinically for me.

"Hyperextension of the medial ligament," he would say, drawing a diagram on a scrap of paper. "Yeah," I would nod. "Twisted knee." "Christ, J. P.," he would say. "Why can't you use the right terminology?"

I would shrug. "Because the guy in Southie or Dorchester doesn't know a ligament from a bicep," I'd say. "And he doesn't care. If White has a screwed-up knee and he can't play, that's all he wants to know."

Challant would sigh. He had studied all this stuff, and could tell you why an ankle would sprain or a knee would blow up, but most of the players didn't give a damn. They wanted quick tape, meal money, and an aisle seat. And maybe, if a championship was won, they'd cut Challant in on a share.

It wasn't automatic. So blown playoffs meant a summer of working another job for Challant, since a trainer's salary averaged maybe half of the minimum $30,000 player's wage. Many of them worked without contract (as Challant did), serving at the pleasure of the owner or the coach. It was easy to overlook their contributions . . . until you got here, and it was Frankie who taped you twice a day. You saw him in the morning, and after lunch (usually cold cuts or salad, because you had to run again), you saw him again. At night, there was a heavy dinner, prime rib, maybe, and a two-hour skull session, Heinsohn lecturing with the chalk . . . every day until the end of the month.

The veterans hate it, and try to avoid as much as they can of it. So today's story—the annual story—is not so much who is here as who isn't. Eighteen names are listed in neat rows on the gym scoreboard, from Cowens to Dabney. Two are missing—John Havlicek and Sidney Wicks. No surprise, really. Havlicek underwent a grueling appendectomy during the summer, and friends who've seen him say he looks skinny and drawn. Besides, he is unsigned, which was nearly a general condition once the 1976-1977 season ended.

In all, six veterans—half the club—had completed their option year in June, and technically become free agents, and only two of them—Steve Kuberski and Tom Boswell—had come to terms much before camp began.

The others, all represented by New York attorney Larry Fleisher, were playing the annual "See You in September" waltz, with Auerbach a not unwilling partner. In the old days, before heavy salaries and free agency, contract signings were casual things, frequently done during an informal chat in Auerbach's office, which was cluttered with memorabilia and bric-a-brac.

Satch Sanders, who'd just negotiated a contract as assistant coach a few weeks earlier, had come armed with a gift cigar and a small sign during his playing days. NO, NOT ENOUGH, it read on one side, and O.K., I'LL TAKE IT on the other. Sanders would recall how Auerbach always changed the subject . . . to the newly arrived championship watches, or his collection of letter openers, or a unique paperweight . . . whenever the conversation seemed headed toward money. Sanders played for thirteen years on eight championship clubs as perhaps the game's best defensive forward. He always signed, but he never got what he was worth.

The new era, with its long-term, no-cut deals and recalcitrant agents, bothered Auerbach, and he seemed to postpone negotiations past vacations, summer camps, exhibition tours, and into early autumn, much as a man would put off oral surgery. Consequently, Jim Ard, the reserve center who'd changed agents over the summer, didn't sign until yesterday. Kevin Stacom, the third guard, signed this morning before coming down.

Havlicek, a well-paid institution at thirty-seven, had no beef with anything except the idea of two-a-day drills.

He would sit offshore in a boat with his fishing gear, the feeling went, until the end of the following week, when he would report in flawless shape with a trunkful of bluefish.

Wicks was another question. The Celtics had purchased him from Portland at the beginning of the previous season, when it appeared that Paul Silas was going elsewhere. He had played well in Cowens's absence, and after Cowens returned, as sixth man, coming off the bench to anchor the "Meet the Press" kamikaze unit that Heinsohn had thrown together in desperation.

Now his contract had ended, and he was back in Los Angeles, working out at UCLA, his alma mater, while Fleisher did the talking back east.

"We had our Chinese lunch," Auerbach is saying today, "and I presented an offer. Larry's going back with it, and I'll be in contact with him. Everything was very nice, the whole process."

Later, and off the record, he is slightly more blunt. "Hey," he mutters, "how much ass can you kiss? Then the guy owns you. I'm not crazy."

Thursday the 22nd
BUZZARDS BAY, MASS.

On a loud day, you can hear the voice as you open the large glass doors downstairs . . . GO THROUGH, GO THROUGH, GO THROUGH . . . before you even climb the gym stairs.

The Hawk is back, with whistle, folding chair, and top-sergeant lungs—a svelter Hawk these days, with the hypnosis and the monster salads he's eating in place of the six meals a day he'd become used to.

Last year, in midseason, when the pressure was building and the road games came in clusters, Heinsohn had packed on so much weight that, at a distance, he appeared to be walking at a five-degree angle off-center. The exact poundage was unknown. "Just say I'm bigger than the average bear," he told a female interviewer, but the whispers had it around 270 or better.

"You know how it is on the road," he says today, with 40 pounds gone and his jersey and shorts fitting loosely. "You get up, have breakfast, get on a plane, and have another breakfast. When you check into the hotel, you have lunch, then sit down in the middle of the afternoon with a player or one of you guys and have a piece of pie and some coffee. Then, you have something before the game and maybe a steak afterwards and a few beers. And I was liking all of that."

Heinsohn knew he could not take another season like that, especially if it was anything remotely like the last one, with people coming and going like minor characters in a Russian novel.

Which is why he pushed for a two-year contract last spring, because he knew that in spite of the near miss with Philadelphia and all the All-Stars on hand, it was going to be a complicated rebuilding process.

Which is why he is sounding worried today. He knew Wicks and Havlicek were not going to be here. But Jo Jo White, last year's Atlas amid the wreckage of midseason, is still having problems with the calcium deposits on his left heel. And Dave Cowens, who had trouble with both feet and his lower back, was advised not to work out during the summer. Now, he wants permission to take certain afternoons off to work on his Nautilus exercise machines back in Boston.

So four of the six-man nucleus Heinsohn used against the 76ers will not be here full time . . . but there is still a mob of veterans, rookies, and free agents fighting for jobs, conditioning drills to run, and a system to teach. "I'll have to be concerned with the people that are here," Heinsohn shrugs. "This is my ballclub."

At the moment, that means Cowens, Ard, and Jeff Cummings, a bright, skinny 6-11 rookie out of Tulane as centers. Freddy Saunders and J. J. Johnson, a thirty-year-old streak shooter whom the Celtics got from Houston in June, are the small forwards. Charlie Scott, White, Stacom, and a mess of rookies—Skip Brown, Bill Langloh, Tom Harris, Mike Dabney—plus free agent Jerry Fort, will be going after the three guard jobs.

But the most fascinating jockeying will be at power forward, where Heinsohn can keep four men, at most. Even without Wicks, who will be guaranteed a spot if he signs, there are four veterans in camp—Curtis Rowe, Tom Boswell, Norm Cook, Steve Kuberski—plus Cedric Maxwell, the loping, limber top draft choice out of North Carolina-Charlotte, last year's Cinderella team.

Rowe and Maxwell are certainties. Boswell, who can back up at center, seems likely to stick. Which pretty much reduces it to a duel between Kuberski, the hardnosed, affable eight-year veteran with two championship rings, and Cook, the shy, hesitant twenty-two-year-old who was last year's top draft choice. One of them will go—and both of them know it.

Tuesday the 27th
BUZZARDS BAY, MASS.

Seven days into camp, with the Grapevine humming with gossip, rumor, and conjecture, and the first camp fight already recorded. Cook, yes, and Kuberski. You could trace it back to the first workout, when Cook doubled up Kuberski with an elbow as they were coming up the floor, jostling for position, Kuberski, angered, had issued a stern warning.

The next time, when Cook caught him with another elbow, punches were exchanged and Kuberski landed a haymaker on the back of Cook's head that left his hand bruised and swollen.

The irony, of course, is that the men don't dislike each other, but neither can afford to be intimidated. Kuberski, nearly thirty, has played for four clubs, and he knows that being released here would probably end his career.

And Cook, sensitive about the rookie hazing he took last year ("Cookie the Rookie," the veterans called him), has come back determined not to play the chump for anybody. Like every non-starter here, is worried about job security.

Everyone sees the transactions column in the morning paper— Herm Gilliam, a starter, has been waived at Portland, Dave Bing, an eleven-year veteran, has retired at Washington, etc.—and they are discussed thoroughly at lunch over salads and fresh fruit.

Today, the word goes, they have decided to bring in somebody. They are bringing in Bing, probably tomorrow . . . which has set off a flurry of rapid mental mathematics among the eight guards. Nobody figures Boston will keep more than four, and that assumes that Havlicek would be used exclusively at forward. White and Scott, starters for the past two years, are immovable.

"I guess that puts the heat on The Bird's ass," Kuberski says, munching on an apple. Stacom . . . The Bird . . . sits down presently.

"They're bringing somebody in," he is told.

"Bing?" Stacom asks.

"How'd you know?" wonders Kuberski.

"I figured they would."

It did figure. At Detroit, Bing had been a consummate playmaker and scorer for nearly a decade, even after a torn retina had nearly ended his career. They'd traded him to the Bullets in 1975, where he'd played two years before coach Dick Motta finally found him expendable.

Last year, when Boston had played down there in February, Bing had watched the entire game from the bench, even after the Bullets had wrapped it up early in the fourth quarter and had sent in the reserves for garbage time. "I don't know what Dave's role is now," Motta would say frankly, after it was over.

So, at thirty-four, he had retired, and was back in Detroit when the call came from Auerbach, who'd known him as a schoolboy in Washington and had liked him enormously. Bing liked the idea of being a Celtic, and the prospect of playing third guard. He would be here tomorrow. And so, the rumors went, would Havlicek.

Just before the afternoon session, equipment manager Walter Randall beckons me over. "Don't tell anybody," he says, softly, "but they told me to get a jersey ready for Bing."

"Yeah," I say. "And the Captain."

"The Captain?" he mutters scowling. "Why don't they tell me these things?"

His calling card is sitting on top of the row of lockers in the dressing room—a large blue denim cowboy hat with the crown festooned with fishing lures.

Upstairs, the Captain is sitting in the athletic department conference room in practice gear . . . the old 17 jersey and black-green sweat pants rolled up to the knees. They will have a press conference for him in a few minutes.

"But first," John Havlicek says, "I want to read that contract, and then I want to call Larry [Fleisher] and read it to him. Just for any changes, additions, deletions. You know."

Just Havlicek being Havlicek . . . which means being precise. The way the story goes, the Funkies (Julius Erving, Larry Kenon, Pete Maravich, etc.) are playing the Straights (Rick Barry, Paul Silas, John Havlicek, etc.) for the World Stylistic Championship. And with time running out and the Funkies trailing by a basket, the Doctah comes soaring in for one of his Mama-of-Merlin, Semi-Levitation Slammers to tie it at the buzzer.

But Erving hangs on the rim, and referee Richie Powers whistles the technical and tosses the ball to Havlicek. Who walks with flat-footed, perfect strides exactly down the middle of the court to the precise center of the free-throw line, bounces the ball once and arches it through the hoop without changing expression or coming within an inch of the rim at any point in its circumference.

"His clothes are all hanging half an inch apart in the closet at home," Beth Havlicek would tell me, when I asked for expert testimony. "Everything from the medicine cabinet to the dresser drawers to the garage is kept that way."

"John was probably born like that . . . I don't think it's something you could learn. He would like the children to be that way. I guess he thinks that's his biggest failing."

"You mean they aren't like that?" I'd wondered.

"Who is?" she'd shrugged, in amused wonder.

For years, Havlicek had been waking up in Portland and Atlanta and Indianapolis and reading the same feature stories, almost paragraph for paragraph, in the *Oregonian* and the *Constitution* and the *Star*. The Bionic Celtic, they would say. Lungs so large they need two X-ray plates. Pulse so low he's barely alive. No sweat glands to speak of. The stories never mention the Closet, though— not that they could be expected to know about it. Yet that has been the real secret of the Hondovian Longevity.

The Closet and the feeding ritual and the turquoise ice basin and the symmetrical suitcase. Simplicity is the true reason, along with common sense, discipline, advance planning, and a touch of eccentricity. You've read birthday tributes about hundred-year-old Irish grandmothers who merely follow the Schedule—do the house, eat a light lunch, say the rosary, and take a belt of whiskey before retiring. John Havlicek has more than a touch of the widow O'Reilly in him.

Do everything sensibly, the idea goes. And do it the same way every day of your life. "Like people take their jackets off, and one sleeve's right but the other's inside out," Havlicek tells me, laying out his 95 theses. "Why not take it off so that both sleeves are right, so when you go to put it back on, it's already right? Or a sweater, pulling it off inside out. Does that make sense?"

"Do you do everything that way?" I would ask him. "Across the board?"

"Yup," he'd nodded proudly. "When I was a bachelor, I'd never leave a dish to the point where it was able to get crusty. I'd always rinse it, so it would come clean more easily. Or folding towels. I'm a nut on that. Or suitcases—especially the kind the Celtics have. If you pack one properly, then if it gets squashed or smashed, everything's symmetrical inside."

"Another thing that bugs me is people who use toothpaste and don't wash it out of the sink. Did I ever tell you how I tore the tips off my fingers at Ohio State? Somebody had been shaving and left the whiskers in the basin. I just got so angry I went over to the paper-towel dispenser, reached in for a handful and . . ."

The anecdotes tended to mark him as a cross between Mr.

Whipple and your seventh-grade hygiene teacher. Hell, he *was* an eccentric. Which is precisely why Havlicek has managed to last fifteen years, night after night, in the most demanding sport ever devised, and why he's signing up for another season.

He *did* arrange shampoos, deodorants, oils, creams, lotions, various utensils, and fan mail in thoughtful order above his Garden dressing stall. But he also knew the requirements, limitations, and possibilities of his own body better than any man who'd ever played the game.

He might have been the only man in the NBA who folded his socks over a coathanger. But he also knew the rules, the court, the players, and the relationships among all three better than anybody who ever lived. That's how he once figured that the lanes at the Spectrum in Philadelphia were two feet narrow—after six teams had played and hadn't noticed any difference. That's how he stole the ball twelve years ago, even with his back turned.

Havlicek knew Hal Greer had only five seconds to inbound, counted to himself . . . 1001, 1002, 1003 . . . and made the move instinctively.

But by dwelling on the idiosyncrasies, you could miss the mere breadth and depth that made them impressive. Where most of us try to clear out a corner and live in it, piling up the chaos and the clutter around us like dirty snow, Havlicek had managed to break down his daily life into a hundred separate and important segments and treat them all the same.

He figured it was easier that way. All it took was the sense to recognize what was essential and the self-control to carry it through day after day until it progressed from chore to habit to instinct.

"In college," Beth Havlicek would tell me, "for a whole year John felt that drinking Coke would cut down on his effectiveness. So he cut it out entirely. If someone told him he had diabetes and couldn't eat sweets again—ever—he'd never touch another one. He has that kind of discipline."

Which brings us to the Tale of the Turquoise Basin, perhaps the ultimate Havlicek-as-Spartan anecdote. In 1976, he tore the fascia in his right foot at the beginning of the playoffs and they said, "Ice it down and maybe . . ."

So Havlicek got himself a turquoise plastic five-and-dime variety basin, dumped in water and ice ("two Hondo handfuls," he would say) and soaked the foot roughly six times as long as they suggested. He wound up missing only three games, played 53 minutes in The Game against Phoenix and earned himself ring number eight.

That was the idea, wasn't it? You did what was necessary, no matter how unorthodox. Three years earlier, when he'd had the bad right shoulder in the New York series, Havlicek had merely invented a left-handed repertoire and helped the Celtics stay alive.

And last season, when fluid built up in the left knee—the one Havlicek used for driving, jumping, everything—and he couldn't shoot normal, squared-off jumpers, he'd devised some Nureyev shots.

"Left-hand hook, right-hand hook, jumping one-legged tip-in," he would tell you, chuckling at the craziness of it. "Off-footed, half-legged jump shot." Yet they all worked, maybe because Havlicek knew they'd have to, someday, and actually tried a few in his spare time. More than anybody since Hippocrates, he'd taken the ounce-of-prevention philosophy to its logical conclusion.

Learn how to do everything, he'd decided. Anticipate anything. Maybe he's just Paul Revere reincarnated, working a few blocks away from his old homestead in the North End. Except Havlicek would have known the British would be coming eventually—probably back-door—and sealed off every Middlesex road in 1770.

Today, he could probably recite every detail of his new contract by rote . . . but it's worth a call to Manhattan, isn't it?

They switch on the lights and grind the cameras as soon as he hangs up, Auerbach and Havlicek both saying how pleased they are at this latest one-year arrangements, and then Havlicek goes out and runs through practice . . . in shape and mentally sharp. What appendectomy?

"You should have heard the rumors," I tell him later, after he showers. "They had to go in through your back, they broke three scalpels on your musculature, they had to tear things open with their bare hands."

"Actually," Cowens says, grinning, "they had to go in through his neck."

Havlicek smirks. "Why didn't you call me? What the hell kind of reporter are you? Really, it wasn't the type of injury that's really serious. If it was a foot, an ankle, a shoulder . . . but an appendix is not something you need."

Back upstairs, they're turning the lights on again for Bing, who has been signed, inoculated and given a high number (44).

"Just like a rookie," he is told.

"Yeah," Bing chuckles, good-naturedly. "That's what I am now, I guess." Still, he is happy to be thought of here, to be given a chance to contribute. He shrugs off the problems at Washington . . . "K. C. Jones was fired, and Dick Motta was hired, and that's it in a nutshell. It's just that simple."

So the only missing link, with three more days of camp to go, is Wicks. Fleisher termed Auerbach's last offer "not acceptable," and they've come to a friendly impasse. "Status quo," Auerbach reports, as the day ends. "I just talked to Larry and he didn't mention it and I didn't mention it. We differed . . . but we differed over spare ribs and egg roll."

Thursday the 29th
BUZZARDS BAY, MASS.

Kuberski wanders into the training room in street clothes after lunch, an impressive-looking arrangement of plastic, tape, and metal extending from fingertips halfway up his right forearm. The hand he rapped against Cook's skull last week is broken, and the verdict is four to five weeks, which would wipe out at least the first six games of the regular season.

"Bert, aww, Bert, you did it," Scott laughs, sympathetically. Kuberski shakes his head in disgust.

"No wonder the sumbitch hurt," he says. "I always thought I was a little mentally tougher than to let a wrist sprain like that kick my ass.

"It got hit again yesterday in practice, by somebody's fist, you know?, and probably cracked it wide open. So I went back to the hospital myself and I said, ah, something is not real cool here. I looked at the X-rays myself, you know, held 'em up, and I could see the damn thing was snapped right off.

"I said, hey, Doc, see this? And he said, yeah, your hand's broke. And I said, yeah, bet your ass. So I'm gonna have some beers tonight . . . like about a thousand of them. Hey, keep in touch. At least they can't cut my ass."

That much is true. A busted hand in training camp is like a million-dollar wound was in Viet Nam. League rules discourage a club from waiving an injured player . . . and with all the competition at power forward, Kuberski knew just how vulnerable he was. So he'll stay on salary until the hand heals, and *que será, será*.

Meanwhile, the variables are decreasing. Heinsohn is happy with Bing, and he's certain to stay. "He sees things," Heinsohn reports, over noon coffee. "He knows things. He understands what we're talking about. Hell, he's an old pro. The question is, at thirty-three, how well can he play? Christ, we've been playing with a guy thirty-seven years old. That's no novelty to us."

When Bing and Havlicek are on the floor together, the Boston backcourt has more seniority than the Senate Armed Forces Committee. And with the two of them, plus White, Scott, and Stacom, no rookie has a chance.

Brown and Harris both seem overwhelmed by the transition from the college game, Heinsohn feels. Dabney and Langloh, whom they say is the best white player ever to come out of Washington's DeMatha High, are injured . . . but still doomed. Only Fort has much of a chance . . . an intelligent, aggressive player who broke his leg prior to last year's camp and played in the Eastern League.

Meanwhile, the phone is ringing regularly in the makeshift office off the gym corridor outside. Ed Badger is calling from Chicago. Don Nelson is interested in Ard if Boston lets him go. "A lot of stuff happenin', a lot of things in the air," Heinsohn nods. "The waiver wire, trades, people calling *us*."

And among the borderline people, a growing tension, with first cuts due tomorrow noon and the exhibition opener at Philadelphia coming Saturday night.

Ard, who shared the starting center job with Boswell when Cowens was gone last year, is more than slightly concerned. Centers have a longer lifespan than most NBA players because of their scarceness . . . but there's nothing that says Heinsohn can't use one of his power forwards in a pinch.

As Ard dressed, I approach Walter Randall. "Randy," I tell him, "Jimmy wants to know if you can get him a concrete block. To drop on his foot, you know." Ard grins. "Yuh," he says. "That's cold, man."

The cuts came early the next morning—Brown, Harris, and Cummings—and nobody is surprised. All three are packed and on their way to Logan Airport before noon. Heinsohn runs through one more session after lunch, then officially breaks camp and sends everybody back to Boston for the night. It is a lovely, liberating feeling to drive back up Route 3 as dusk is falling, with two weeks of sea gulls, canal fog, and liniment behind. But there's also a vaguely unsettled feeling, too—somewhat like taking off on the road to London in some old Joseph Fielding novel. Lot of highwaymen, wenches, and the King's soldiers out there, and no shot at turning back.

The plane for Philadelphia leaves at 9:00 A.M. Saturday.

OCTOBER

When Are the Celtics Gonna Play
Like the Celtics?

Tuesday the 4th
PORTLAND, MAINE

The Buffalo Braves (or leftovers thereof) are the *plat du jour* tonight at the Cumberland County Civic Center, but for lunch, Cowens has arranged a feed of lobster and fresh fish, gratis.

Five minutes after we arrive at the motel lobby, a Greek friend of David's, who used to run a pizza place in West Newton, shows up with two large cars and seven of us pile in—Kuberski, Ard, Havlicek, Saunders, Cowens, and Harvey Robbins from the Quincy *Patriot-Ledger*.

A table is waiting at a dockside restaurant, and steamers and beer are brought. Havlicek samples a Heineken, and sighs contentedly.

"This is good," he pronounces. "Dutch. You know, the French can't make beer worth a damn. But if you ever get to the Ivory Coast, try Flag beer. You'd like it."

Eventually, they bring out a massive four-pound lobster for him and a camera, and take Havlicek's picture with a bib around his neck, the drawn butter in front of him, and the waitresses smiling on either side.

Saunders, who grew up in Columbus, Ohio, as a minister's son, looks worried. "Lobster?" he wonders. "The Bible says no, because the lobster is the scavenger of the sea. Like a pig, you know?

Ard raises his eyebrows. "And a chicken."

"Chicken?" Saunders says, mystified. "The Book doesn't mention chicken."

"Yuh," Ard says. "All I know is they use chickens to clean up around barnyards."

Saunders, troubled now, shakes his head, and says he'll check back with the Book.

Ard and Havlicek, both passionate fishermen, begin talking about haddock and sole and cod and where you can find them off the New England coast.

"Yeah, cod," nods Kuberski, who grew up Catholic in Moline, Illinois. "On Fridays, we used to have a lot of fish sticks and baked macaroni. That was all I ever saw of a cod."

"How about carp?" Saunders asks.

Carp?

"Hey, in the ghetto, that was the only fish we knew," he says. "Have it all the time." Saunders liked to talk about Columbus, and "the Bottoms," the dead-end area he grew up around, where only street basketball and his father's large fist kept him off drugs and out of trouble.

He was easily the funkiest Celtic, loose and fancy-free, carrying a large cassette player and talking in a high-pitched patter, giggling every 40 seconds or so for one good reason or another. Experience had taught him that you didn't make advance plans.

He was playing for Southwestern Louisiana when the school was slapped with the harshest penalties ever laid on by the NCAA— including a full year without any team at all. So most of the varsity players packed their bags and left . . . and Saunders wound up at Syracuse. Phoenix drafted him, and he played there until an elbow injury made him expendable early in his second season.

He turned up as a free agent at Buzzards Bay in the fall of 1976, and merely survived every cut, playing enthusiastically, rebounding well, and hitting his ghetto special—a bizarre jumper that he would launch from the baseline, legs atwitter, the ball cocked over his right shoulder.

Heinsohn always mentioned him in his postpractice analyses last year, yet nobody underlined him as a serious candidate. "My people would say, 'Are they talking to you? what are they saying?' " Saunders would say. "I said, 'They aren't saying anything.' So no news was good news to a certain extent."

He asked no questions, climbed aboard the plane to Indianapolis for the season's opener, and woke up with a job. Some friends, watching the evening news back in Boston, called him. "They said 'Congratulations,' " Saunders said. "I said 'For what?' They said, 'Glenn McDonald got cut.' I said, 'Yeah?' And that was it. I came to the locker room, Mac wasn't there, so I knew."

He wound up starting at small forward for the second half of the season, after Scott broke his wrist and Havlicek was moved to guard, and at the end, they named him the Unsung Hero. Now, Saunders has survived again, and the only questions he had concerned crustaceans.

Wednesday the 5th

HARTFORD, CONN.

Philly Redux tonight . . . and walking down to the Hilton with the luggage, you can see the 76ers bopping along Asylum Street on their way to the Civic Center, dressed in their red warmups, with leather bags swinging on their shoulders.

Dawkins, Free, McGinnis, Collins . . . all of them strutting and joking . . . like a Center City YMCA team off to crush some crosstown turkeys. All of them except Steve Mix, who is walking in street clothes on the other side of the street, his uniform in a suitcase. I'm not with *those* suckers, his expression says.

Later, as I'm having dinner in a Civic Center restaurant, Celtics promotions director Mike Cole comes up, anxious and apologetic. "There's going to be a press conference downstairs," he says. "We've been looking all over for you."

Auerbach is already in the press room when I come down, along with a gaggle of writers from Boston, Hartford, and New Haven, and he looks outraged. The cigar smoke rises in a cloud above him.

He is canceling the deal for J. J. Johnson he made last spring. Period.

"In thirty-one years, I've never seen such outright misrepresentation," he is saying. "Houston told us some things that were very, very different from what happened. When you make a deal, they're supposed to send you the papers. For some reason they never did, so we called them during training camp. And when they sent us the contract yesterday, I blew my top. I was shocked. It was entirely different from what we had agreed upon. I'll never sign it. Therefore, John Johnson is still the property of Houston, as far as we're concerned. He's a hell of a kid, but we would consider very few cornermen in the league under those conditions."

What conditions? Auerbach isn't saying. At least not to the general populace. But later, Jeff Cohen, the assistant GM, comes over. "Got a minute?" he says softly. "Red would like a word with you."

Out in the corridor, away from the crowd, Auerbach lays it out. "Look, here's the story. They didn't say he had a two-year, no-cut, $75,000 now, $75,000 later each year. I'd be crazy to go for that."

The deal was made over the telephone between Auerbach and Houston president Ray Patterson, as most are in the NBA. And Patterson, when I call him, remembers it differently.

"I really think Red wants to believe what he says so much now that he really believes what he says," Patterson is saying. "To assume that J. J., who was chosen seventh in his draft year [1970, the best in NBA history] and is a seven-year veteran, would not have a no-cut contract doesn't make sense for a man of Auerbach's experience. And even if I wanted to misrepresent the deal . . . which I didn't . . . we had a conference call with the league office, and they have a copy of the contract."

The whole thing is hung with obvious . . . and unanswered questions. Why did the Rockets wait so long to send the papers? Why didn't the Celtics insist on seeing them before Houston used Boston's second-round draft choice (the other end of the deal) to choose Larry Moffett two days later? Why couldn't Boston have asked the league to send a copy of Johnson's contract via Xerox telecopier?

Because, Celtics people explain, Auerbach has never done it that way. He's always reached for the phone and talked deals with his peers as casually as you might buy a stick of pepperoni. You gave a man your word and he gave his, and when he got around to it he sent the papers along. Besides, it was only an eight-team league back then, and if you screwed somebody the word got around and you were frozen out.

The problem is, nostalgia aside, that it isn't 1956 anymore. There are twenty-two teams and most of them have owners who don't know a basketball from a bagel. And with the enormous salaries, free agency demands, and more litigation than ever, everything should be down in writing and checked by a lawyer before anything changes hands.

"I feel sorry for a situation where you can't believe what people tell you," Auerbach says, grumpily. But then, that's why loan sharks keep a few leg-breakers around. Not everybody remembers the terms.

So the league will have a hearing, and Larry O'Brien will decide. And if the evidence is threadbare, the joking goes, O'Brien will play Solomon, prepare Johnson for the sword and see which side bursts into tears.

Johnson, meanwhile, is left in the middle. He'd shown up at Buzzards Bay on time, as he was supposed to, and had worked hard to adjust to the system, despite a nagging hamstring pull that had him in tape almost from the start. Now, most clubs had broken camp and were firming up rosters, and he was sitting in his new apartment, odd man out.

I call him there, and can hear a baby crying in the background. "I wasn't aware of anything," he sighs. "They called me up when the deal was made. Tom Nissalke told me I'd been traded, so I talked to Red and I talked to Tom Heinsohn. And I didn't know what they knew or what they didn't know. I'm just caught up in the middle of it, and I don't think I deserve it.

"I didn't make the deal. It wasn't my duty to see that anything was carried out. It's like shattering news, still. I didn't take anything for granted. I can't afford to. I said, by God, I've got to run hard in training camp, because a couple of times Frankie told me not to practice with the leg, you know, and I said, no, I gotta go. I don't care if it falls off. I've talked to my attorney, but I don't know what's what yet."

I wish him well, hang up, and go out to cover the game, which Boston wins, 109–103, with a healthy Cowens and White.

In the morning, there is a bus going to New York for tonight's game with Washington at Madison Square Garden . . . and the itinerary says we're out of here at 9:15, American Airlines, from La Guardia tonight. The itinerary also says we're coming back Saturday morning for another Garden date with the Knicks. So why don't we just stay here Friday, work out, and avoid all the back-and-forth?

The Knicks pay the expenses, after all. So it's not coming out of Auerbach's pocket.

The more intriguing theory is that Auerbach simply doesn't like Manhattan . . . the Knicks, the Garden, the hassle, the atmosphere, the distractions—especially the distractions . . . the city women, and the 4:00 A.M. bars.

Bill Bradley, New York's marvelous forward, wrote about how Auerbach and Knick coach Red Holzman would feud in the old days, bitching about dressing-room accommodations and shooting schedules . . . once even arguing about which club would board a plane before the other.

Whatever, Manhattan is a one-day thing, even now. "We never used to stay here," Heinsohn is saying. "Come down in the morning, play, and boom . . . you're home."

Once, I was told about the place the club would stay when Auerbach was coaching, a cut-rate salesman's hotel near Times Square because it was convenient and Auerbach supposedly knew the proprietor.

"You wouldn't believe it," the storyteller would say. "The world championship Celtics, legends like Russell and Cousy walking into the lobby with the threadbare carpets and the smudged windows."

Now, the club stays on the East Side, checking into the Summit just long enough for a four-hour nap. They're at the Garden by 5:00 today, play the Bullets at 6:30 in the first game of a doubleheader—beaten 118–115—and are on the way to La Guardia by the time the Knicks and 76ers are going up for the tap.

Back again—and the *Daily News* is saying that the Knicks have signed Cleveland guard Jim Cleamons and shipped Walt Frazier out there as compensation.

Clyde . . . of the circular bed Clyde, the Rolls-Royce Clyde, the ceiling mirrors, the wardrobe, the ladies, the impeccable cool.

Can there be a Clyde in Cleveland, home of Babbitt and Howard the Duck, of a river that catches fire, of February blizzards sweeping in from Lake Erie? Euclid Avenue is not Broadway . . . and in the dressing room, the Celtics are chuckling about it.

"They deserve each other," mutters Cowens, who owns neither a Rolls nor a mink coat. "Whoaa," Scott roars, delighted. "Headlines. I can see it: CLEVELAND, CLYDE DESERVE EACH OTHER—COWENS."

Upstairs in the press room, I sit with Heinsohn over coffee, hashing out a preseason assessment. He is guardedly optimistic . . . hell, it can't be any worse than it was last year.

"Last year," he says, "it was hey, wake up, wake up, when's the alarm going to go off? We were going in nine different directions. There was no cohesiveness. The chance of being cohesive was zilch. We had five new ballplayers, two of whom didn't know what the hell we were doing. Wicks and Rowe missed our training camp. Saunders was a free agent, Cook a rookie, Boswell was in his second year. And a lot of other teams got stronger, too, in relation to us."

Now, he thinks, the guards are better. Cowens is back, and Saunders is playing better at small forward. Power forward is the worry. "We've got good personnel to run, if we can rebound," Heinsohn says. "The big thing right now is the boards. All the other teams seem to have three or four monsters in there bangin'. We don't really have a big team. Philly's playing a front line with big people. Washington has a tremendous front line, and the Knicks have that potential, too."

"Almost every one of those teams can move a 6–10 guy in at power forward. Hell, our center is only 6–8. Rowe is not a big man [a short 6–7], and we're going to be rebounding against centers now."

Wicks, who knows the system and did the rebounding in Cowens's absence last year, would be one answer, but Heinsohn is openly losing patience with him.

"I think he's being foolish," Heinsohn is saying. "Last year, we didn't have any alternatives. We had nobody else. Sidney's a hell of a player, but he's not the all-time superstar of the century who's going to change the destiny of your ballclub. The more we get into it, if one or two of these guys start sticking it to somebody, then the hell with him."

So we walk down onto the floor—and the Celtics take a fantastic beating, 131–103, right from the tap. New York puts seven men in double figures, Lonnie Shelton hammers Cowens in the pivot, and Boston never gets closer than seven points all night.

Later, Heinsohn is fuming. "So much for experimenting," he says. "Not one single thing was I pleased with. Not one person. Our defense was very poor, nobody was going to the boards, we didn't talk. I've seen enough."

Well past midnight, over steak and onion soup at the Brasserie on 53rd Street, I spot Heinsohn walking out with his parents. He sits down, and we talk over coffee until half-past four. The Hawk is grim now. Cowens is playing without intensity, he feels, and Heinsohn is worried that the game may not intrigue him any longer. He'll have a talk with him. Saunders's defense is disappointing . . . there could be problems at small forward. And power forward is a washout. Wicks, overnight, has become a desperately valuable commodity.

Later, the talk ranges from the Johnson snafu to the concept of free agency to the Tax Reform Act of 1976, which whittled down the last great deduction—the depreciation of ballplayers. Heinsohn loves to theorize, and he tosses the numbers and formulae around easily. He is worried about the idea of deferred payments, and the way everybody has been embracing them as fiscal lifebuoys. Walking out into the cold rain, we decide that the league is doomed long-term. You can develop great foresight in Manhattan just before dawn.

They give you most of the day to pack and tie ends together because the flight is a bitch . . . worse than the Coast, and every bit as long as the overnight to Paris. Two and a half hours to Atlanta, a 90-minute layover, two more hours to San Antonio, and all of it only one time zone west.

They hold the tickets inside the Ionosphere Club at Logan, where self-styled VIPs pay $25 a year to have Scotch and Spanish peanuts behind closed doors. One by one, the players wander in, wearing coats and ties this year (no leisure suits or disco creations, by club edict). When Cook steps through the door, Heinsohn winces, and calls him aside.

A few moments later, Cook leaves, shoulders slumped, and walks back down the corridor, out of the building and the NBA. His luggage will arrive in Texas, on schedule, at 9:35 P.M. Meanwhile, as we board the jet, the rumors spread. Scott has heard that Wicks is moving his wife and daughter into a Boston apartment. Challant was told to bring the 12 jersey with him. Fleisher sounded optimistic on the phone today. Anyway, why waive Cook, a power forward, unless you were bringing in Wicks?

Somewhere over Virginia, Maxwell mentions it to Boswell, how surprising it is that the Celtics would cut a first-round pick before the first game of his second year. Boswell nods his head, grinning. "I told you, Bread, this league is cold-blooded, man. I been through it. So I just go from day to day, Chief. I don't worry."

It's better that way, especially on the day before the opener. Last year, Boston completed the three-way deal that brought in Rowe two hours before the flight left for Indianapolis and the first game. That time, Glenn McDonald had been Norm Cook. He made it to the hotel in Indiana before they cut him.

In Atlanta, a phone call confirms what most insiders had already guessed. Larry O'Brien has nullified the Johnson deal, penalized Boston two second-round draft choices, and sent Johnson back to Houston, where he'll play against the Celtics Thursday night.

Boswell was right. Flow with it. Go where the plane ticket says, and put on whatever uniform you find in the locker.

It's after ten by the time we reach the Hilton, and Mexican food is the answer. Five-minute drill, the Captain orders. Open the door, toss the bags in the room, rip off the necktie, meet in the lobby. Out on South Alamo Street, Ard, Maxwell, Rowe, Bing, Havlicek, and I pile into two cabs and head for Mi Tierra, the all-night ("We Never Close") cafe and bakery in the middle of the old produce market.

"Lot of Mexican people in California," says Rowe, who casually orders guacamole, beef enchiladas, and a couple of bottles of Big Red over ice. Maxwell, who grew up in east Carolina, is softly horrified. "I'll have French fries and a soda," he tells the waiter, but is gradually coaxed into an order of beef enchiladas.

Platters of beef nachos—lovely, hot, and messy—are brought, and the stories start to roll out, about college days and old NBA folk heroes, like a fraternity bull session. Rowe reminisces about UCLA and the mystical advantage of playing at Pauley Pavilion, where they lost two games during Rowe's three varsity years.

Maxwell talks about a game against Centenary, which seven-footer Robert Parish dominated. "I mean, he got *up,* man. But we won, by two."

"Where was the game?" Ard asks. "Charlotte," Maxwell says.

"Yeahhh," Rowe snickers. "You think they might have won if you didn't have *your* people there?" Maxwell ponders this for a moment. "I think so," he decides.

The talk turns to Reggie Harding, the legendary seven-foot center who played for Detroit and wound up dead from a bullet while trying to rob a liquor store. Bing is the acknowledged expert here, of course, and he tells the tale softly, with fine timing, a marvelous raconteur . . . almost scholarly with the gold-rimmed glasses.

"I think he scared Dave DeBusschere [the player-coach] a little bit," Bing remembers. "One time, after he'd just been released from prison, he came into the locker room and said, 'Big Fella's gonna get some time tonight.' Most of the people shrugged, you know, so Reggie pulled out a gun and laid it on the table. 'Yeah,' he said again, 'Big Fella's gonna get some time.' "

"Did he?" Rowe asks.

"He did," Bing nods solemnly. "He did."

Havlicek, at the other end of the table, giggles. "I heard he went around twice to a local store to rob it," he says, "and was shot twice by the owner. 'Why do you keep going back there, then,' they asked him. 'Cause I know he won't kill me,' he said."

Afterwards, the night is warm, and we walk back to the hotel along the deserted streets, passing the one-story buildings, the bail-bond storefronts, the open squares. The only sound is the screech and flap of unseen birds overhead, obscured by huge dark trees. There is a lazy, eerie peace about all of it, a stopped-motion feeling. Won't last long, I figure.

Wednesday the 19th
SAN ANTONIO, TEX.

Wandering along the Riverwalk, the cafe-lined canal that twists in a loop through downtown, and stopping every few hundred yards to make ritual calls to Auerbach and Fleisher about the Wicks negotiations. Something is happening . . . but what? It's 3:00 already, with game time at 7:30.

Turn into the hotel lobby . . . and Wicks is there, leaning over the counter, checking in. "Hi, Sidney," I say. He turns . . . "Hey, man," automatically . . . then sees it is me, and goes stone-faced, turning away, as the bellman takes his bags.

We do not get along . . . haven't, not since I joked in the Portland press room a year ago about his 'mysterious' nightly 18 points and 12 rebounds and woke to find myself quoted in the morning paper. He will go upstairs, and sign a multiyear contract, guesstimated at $1.5 million for five years, in Heinsohn's room, and the Hawk will press him into service immediately, playing him 23 minutes in a running game, until Wicks goes glaze-eyed and open-mouthed. "Gotta get him into shape," Heinsohn shrugs.

The evening turns into one of those crazy HemisFair shootouts, with the local blend of good ole boys, Meskins, and Air Force personnel hawlerin' every time the Spurs touch the ball. San Antonio leads throughout, by 15 points early on, before Cowens throws in 10 straight points and drags Boston back into it at the beginning of the fourth quarter, losing by only three now.

A year ago, this would have been the unspoken signal for a San Antonio collapse—"It used to be, heck, here come the Celtics again, and bingo," Spurs coach Doug Moe would say. "You got Boston here, and you lose six straight to 'em last year, and they get it down to three points at that time in the game. We'd had that experience before."

This time, San Antonio hangs in, and the last few minutes are turbulent and dramatic. Moe is coatless now, mouth agape, wandering to midcourt. Heinsohn is doing pirouettes on the sidelines, screaming at Tommy Nunez, the Chicano referee that some Celtics call "the lettuce picker." George Gervin, the loping, limber "Iceman," is swinging from the rim, and country fiddle is blaring from the loudspeakers.

Finally, Gervin launches a bomb that just beats the 24-second clock, Scott fouls out guarding him, and Mark Olberding, the Spurs' twenty-one-year-old baby bull, drops in the two free throws that end it with 11 seconds left—San Antonio 114, Boston 109.

Later, the Spurs are whooping and joking like some undersized high-school varsity that's just taken down the state champs on the first weekend of the season. "They'd beaten us so many times." says Larry Kenon, the irrepressible Mr. K., "that we knew they weren't going to die. But this time, we weren't going to either."

They learned something tonight: You can beat Boston down the stretch. No great revelation, certainly . . . unless you'd been in this locker room in April, when San Antonio had just been taken out cold in two playoff games, beaten each time in the final 12 minutes.

Twenty minutes after the final buzzer, Gervin is still wearing his silver uniform, bouncing down the corridor that leads to the lobby. He is grinning like a maniac. "Can't lose 'em *all,*" he yells.

The wakeup call comes at half-past eight, and we're on the plane well before eleven, with Cowens reading *The Wall Street Journal* next to me. He keeps a stack of them back at his office for reference. "Even if I don't read 'em right away," he says, "I know that there's a lot of valuable information in there that will be useful when I get around to looking through them."

He takes that approach with almost everything. When he went through Florida State on a scholarship, the school reclaimed the criminology books he'd been issued as soon as commencement rolled around. So Cowens went out and bought all the books again on his own. Why waste four years of study? Why not read what's there to be read?

Like contracts. At dinner in Portland last year. Stacom mentioned that he'd never really gotten around to reading his . . . and Cowens was horrified.

"You mean you don't know what obligations you have?" he asked him. "You don't know what they can make you do? How could you sign something you never read?"

It is the original Kentucky frontier attitude—a man should learn the limits of his freedom, and who imposes them, and ask questions accordingly.

"Like when I was having my contract drawn up," Cowens is saying. "You know how there's a lot of stuff in there about misconduct? Well, I asked them, what does that mean? Does that mean I can't go out and hang a moon at somebody on the street? I want you to define 'misconduct.' I want you to put in there what sports I can play and which ones I can't."

Cowens wanted the whole contract done that way, including a leave-of-absence clause, and whenever Auerbach would balk at something ("I don't know if the Commissioner would go for it"), Cowens would say, "Put it in. We'll see if the Commissioner goes for it."

That was how you put a contract together, Cowens felt. That was how you did anything that required your services and paid you a salary. And now, as Boston's player representative, he couldn't understand why most of his teammates were so casual about things that could take money out of their pockets.

"I'll go to a meeting," he says, "and bring back information from Fleisher, and most of the guys don't care one way or the other. All they're worried about is today."

So while they're playing cards, he's reading the *Journal*. Or saving it in a corner in Wellesley.

The workout at Houston Baptist University is optional, team publicist Jim Foley is saying, but if I can find my way out there in half an hour, the Rockets' new reserve small forward might still be around, running wind sprints. Which he is.

"Got to get back in shape," J. J. Johnson tells me, panting, "and learn the new plays." For two weeks, he says, he'd been sitting in his Brookline apartment with his family, watching the baseball playoffs and World Series on television and running up and down the hallway while they determined his fate in Manhattan.

He got the word along with everybody else Tuesday evening, boarded a plane at Logan Airport yesterday morning, and found himself in a red-and-white uniform for the home opener with Chicago last night. Saturday, he'll be launching his old baseline jumper against the Celtics. No hard feelings.

"Even if I had hard feelings, what good would it do?" he shrugs. "It's history. Passé. I've got nothing against the Boston people, Tom Heinsohn or Red Auerbach. No ill will. I've got a job to do." We shake hands, and he goes off to pack for the flight to Kansas City, which leaves at dinnertime.

By Saturday, he will be gone—again—traded to Seattle for— what else—two second-round draft choices. He will get on a plane while the Celtics are playing Houston, and will come off the bench at the Coliseum Sunday night and play against the Spurs.

No airline restaurant guides or word-of-mouth necessary tonight. The Captain knows where he wants to dine. "Elan," he tells the cabbie, crisply, and within 10 minutes, four of us are deposited at the door of the city's most exclusive supper-and-disco establishment.

It's members only, and several hundred dollars a year, but Havlicek walks directly to the desk and tries the humbly confident approach while Ard, Stacom, and I strain mightily to remain inconspicuous.

"Excuse me, but we're with a professional basketball team from Boston, and we're here for a few days," Havlicek begins, softly. "And we were wondering if we might possibly avail ourselves of your hospitality tonight . . . maybe have a meal, drink a little wine, and listen to some music. Could I leave a name, and maybe if you have a table open . . . that's Havlicek. H-A-V . . ."

The hostess, in her twenties, blonde, and exquisite, glances up abruptly. John Havlicek, the mouth says, wordlessly. It takes maybe 30 seconds to get a table for four and a round of drinks. A letter of introduction from H. L. Hunt himself couldn't have been more effective.

Havlicek looks at the surroundings—exposed brick, plants hanging everywhere, heavy napkins, good silver and crystal—sees escargot and steak on the menu, and nods his head, satisfied. He loves the road.

Most of his teammates, thinking about the forty-one plane rides, the droning monotony of elevators and Sheraton-Hyatt-Marriott double beds and grim winter weather, usually settle for a room-service sirloin and salad and switch on the television.

But after sixteen years, Havlicek still gets excited about driving out to see the Rockies or fishing for Oregon trout. He will arrange the hours carefully on a one-day stop to New Orleans so he can have a sumptuous lunch at Galatoire's, midnight beignets and coffee at the Café du Monde, and still squeeze in his pregame nap. This has led to such innovations as the two-minute hotel arrival drill, and the inspiration for the NBA Restaurant of the Week, a minireview which I include among my Sunday basketball notes.

Normally, Havlicek will ask for veal . . . "If I were going to the gallows and could have one last meal," he muses, "it'd be some kind of veal, basically, with an Italian influence somewhere along the line."

But tonight, he sees a 23-ounce porterhouse, and decides it would go nicely with the escargot and a carafe of red wine. We all wind up with steak, a tableful of onion soup, marinated herring and spinach salad placed here and there.

The conversation ranges from fishing holes to the energy crisis, while the disco music floats down from three separate tiers. Finally, the check is called for, and Ard collapses into a mock coughing fit when he peeks at it.

"I saw a 1," he says, as we wander upstairs. "And then I saw a 4. And I said, 'Yuh.' " As in $140. Meal money in the NBA is $25 a day. Not quite enough to play Dionysius . . . and this place is Dionysian. Backgammon tables line the walls, and gowns and three-piece suits are everywhere. Nobody would ask you for an autograph here, which Havlicek (whose signature is elaborate) appreciates.

He prefers to remain in the background, sipping at a white wine and soda and watching people glide up and down the stairs. "Ready?" he says, before midnight . . . and we're gone.

Saturday the 22nd
HOUSTON, TEX.

The Celtics weren't here much longer tonight, not in any real competitive sense. Moses Malone, Houston's monster rebounder, rammed in a dunk right from the tipoff, the Rockets went up 11–0 in less than three minutes, and it was gone. It was one of those bizarre NBA evenings where you score 10 points in a row and don't get a thing for the next four minutes, where you need six straight baskets just to get back to within 12 points. One of those games where you achieve your big objective, keeping Houston's 7–0, 6–10,

6–8 front line off the boards, outrebounding them solidly . . . and it doesn't mean a damn.

The Celtics are merely beaten like a drum from start to finish, trailing by 20 at halftime, by 83–69 after three quarters. "We kept pecking away and pecking away," Heinsohn shrugs later. "And we still never got it below 10." So much for five days in Texas, shakin' it all down.

Monday the 24th
DETROIT, MICH.

You can hear the yelling out in the hallway, through the closed doors. Deep, angry, Union City, New Jersey, yelling. And you don't hear anyone else's voice. Heinsohn wants the floor to himself tonight . . . and nobody's giving him an argument about it. Detroit 100, Boston 85, it was, and we're talking about a nine-point third quarter that wiped out a seven-point halftime lead and made it 69–58 for Detroit going into the last 12 minutes.

The tirade lasts a good 10 minutes, as the security guards raise their eyebrows and grin a little self-consciously. Later, Stacom will say that everyone came in for some fire, even Ard, who never got off the bench. "Sitting without intensity, I guess," Ard says. The dressing rooms at Cobo Arena are subdivided into three sections, and a few Celtics are dressing silently in each, answering questions in whispers.

Heinsohn sits in the middle of the largest one, sprawled across a folding chair, and he talks in the short, precise sentences he uses when he is furious.

"We don't want to win the goddamn game," he mutters. "We played very tough the first half, and we came out in the third quarter and rolled over and died. We played dumb, nonhustling basketball. We have people who aren't thinking out there. We have guys who don't want to get up and work hard on people. They're half doing it and half not doing it.

"We got to get our heads together and say we're gonna play tough basketball. We think all we have to do is send our jerseys out there, but these goddamn teams are waiting for us. There's reason to be disorganized at this point in the season, but not to play without intensity.

"And I'll be a pig's ass if this will continue. They'll drill until it comes out their ass, and I don't give a shit."

As the writers turn away, one Celtic comes up, wearing the expression of a schoolboy who'd just been called into the principal's office.

"What'd he say?" he wonders. "That the ball just wouldn't go in the basket?"

The season's barely started, and there are new people, and this *is* the road . . . but on the other side of the building, Bob Lanier, the Piston center, has noticed something. "Boston isn't the team out there they were before," he says. "Usually they keep coming at you, but right now they are not doing that."

Tuesday the 25th
HARTFORD, CONN.

It is not precisely the moment for levity and light conversation, but nobody's mentioned that to the middle-aged salesman with the briefcase and hot-combed hair. He's unaware of all the bad karma converging on the sidewalk outside the terminal here at Bradley Field. Three straight losses, a brooding Hawk, a 6:15 wakeup call in Detroit, an Allegheny flight here, and the thought of a game with Atlanta tonight at the Civic Center, where Boston will play six times during the season.

The players hate the whole idea of Hartford—the two-hour bus trip each way from the Garden, the day spent in the hotel room, the lukewarm fans. A road game in Chicago is all it is. But now, our Mr. Polyester slides up to Cowens as he's waiting for the bus.

"When are you guys gonna stop losing?" he wonders.

Cowens stares at him. "When," he says, "are you gonna stop bustin' my balls?"

Later, as the bus pulls out for the 20-minute drive downtown, Cowens shakes his head. "Businessmen," he mutters.

Hell, the losing is gonna stop tonight. Haven't the Hawks beaten Boston only four times in seven years away from home? And didn't owner Ted Turner and coach Hubie Brown dump half of their highly paid losing roster over the summer, planning to start fresh with a small nucleus and a bunch of scrappy hustlers?

Down at Newport, where Turner (Captain Courageous!) was defending the America's Cup, we had joked about it. "Just like Sodom and Gomorrah," Turner had promised. "You know, where the Lord says, 'I hate it, I can't stand it, I'm gonna wipe it all out and start over.' I don't mind losing . . . but I'm gonna lose with guys making $30,000 a year instead of $300,000. Hell, the incentive's there. Play well, and you make $70,000 next year. If you don't play well, you'll be back at McDonald's, rustlin' up egg McMuffins."

Turns out he was serious. Turner kept five veterans, and filled out his roster with journeymen, and free agents nobody else wanted. John Drew and His Hungry Strangers, you could call them. "If we win 40 games this year," Brown had told them, only half in jest, "we'll all go in the Hall of Fame."

Tonight, Atlanta is clearly out of the game twice, losing by 30–14 in the first quarter and 66–50 in the third. But Brown, who grew up hungry himself in Elizabeth, New Jersey, and is somewhat of an evangelical screamer and motivator, has the Hawks scrambling.

They dive for loose balls. They press maniacally. They trap and zone on defense, looking for turnovers and steals they can transform into easy baskets. And they make sure that Drew, their silky twenty-three-year-old shooting forward, gets the ball.

With 20 seconds to play, Boston's lead has been whittled down to 107–103, and the Hawks have the ball, with Brown hollering instructions.

Three shots are taken, missed, and taken again. Finally Rowe grabs a rebound and feeds White, sneaking away, for a layup that ends it. Brown, howling that Rowe stepped out of bounds as he was coming down with the ball, gets himself thrown out. White converts the technical foul, and the final is 110–103. No champagne is uncorked in the Boston room afterwards.

Friday the 28th
PISCATAWAY, N.J.

Until tonight, this has been merely a bizarre address for a sad team, a temporary mail drop that the newly moved (from Hempstead, Long Island) Nets can use until owner Roy Boe builds his dream castle in the Jersey Meadowlands a few years from now. We used to joke about Piscataway on bar stools in September. Now we have to find it. Somewhere near New Brunswick, the wise men say. Fly to Newark, rent a car, drive south on the New Jersey Turnpike, and hope that the urchins haven't knocked down or twisted around the signs that point you towards the Rutgers gym.

Somehow, it all works, and less than an hour later, the building looms up out of the darkness, an impressive college facility (seating 9,000) with a college team waiting inside.

Boe's Jests, a Newark paper calls them . . . a scruffy band of gypsies the Nets have decided to go with until solvency—currently about $7 million away—looms. They finished dead last in the league last year, losing 60 games, and have lost their first four now.

Kevin Loughery, who once coached the worst professional basketball team in history for a while (the 9–73 1973 Philadelphia 76ers), works here now, and two weeks into the season, has already decided that his new running game is not going to work. The Nets will play deliberately, and hope for the best.

Which, early in the second quarter, is Boston 49, New Jersey 35 . . . so Loughery sits down most of his regulars and goes with a hodgepodge that would delight any collector of NBA minutiae.

Bobby Carrington, who'd had a job collecting bills and repossessing cars for Chrysler, came here for one last shot before giving up on a career. Bubbles Hawkins had been on the Golden State scrap pile ten months ago. Dave Wohl was picked up for a fourth-round draft choice last winter. George Johnson had played center for three clubs since January. And Mark Crow was the 111th player chosen in last spring's NBA draft.

No All-Stars there, but Loughery said, Hell, why not? and sent them out to throw a zone press on the Celtics veterans and see what happened.

And what happened was an incredible self-immolation, as Boston threw the ball away twenty-four times, had eight shots blocked, and looked as baffled as a bunch of high-school freshmen seeing a system defense for the first time.

The 16-point lead became a seven-point deficit in less than seven minutes, as Heinsohn watched in angry disbelief and the fans roared in delight. Boston never saw the lead again, trailed by as many as 14 points in the fourth quarter, and lost, 116–109.

"You know," Havlicek would say, softly, "you should be able to remedy something like a zone press with a timeout. We've seen that thing a lot of times, and there's no reason why it should bother us as much as it does."

Not thirty-year-old veterans. Not Celtics. Around the country tomorrow, they won't be talking about this as a Nets renaissance, but an amazing (and amusing) Boston screwup.

"What was the Celtics' problem tonight?" someone asked Bernard King, the rookie forward who scored 30 points and had dunked over Cowens at one point.

King looked incredulous. "The problem is, they were facing the New . . . Jersey . . . Nets," he replied, with visible pride.

"Whoo," hooted teammate Darnell Hillman from across the room. "Listen to the young man."

Saturday the 29th
CLEVELAND, OHIO

The morning flight out of Newark is a short one—80 minutes—and the bus for suburban Richfield and tonight's game with the Cavaliers won't leave until five, so Havlicek suggests a hearty lunch somewhere.

The hotel—Swingos' Celebrity downtown—has a gourmet restaurant with good veal, but Havlicek says that Cowens, who likes natural foods, knows of a place nearby, on Euclid Avenue, which turns out to be the Govinda Restaurant, offering as much pure vegetarian fare and Hare Krishna dogma as you can digest for 99¢.

Today's special—whole wheat bread, papaya juice, wild rice, tamarind tea, halvah, and a gloppy green concoction called potato prep—is listed on a blackboard, and is served up by a pallid, top-knotted New York refugee who recognizes Cowens immediately, and is a little astonished to find him here.

"Hey, buddy, you look as though you could use a little sun," Cowens tells him, grinning. "Does Bill Walton ever come in here?" Walton, Portland's superb center, has been an unabashed—and unabridged—vegetarian since his UCLA days, to the point of calling his early teammates "dead-flesh eaters."

Cowens isn't nearly as religious about it, and he frowns when he's labeled a vegetarian. "I eat *GOOD* food," he'll tell you, meaning raw or lightly cooked vegetables, selected meats, and fruit and honey instead of sugary soft drinks and candy.

Last year, before a game on Long Island, he'd eaten half a chocolate bar, and it had affected him like a jolt of uncut adrenaline. "Remember how I was running around crazy and waving at people during warmups?" he would say. "Well, that was the first time I'd had a piece of candy in a year."

Havlicek, remembering Cowens' dietary habits as a rookie, would smile at the change in him. "Dave, what'd you eat tonight?" we'd ask him back then. 'Uh, bologna sandwich, can of corn, couple of beers,' he'd say."

Now, upon light prompting, Cowens would give you the full analysis—how the body was a machine that needed to be properly exercised and fueled, how the enzymes worked, and how one's daily intake of starches, sugars, fats, proteins, etc, affected all of it. It wasn't a matter of pop sociology or Eastern religion. It just made sense, especially if you were making a living with your body.

Stacom, who'd been brought up on simple salad-steak-potato concepts in Irish Queens, stared at his potato prep, and shook his head doubtfully.

"But, Dave, I'm used to bulk," he is saying. "A big piece of meat . . . something. Don't you feel weak eating this kind of stuff?" Cowens hadn't thought of it. "Whales don't eat meat," he reasons. "Elephants don't eat meat. Maurice Lucas [Portland's 6–9 power forward] doesn't eat meat. What do you mean, weak?"

Before we leave, Cowens has the proprietor step out on the

sidewalk and takes his picture in front of the door. He is thinking of opening his own natural-food place, and is doing a little informal research wherever we go.

Later, we walk across the street to a health-food store for free samples of vitamin E and big bags of natural nuts. "If you win tonight." I tell Stacom, "I've got my lead all written. *Fueled by the pure vegetables from the Great Lord Krishna, the Boston Celtics . . .'* "

Lost, as it turned out, 103–98, as Walt Frazier scored 22 points. He likes it out here, is looking for a condominium, and planning for the playoffs. "This is about what I expected," Clyde says after the game. "Except I couldn't believe how expensive it is to live here. I saw condominiums that were more expensive than in New York. And no view, man. Nothin'."

Back at the hotel, around midnight, Eddie Gillooly, the *Herald-American* writer, and I spot Cowens in the restaurant, finishing off an order of escargots and a monster salad. Naturally.

Sunday the 30th
EN ROUTE TO BOSTON, MASS.

"I've had enough of the road," Tommy Heinsohn is saying, grumpily, over his second cup of coffee at Hopkins Airport. What I like to term the Jack Kerouac Memorial Road Trip will officially end at 11:16 A.M., when the Celtics arrive home with wrinkled clothes and psyches, and their worst start (1–5) in seven years.

It is now nine o'clock, and Heinsohn and I are having one of our formal weekly review-and-prognosis sessions. The Hawk, of course, is the hemisphere's foremost coffee-shop philosopher, hunching over his mug for hours ("Ah, dear, a little more here, if you would"), the big hands describing ellipses and trapezoids in the air, the deep Jersey voice painting word pictures.

A player's game is compared to an unbalanced spaghetti sauce, with too much oregano and not enough salt. He will talk about the difficulties of getting Romeos to play Macbeths, liken his club's vanishing consistency to that of Bigfoot . . . did we really make those tracks? He will fill the off-days with Henry Clay and desert mirages and Ebenezer Scrooge, in darkened buses, deserted airport corridors, and busy hotel lobbies, twenty-four hours a day, on deadline and demand.

This morning, thinking back on a month-long trail of predawn wakeup calls and full upright seatbacks and tray tables from Dayton to San Antonio to Piscataway, he mostly feels numb.

"Right now," he says, "we have the mental and emotional feeling of having played fourteen games . . . fourteen straight games . . . on the road. And I'm getting tired of hearing people in the stands saying, When are the Celtics gonna play like the Celtics?

"I liked some of the things we did last night, especially on the press. We were finally playing a total upbeat game with pace. What disturbed the hell out of me at New Jersey was that we paced ourselves. We were getting our ass whipped, so everyone put it in gear after 43 minutes and put on a full, gambling press. And at the end of the game, nobody was tired. What the hell were they doing the other 43 minutes?"

He talks wistfully of 1974, when he had a full kamikaze going from the opening tap. "What we did was the sledgehammer effect," he says. "Just keep coming at 'em. Now, two teams did that to us last week with a zone press . . . Atlanta and New Jersey . . . and kicked our ass with it. Our problem is that we haven't played a total upbeat game in over two years.

"But now, I'm gonna press everyone. Everyone's gonna press, so they better get used to it. Because I've tried everything else. I've tried to play what appear to be the top guys on paper, and get cohesion with that group, and we haven't won with that."

So he'll set up shop at the Lexington Christian Academy, the suburban school where the Celtics schedule their off-day work during the season, "and just play fast break-and-press basketball and put all the plays in." And the Celtics will enjoy the comparative luxuries of four straight games in the Garden . . . with no more airports until November 12.

NOVEMBER

Catcalls from the Balcony

Wednesday the 2nd
BOSTON, MASS.

By now it has become a Pavlovian chain reaction, coming around nine o'clock on these disappointing evenings. Tom Heinsohn glances at the scoreboard—VISITORS 60, HOME 46, it tells him tonight, with the third quarter almost gone—stares at the rafters in exasperation, then looks along the bench until he sees his new cattle prod.

"Max," he hollers, and Cedric Maxwell comes loping down, shedding his sweats, elastic and eager to get something started. "The Cornbread Man," they call him here, after his Carolina nickname, and no rookie has stirred local imaginations like him since Dave Cowens.

Red Auerbach had seen him eighteen months ago at Madison Square Garden, an odd collection of arms and legs who could shoot and dribble and rebound and run. He played for one of those hyphenated Southern schools—University of North Carolina–Charlotte—that pop up in the small print of your Sunday newspaper and start beating people . . . good people . . . in New York City.

Auerbach had tucked Maxwell away in his memory file and hoped nobody would remember him on June 9, 1977. And when

Milwaukee had grabbed Tennessee's Ernie Grunfeld (whom the Celtics had wanted), Auerbach had called for time, riffled through a few notes, and drafted Maxwell.

His first trip to the Garden had terrified him. Auerbach and Heinsohn and Tom Sanders had been sitting in Auerbach's office, chatting and joking, and when Maxwell had walked in, there had been complete silence. The Cornbread Man had wanted to turn around and go back to North Carolina and forget the whole thing.

Instead, they had given him the traditional induction, beginning at a Chinese restaurant in Brookline with lobster and smoke from a long Auerbachian cigar.

"I'm allergic to seafood," Maxwell had remembered, suddenly. "What if I swell up?"

Later, down on Causeway Street, they had him take off his suitcoat, vest, and shirt and pull on a white team jersey. "Take him upstairs," Auerbach would say. "I want him to see the court and the dressing room, and all that. And give him some shoes, socks, T-shirts . . . whatever he wants."

Disney used to love stories like this. So did the Brothers Grimm. Maxwell had come out of Kinston, North Carolina, a town of 22,000, with tobacco fields and a big synthetic fiber plant on the Neuse River near Camp LeJeune. "It's not a big river," he would tell you. "Just a small stream that you might go fishing in. You might see Tom Sawyer coming down it in a boat."

Maxwell had been cut from his high-school varsity as a junior. None of the Tobacco Road people—Duke, North Carolina, Wake Forest, or State—were interested. East Carolina, a few miles away in Greenville, offered him a half scholarship, but only UNCC really wanted him among major colleges. "There was really no choice," Maxwell would say.

So he went off to Charlotte and a gym they called "The Mineshaft" and played in the Sunbelt Conference against the likes of Jacksonville, Georgia State, and New Orleans. A new coach came in at the beginning of Maxwell's junior year, built the offense around his oversized hands and rubbery inside moves, and watched UNCC go all the way to the NIT finals in Manhattan, which is where Auerbach discovered him.

A year later, everybody knew Maxwell. He was Cornbread now,

named after a character in the movie *Cornbread, Earl and Me* (played by Golden State's Jamaal Wilkes), who loved orange soda and summer basketball.

And he brought the 49ers (because the school was located on Route 49) to Fantasyland, the NCAA Final Four, where they came within a last-second dunk of upsetting Marquette and playing for the title against North Carolina, their high-rent cousins from Chapel Hill.

And that was Maxwell you saw, gangly and grinning, galloping across the pages of *Sports Illustrated,* the funky team symbol. It got him more plates of cornbread at more banquets than he ever thought existed; actually, he would say, he detested the stuff. But it also got him a Celtic jersey. "The same green and white I was wearing in school," he said.

Here, Maxwell plays the same way, running in three directions at once ("like Ray Bolger in *The Wizard of Oz,*" Heinsohn would marvel), and setting up down low. All you had to do was get the ball anywhere near him, and the hands would take care of the rest. Either Maxwell would twist, turn, and fling the ball in, or he would draw a foul, crashing to the floor in a tangle, then springing back up, his eye on the free-throw line. *That,* Heinsohn would proclaim, was a gift. You didn't teach instincts like those.

The veterans had accepted Maxwell quickly, shortening the nickname to "Bread" and including him in their card games. He would hunch in an airplane seat in his three-piece brown suit, a tweed country squire's hat pulled down over his ears. And when the stewardess came around with the small bottles of complimentary liquor, Maxwell would carefully stuff them into his traveling bag and continue playing.

He lived the life of the bachelor rookie up here, staying at the airport Hilton until he moved into a Brookline apartment, and eating typical rookie fare . . . which horrified John Havlicek, who could recite his own last twelve meals for you down to the ounce.

"They told me what he eats," Havlicek would tell me, "and most of it you put in a toaster. And before a game, I've seen him drink grape sodas with a couple of Butterfinger bars on the side."

It didn't seem to affect Maxwell on the court. Tonight, after Heinsohn sent him in to light a fire under a few veterans, Maxwell wound up with 15 points, seven rebounds, and the evening's MVP award in 16 minutes. And Cavalier coach Bill Fitch had to call three timeouts in the final 47 seconds, after his lead had shrunk to a single point.

So if the entree was the same sad shepherd's pie the Celtics had served up in six different cities last month—a 104–101 loss when the buzzer sounded—the dessert had been different, at least. Cornbread with whipped cream. An acquired taste, hopefully.

Friday the 4th
BOSTON, MASS.

He hears the boos whenever he stands up to pull off the sweats ... you *KNOW* he hears the boos, even though Sidney Wicks walks along the sidelines with his head up, eyes flashing, like some Nubian warrior coming in to set things straight.

He plays his minutes as sixth man in relief of Curtis Rowe, he returns to the bench and when Tom Heinsohn calls for Wicks again, it all begins anew. Not the outraged howl that greets bad calls, but an audible negative undercurrent, a prolonged O-O-O-O-ugh that says naww, not *HIM*.

It began as a rude murmur in the home opener with Cleveland, but you hear it nightly now, and finally Heinsohn explodes. "I wish people would get off Sidney Wicks's ass and let him play," he tells us, loud enough for Wicks, dressing across the room, to hear. "Get off his tail. I want you to print that. They're trying to make Sidney Wicks the scapegoat now for everything that's happened, and he isn't the scapegoat. He's done everything I've asked him to do. He carried this ballclub last year. This is the modern era of basketball, where he's entitled to do what he did negotiating for a new contract. The fans ought to be for him, not against him. They're doing the same thing to him that they did to Finkel and it's not fair."

Hank Finkel was the unrefined seven-foot white center who'd bridged the one-year gap between Bill Russell and Dave Cowens, playing earnest if not exceptional basketball. As the Celtics had faltered, slipping from a championship season to their worst ever, Finkel had come in for most of the individual abuse. He's a stiff, the feeling went, and look what the hell's happened. Now with Russell . . .

By 1975, after Cowens had established himself gloriously in the pivot, a championship had been won and his own role had diminished to a handful of reserve minutes, Finkel had become a sympathetic figure . . . mock-heroic, actually . . . with every basket and rebound now cheered wildly. At least the guy tried . . .

So the public perception was variable, frequently depending upon the man you replaced. Wicks had succeeded Paul Silas, and the comparisons were obvious, and always to Wicks's disadvantage. Silas had been a scrapper, a rebounder and defender who relished the unrewarding inside work that made the Celtic system go. The most underrated player in the game, Bostonians had said about him . . . so often, in fact, that Silas had nearly become overrated. But the record spoke for itself. Silas had played four years in Boston, and there had been two titles to celebrate.

Auerbach, introducing Wicks at a luncheon in the fall of 1976, had sworn it could still be that way. Hadn't Wicks played for consecutive NCAA champions at UCLA in 1970 and 1971? Hadn't people who'd seen him dominate Jacksonville's 7–2 center Artis Gilmore in the finals called him the greatest college player they'd seen? Forget the five years with the Trail Blazers and all the losing.

"A lot of people were apprehensive about Charlie Scott," Auerbach would say, when the question of attitude was brought up. "Hell, he's happy, we're happy, he's playing great ball. All he wanted to do was win a championship and get a ring. Same with this guy. This guy knows what it is to win, and he'll pay the price."

The price, though, was payable in a different currency than what Wicks had expected. He had been a marvelously fluid scorer at Portland, averaging better than 20 points a game, and they had looked for him there, making sure Wicks got the ball where he could do something with it. It was not that way in Boston.

Jo Jo White, Charlie Scott, Dave Cowens, and John Havlicek could all score. What was needed was a man who could complement Cowens on the boards, play some defense, and get his points where he found them. A Paul . . . of course . . . Silas.

So the seeds of the disaffection had been there from the start, even though Wicks had played marvelously during Cowens's absence and led the club in rebounding. He was still a newcomer, and as such was placed on the same kind of stylistic probation that Scott had had to endure. He wore the green jersey, but was he a Celtic? Did he move without the ball? Did he dive for loose balls? How many contested rebounds did he get? Would he set a pick? And if not, why not? Why does he wear the headband? Silas never wore a headband. And Cowens . . . we heard Cowens doesn't like him. Cowens and Silas were like brothers.

When Wicks sat out training camp as Larry Fleisher negotiated with Auerbach, you heard the comments on the radio talk shows. What the hell does the guy want? Who does he think he is . . . Havlicek?

The booing had started right away at the Garden, when it became obvious that the team was far from being ready to play, and that Wicks wasn't anywhere near top physical condition. He'd shrugged it off—he'd been booed in Portland, too, when it became obvious Wicks wasn't their black Moses, come to lead them out of the expansion wilderness.

It's just a matter of time, Wicks has been saying cheerfully, night after night, until the fans come around to my side. Meanwhile, loss follows loss—it was Denver 109, Boston 107, tonight—and each one has been draped around Wicks's neck like a stinking albatross. All he has to do is stand up to know that.

Monday the 7th
BOSTON, MASS.

Jimmy Ard was released today, a casualty of the new eleven-man roster limit that takes effect next week. "Before practice Hawk said, 'This is what I have to do, I'm doing it, I'm sorry,' " Ard says, when I reach him at home. "Boom. Like that."

He has no immediate plans, he says, but several options. He could go back to the University of Cincinnati, where he was an All-America center and an ABA bonus signee, and finish up the eighteen hours he needs for a marketing degree. He could play in

Europe . . . they can always use an experienced big man there, and Ard can speak a mouthful of French. Or he can stay in shape and wait for somebody, somewhere, to tear up an ankle or break a hand.

At twenty-nine, he is still a worthwhile commodity in a league that deals in commodities, and he has never had any illusions about his limitations.

Jimmy knew he couldn't run with a Bill Walton or shoot with a Bob Lanier. But he would rebound for you and fill a lane with anybody. And he was always cheerfully on call, no matter how few the minutes, or when they came.

Two years ago, when Cowens had fouled out in the classic fifth playoff game against Phoenix and it had come down to a third overtime, the minutes had come in one pressurized cluster, as Heinsohn motioned Ard off the bench.

And he had set up three baskets with a steal, a jump ball, and a rebound in the last two minutes, and dropped in the two free throws that finally won it. Two days later, he was drinking champagne in Arizona with the rest of them. LIFE WOULD BE HARD, the Garden banner reminded you the following autumn, WITHOUT JIM ARD.

Around the league, his dismissal has been greeted with a universal shrug—just another one of Big Red's backups—but hopefully the true Celtic archivists, who standardize Celtic virtues, will remember his wit, his intelligence, and his unselfishness. Because his teammates, with whom he's played since 1974, seem to have already forgotten him.

In another season, a bunch of them would have come over with beer and sympathy for an informal Irish wake. Two days after word came down, only Bing, the newcomer, had called to offer condolences.

Wednesday the 9th
BOSTON, MASS.

The sound is surprising and ugly after all these years, and it starts earlier every night, billowing down from the cheap seats as soon as the first quarter ends.

It falls halfway between fan disappointment and consumer dis-gust—B-O-O-O-U-U-G-H—and it comes from people from Med-ford and Dorchester and Brookline who look at the green jerseys on the floor and the title flags above and for the first time see no link.

You could hear it frequently tonight, until most of the 11,000 customers simply threw up their hands and reached for their coats with six minutes to play and the Celtics trailing San Antonio by 17 points.

It was a taunting, sniggering crowd, not entirely without justifica-tion. The Spurs had never won in this building, but from the beginning, they moved the ball around like the Globetrotters and let it fly, their success assumed. After 12 minutes, they led by 11 points. With less than three minutes to play, the margin was up to 25. You could see Auerbach across the floor, steaming in his loge chair.

And now, when the buzzer sounds, he busts through the crowd and into the dressing room, and goes into one of his old-time religion tirades. Quitters, he calls them, singling out Havlicek and White. It is one of his favorite psychological ploys, dating back to his coaching days. You landed on the people who could take it, regardless of the degree of guilt. They absorbed the heat, but a collective point was made.

Tonight, Havlicek, who played four years for Auerbach and learned to dismiss his bluster, shrugs. But White, humiliated, stands up and shouts back, "O.K., then, I quit."

After a while, his rage spent, Auerbach emerges, tight-lipped and dour. White is sitting in his corner, reluctant to talk. "John, I don't know, man," he whispers, as I approach. "I'm just like you."

Across the room, Cowens sits back, weary and puzzled, hunched in his cubicle. "I'm confused," he says. "I lie awake nights thinking. I try to think back to other teams I've been on, other situations, but I've never been a part of a situation like this. We've got to get mad. We've got to play harder. We've got to intimidate people if we have to. Because I'm fed up with losing. It's embarrassing."

They are not used to this. Five straight losses, three of them in the Garden. Eight in nine games, by far the worst start in franchise history. The derision from the balcony. Auerbach hollering at them.

Scott, who has little use for happy talk in general, smiles sadly. "One loss has nothing to do with another," he says. "Or shouldn't.

You can say you are ready. You can say you want to play. But getting out there and doing it is something else."

When the crowd thins out, I go over to Havlicek and ask him if he can find a parallel, anywhere, in his twenty-four years as a player. "In high school one time, we were 4–19," he says. "But we didn't have a gym."

Thursday the 10th
BOSTON, MASS.

White is not at practice this morning, and nobody will say much about it. "This is not an excused absence," Heinsohn says, curtly. "Better ask Red."

Auerbach is in his office, preparing to leave for a speaking engagement in Rochester. He dips into his cigar box for a handful, and says he is fining White, and that it will be substantial. Anything beyond that will be up to Jo Jo, he says. "All I know is, he missed practice."

Later in the afternoon, I call White in his apartment, a few blocks from the Garden. Soft jazz is playing in the background.

"Going to play tomorrow night?" I ask.

"No," he replies, barely audibly.

"And after that?"

"I've really got nothing to say right now. It depends on them. It's a lot of different things, but I'd rather not say anything now, until I talk with them. I don't want to make it seem as though it's just a matter of me walking away."

Does this have anything to do with what Red said after the game last night? I wonder.

He won't comment, but some of the other Celtics feel it does. White is proud and sensitive, with an almost Oriental concern for face. You do not call him a quitter, even for effect. Especially in front of his teammates, some of whom call him "the Chief."

He enjoys the nickname, and the unspoken deference that comes with it. Hasn't he been here for all of it, coming in as a rookie as

Russell was going out? Wasn't he a building block in the Reconstruction, sitting in the front row of the two championship team pictures, winning the MVP Award for the 1976 playoffs? Hadn't he played in more than four hundred consecutive games, pulling on extra socks over his sore heels and shuffling out, his face impassive, for another night of pushing the ball upcourt?

They said he'd be the next captain, once Havlicek retired, and it made sense, because he was as much of a Celtic symbol as any of them. White was durable and poised, supremely self-confident. And he dressed like a European, out for a night of the theater and a midnight discotheque.

In Manhattan, they talked of Clyde and his wardrobe, his furs and leather, but White was far more understated and classical. His shirts were crisp and fresh, his suits dark and marvelously cut, the shoes gleaming. If it was chilly, he would drape a long, impeccable leather coat over his shoulders, and step lightly into the street.

"He looks better in a T-shirt than most men do in a tuxedo," Bob Ryan would say of him, and it was true. He was Jo Jo, the 'Gyptian, the Chief. "Make sure you stop by his locker after each game," Ryan would counsel me, before I assumed the beat. "You don't have to use what he tells you, necessarily. But he likes to be consulted."

Heinsohn had sensed that upon becoming coach, and he'd taken care to treat him with a lighter touch, defending him when some of the older veterans complained about what they saw as his incomplete sense of team play. You criticized White best if you did it indirectly—and in private.

That was not Auerbach's way, not when a team of well-paid professionals were throwing away games in the first 12 minutes in front of loyal customers.

"I got mad because they lost their intensity and didn't have enough pride to come back and work hard at the end of the game," he tells me, on the way out the door. "It was execution, a lot of it, and attitude. They all want to play a lot of minutes, but they're relying on their reputations. And there are guys coming in, making one-fifth of their salaries, who are eating 'em up. And instead of reacting and getting mad, they're looking for crazy reasons. The guys that are hurting us at this point are the old pros. The old pros are not doing it. They're being intimidated by young, scrappy kids.

They didn't go down fighting last night, and I'm not used to this kind of shit."

So there will be changes made tonight, Heinsohn announces. If White does not turn up, Bing will start alongside Scott. And Maxwell, who came in for 15 minutes against San Antonio and scored 13 points, will walk out for the tap-off instead of Havlicek, who'll return to his sixth-man role.

"We didn't panic when it was 1–6," Heinsohn says. "But now it's 1–8 and we're gonna make some changes with people who want to work hard.

"Just because they made All-Pro—and I'm not directing this at any one player—doesn't mean they're gonna be a starter for us. We are not going by the paper, which says this guy should do this and this guy should do that. I want to see it, and I don't care who has to sit down. I think I've been very patient, but I am gonna find a way for this ballclub to be effective, and to win.

"So we're gonna work on our fast break again, and try to get some movement without the ball instead of standing around. We have it for one game, and then we don't have it anymore. Like, what's that North American animal that people see . . . and don't see? Bigfoot? Well, we see footprints in the snow, but we aren't sure we left them."

Friday the 11th
BOSTON, MASS.

The man from *Sports Illustrated,* just in from Philadelphia and another postmortem on fired coach Gene Shue, was hovering around the Captain's locker two hours early tonight. John Havlicek had guessed he might be. "Hey, another wolf is out," Havlicek chuckled, shaking hands with Curry Kirkpatrick. He had heard the same distant baying as everybody else.

It had been spewing up out of wire-service machines and landing on the front pages of sports sections from New York to Los Angeles for two full days. And they were treating it as if the British royal family had been turned in for public drunkenness.

White was bailing out. Havlicek was sitting down for—gasp!—a rookie. Auerbach was calling his veterans quitters in November. What the hell was going on up there in the Land of the Legend, anyhow?

Nothing that couldn't be cured for one night, anyway. White came back and played brilliantly, scoring 23 points and handing out half-a-dozen assists. Havlicek said he didn't mind sitting down for Maxwell, who scored 21 points, grabbed nine rebounds, made three steals, and blocked three shots in 39 minutes. And the Celtics—praise the Lawd—finally got something at home, a 109–103 decision over Buffalo. What problems?

White had turned up in the dressing room shortly before six o'clock, to light ribbing. "Out of retirement, huh, Chief?" Rowe said, grinning. White merely smiled.

He'd had the meeting with Auerbach during the day. "A short one," Auerbach would say. "And we talked a bit. It all evolved from the fact that Jo Jo was emotional at the time and wanted to do something to shake up the ballclub and get people to recognize their responsibilities. We shook hands, and that was that. It was as though he'd never left."

Afterwards, I check in with White.

"Short meeting, huh?"

He looks up, puzzled. "Short? Two hours?"

"Red said it was only about 10 minutes."

White smirks. "What did you expect him to say?"

It was a psychological ploy, White says, his talk of walking out. He wanted to do something dramatic, something that would shake his teammates out of the doldrums and galvanize them.

"I played my hand," he says, "and that was the trump. I just hoped Red would read me like I read him. It was a bit of a standoff for a while, because we both have our pride."

White knew he wouldn't be suspended—even the fine might be ignored—once he'd had a chance to hash it out with Auerbach. And Auerbach, who'd drafted White out of Kansas eight years before and knew his temperament, was certain that White wouldn't walk out on his Iron-Man streak of consecutive games, the longest in the league.

And the evening ended with the kind of drama they used to throw into the final reel at MGM. With three minutes to play, the game still in doubt, and Scott gone on fouls, White simply took control, put 10 points on the board, and ended it. Stylishly.

For his curtain call, he chose three variations on his full-tilt layup—an unbroken, swerving sprint towards the hoop with an airborne twist, a quick cut, and the traditional Boston Back Door, with White suddenly appearing underneath like a Looney Tunes cartoon character, coming up with the ball and flipping it in.

The Braves, who'd erased debits like 39–22 and 65–54 and once actually saw the lead, never had a chance to take a breath. Down the hall, coach Cotton Fitzsimmons sighed. "It certainly wasn't a good time for us to come into the building." Not with the call of the wild in the distance.

Sunday the 13th
MILWAUKEE, WIS.

Simply no end to milestones this weekend—a road victory only twenty-six days into the season, yet! Celtics 127, Bucks 119, at the Arena tonight, with a ravenous grab for stat sheets in the Boston room afterwards. And for once, there was a plum for everyone.

Eight men found themselves in double figures at the end, and none of it was garbage-time frosting. Heinsohn, looking like a man who'd just received a plenary indulgence from the Pontiff himself, sighed, then grinned broadly.

"One of *our* kind of victories," he would say. "Everybody did something. Everybody functioned. The fast break, the movement, things were happening. Now if we can only keep it up about another two months . . ."

It was a flashback to the early seventies, when Boston played that kind of game so frequently that it was easy to take it for granted. Everybody from Cowens to Wicks managed to materialize with precisely what was needed at exactly the right time, not unlike the Merry Men dropping out of trees and vaulting from behind rocks to give Robin Hood a hand.

When the Celtics fell behind by 10 points in the second quarter, Maxwell loped off the bench to drop in two free throws, make four layups, hit a jumper from the top of the key, sweep in a hook, give layups to Wicks and Cowens, block two shots, and make a steal . . . all in 10 minutes.

When Marques Johnson, the Bucks' graceful and muscular rookie, threatened to tear the game away in the final quarter, here came Wicks to shut him down.

And when the Celtics needed a basket to get it into overtime, Cowens merely sent Havlicek back-door—the quintessential Boston solution—with 34 seconds left. Two jumpers by White busted it open almost as soon as overtime began.

Down the hall, Milwaukee coaches Don Nelson and John Killilea shook their heads, all too familiar with the pattern. They've created somewhat of a Celtics West approach out here, with the fast break, the opportunistic defense, and the role players, from inside rebounders to outside shooters to red-haired centers. Beating Boston at their own game has become a passion with them, and both men are glum afterwards.

"I don't know what *their* problem's been," Nelson says.

Friday the 18th
BOSTON, MASS.

Lloyd Free had remembered the sound from Game 3 of last year's playoffs here, the derisive *SHO-O-O-O-T* that tumbled down from the Garden balcony whenever and wherever he touched the ball. So Lloyd Free came out early for his pregame warmup tonight.

"When I came here today, I figured if they said, 'Shoot, shoot' again, well, I was gonna shoot it for them," he is saying, after another one of his 1812 Overture productions. "And I guess it worked, 'cause I didn't hear anything after I made a couple. Except maybe 'Don't shoot.' "

And after the howitzer fire and church bells had ceased, Free had himself 29 points and Philadelphia—now the Brotherly Love quintet under new coach Billy Cunningham—had themselves a 121–112 victory that dashed a pail of cold water on the Boston resurgence.

Nobody here had to be reminded that it was Free who'd won the two most important games of last year's playoff series (the third and the seventh), simply by doing what he does best—tossing in high, arching bombs. *FRE-E-E-E-E-E,* PA announcer Dave Zinkoff would shriek, when he was putting them up at the Spectrum, where he is a funky folk hero, along with The Doctah and Darryl Dawkins. "The Prince of Midair," they call him.

Here, where the pick-and-roll is considered an art form and rocket launchers are made to feel ashamed, Free is damned as a shooting Sodomite, the symbolic conductor of this strut-and-glitter pregame show that passes for a professional club.

Bob Ryan, who preaches five-man basketball with the zeal of a Baptist revivalist and the logic of a Jesuit professor, detests Free and everything he represents. In Ryan's running list of the Five Most Hateful Humans, Free ranks second, behind Adolf Hitler.

Actually, Free is a perfectly affable person—a twenty-four-year-old jumping jack guard who came out of the Brownsville section of Brooklyn, and is going prematurely bald. He plays street ball with ghetto kids, talks with enthusiasm and wit after games, and, he says, is quite friendly to the elderly.

If you look it up, you will also find he averages more assists per game than Havlicek . . . a great barroom bet. Mostly, what he does is torture Boston, who has no guard that can stop him. Not White, not Stacom, not Scott. Tonight, Free gets 14 points in the second quarter, then comes on with 13 more in the last nine minutes to tear it wide open.

And each time, the crowd reaction is the same . . . a mocking *SHO-O-O-O-O-T* as Free scrunches down behind a pick and prepares for the launch, and a deflated *U-H-H-H-H* as the ball drops cleanly, 30 feet away. Something is going wrong in the Standards and Practices Division of professional basketball, Bostonians feel. And the 76ers, with pats on the rump from Cunningham, are pulling farther away in the divisional race.

Friday the 25th
BOSTON, MASS.

There was a time when this game would have been preceded by a twenty-four-hour period of prayer and fasting, impassioned debates in the college saloons along Commonwealth Avenue and fistfights in the Garden balcony between quarters.

You never had to ask when the Knicks were coming to town. They were always here, in the symbolic guise of the B.U. sophomore from Queens. He was the one in the corner proclaiming, with nasal authority, that the 1973 Knicks (The Open Man!) made all that Boston team-minded dogma seem simple-minded by comparison.

Cowens? Give me Willis. Havlicek? Bill Bradley, the Rhodes Scholar. Silas? I'll take DeBusschere. It was the essential Red Sox–Yankee clan war moved indoors and intensified, because the meetings were fewer (seldom more than eight a season), and because the playoff system, for three straight years, brought them together with the conference title at stake.

The B.U. sophomore is still here—as a second-year law student—and there is still an occasional gallery brawl, but the competitive quality that gave the rivalry (the oldest in the league) its edge has vanished. New York has missed the playoffs two straight years, coach Red Holzman (the Manhattan Auerbach) has been dismissed, and the Gulf & Western people are spending money wildly to recapture what has gone. Lucas, DeBusschere, Bradley, and Reed (the new coach) have all retired. Walt Frazier has been sent to Cleveland. The only ring-wearing survivors are Earl Monroe and Phil Jackson, and both are in their thirties. Time passes on 33rd Street just as it does here.

Still, the sight of the orange-and-blue shirts, the presence of Reed and Monroe, and a capacity crowd divided between True Believers and Nasal Authorities is enough to stir the ashes for one night, especially since there will be no rematch here until March 5. A twenty-two-team league with equality for all will do that to a rivalry.

For 24 minutes, it is Hibernian heaven. The Celtics, who've now put together home victories over Atlanta and Houston into a modest four-of-six streak, come out running and roll up 69 points (and a 19-point lead) at halftime. The shooting is a fat and sassy 56 percent, and seven players have at least eight points apiece. Heinsohn, delighted, makes the mistake of mentioning it to them.

"A super first half," he will groan later, "and then we pull our own plug. We had played rock 'em, sock 'em, the best half of basketball all year. And we come into the locker room and say, hey, terrific, great half. And it all stops."

And "The Magic Show," courtesy of Mr. Monroe, begins, giving Garden running scorekeeper Happy Fine a chance to dust off some rare terminology. Overhead runner. Driving fallaway scoop. Whirlaway layup.

After three quarters, "the Pearl" has 17 of his 37 points, Cowens is wearing five fouls, and the lead has shrunk to 93–90. And suddenly, it is 1973 again, and 15,000 people are on their feet for the last 12 minutes. Make that 17. It goes into overtime, naturally, after Boston has the ball for the final 44 seconds and gets only two forced jump shots, one by Sidney Wicks as time runs out.

All of which makes caution the byword in overtime. But as New York lets the 24-second clock expire one time up the floor, and gives up the ball on an offensive foul the next, Charlie Scott makes a twisting bank shot, Cowens adds a tip and two free throws, and it's 117–111.

Should be over, right? So Boston lets the 24-second clock run out on themselves, Bob McAdoo cuts it to 119–117, and Jo Jo White fouls him in the backcourt with 12 seconds left. Tie game. Again.

So John Havlicek inbounds to White, who looks for Cowens for a "special," and winds up getting fouled by Jim Cleamons. "Terrible call, naturally," Monroe says. Cleamons is a little more vehement about it. "Why didn't they have the guts to call it earlier in the game?" he fumes later.

"If it's not going to be a foul in the first quarter, it shouldn't be a foul in overtime. If I'm holding and pushing him, yeah. I can't impede his progress. But I just had my hands on him. That's not a foul in the NBA. It won't be tomorrow."

So White makes the shots, Monroe misses at the buzzer, and the B.U. sophomores have something to mull over for three months.

"Hell of a way to win a game like that," Cowens says. "On a silly-ass foul in the backcourt. Still, you don't want to disappoint all those New York college students. Gotta keep 'em coming to the ball game."

Saturday the 26th
KANSAS CITY, MO.

The sanity always seems to hold up as far as O'Hare Airport, until we have to change planes for the Heartlands. And then, it's as though the Celtics fall through some distorted mirror on the edge of the Land of Oz, and end up spending a macabre evening in an echo chamber in the middle of the stockyards.

Last year, on the way to a one-night stand here before a week on the Coast, Norm Cook got himself lost in the maze of O'Hare lobbies during the layover. They had to hold the flight and bring him out onto the tarmac as the jet was backing out. When the bus pulled away from the terminal at Kansas City International—a good country drive from the city—Dave Cowens was in an airport rest room. The cab fare was $20.

And 30 minutes before tapoff at Kemper Arena, Tom Boswell came bouncing, barechested, into the press room, looking for a dime to phone the hotel. His jersey was still in his room.

Tonight was just the second reel, as the Kings, losing for 35 minutes, brought down Boston in the last 49 seconds, 110–108, and completed a daffy day that caught up everybody, from Cowens to Kansas City guard Lucius Allen, in its weird tangle.

Cowens, who apparently had his luggage (and uniform) stolen along the way, wound up wearing number 54 with a high-cut sneaker on one foot and a low-cut on the other. "It's gone," he would shrug. "I don't have anything. Nowhere to be found."

And Allen, driving casually along Interstate 70 to the arena, found himself in the middle of a freak ice storm, slammed through a guard rail and ended up being towed, as the game went on without him.

"The police told me there were maybe fifteen accidents already ahead of me," he said later, "and probably twenty behind. I didn't think I was going to make the game, because everything had to move so slowly."

So Kansas City wound up sticking rookie Otis Birdsong in the starting lineup, and using chunky forward Bill Robinzine when power man Richard Washington sprained an ankle in the first quarter. And the Celtics led comfortably throughout—or until Allen scrambled into his uniform and turned up on the bench 15 minutes from the final buzzer.

Under his direction, the Kings scored the next 11 points, took a 91–86 lead, then rallied again in the last minute, with Birdsong writing the final two paragraphs.

They sounded suspiciously like Lewis Carroll, but then, many visits to this place sound that way. The road record is now 1–7, and Heinsohn was so furious afterwards that he moved his folding chair into the corridor and conducted his postmortem there.

"We played a strong first half again," he said, "and then we folded our tents again. We missed key baskets. We never made an important shot. When we get everybody involved, we play well. When we don't . . . I'm not very happy with this."

When we hit the parking lot, the ice is half an inch thick on windshields and highways. Virtually every decent restaurant is closed, and nobody, absolutely nobody, is on the streets. Atlanta and 70-degree weather never looked so good.

Tuesday the 29th
ATLANTA, GA.

They no longer have anything to say about these persistently flawed evenings. They no longer know what to say. They come out of the showers after another empty second half and dress quietly and speak in whispers, if they speak at all.

How do you explain a veteran basketball team, chock-a-block with scorers, that shoots 73 percent in the first half and leads by 13 points—and scores 37 points the rest of the night?

How do you explain twenty-nine turnovers and only three offensive rebounds in one evening, and just one basket in seven minutes during the final quarter? How do you explain a 108–101 loss to a group of Hawks who had three starters hurt and a reserve guard missing?

"I don't know," Dave Cowens murmured, after the Celtics lost their eighth road game in nine tonight. "I just don't know."

This was a game that should have been chalked up on the plane down from Kansas City. Boston had beaten these people 131–105 at the Garden two weeks ago, when they'd thought they'd turned the corner. They'd had two days of rest here.

And in the last five minutes, when injuries and foul trouble had forced Hubie Brown to put a crazy-quilt lineup of Tom McMillen, Ron Behagen, Claude Terry, Tony Robertson, and John Brown on the floor, it was there for the taking.

All but Brown had been considered excess baggage elsewhere. All but Brown had played for a different team last year. But when the crunch came, they outrebounded the Celtics down the stretch, outsmarted them, and outscored them, 35–20.

It enraged Heinsohn, who had another sputtering session in the Omni hallway. And it pushed the elder statesmen among the squad deeper into confusion and depression.

They think they have been going out enthusiastically and working hard. Hell, the halftime scores tell them that. They do a full Dale Carnegie in the dressing room during intermission, with constructive criticism, whacks on the rump, and mutual reinforcement for all.

And then they come out for the third quarter and it all vanishes in a vapor trail. Balls are thrown out of bounds. The rebounding dries up. The 24-second clock ticks down to the dregs and Scott or White is still pounding the ball at the top of the key, waiting for some-body—anybody—to move. Three minutes pass without a basket. Seven minutes. And an 81–73 lead becomes a 90–84 hole, as it did tonight.

The season is nearly a quarter gone now, and Boston will step off their Delta jet tomorrow noon with a 6–12 record and not a single road victory in regulation time to their credit. And Philadelphia, which few Bostonians even consider a true basketball team, is eight games ahead in the Atlantic division race.

On the way to the press room, I pass Havlicek in the showers, standing alone.

"I used to think I knew something about basketball," he says softly. "Now, I don't know."

DECEMBER

Two H-a-a-ppy Guards

Friday the 2nd
BOSTON, MASS.

They had come—11,000 of them—because it was Friday night, because they were giving away team pennants, and because there was a victory over Chicago here two nights ago that might have signaled an awakening.

They had left—most of them—with six minutes to play, grabbing for coats and tossing curses over their shoulders. The booing began well before halftime, when the deficit was already 57–39, and they never really stopped.

Hadn't the Seattle SuperSonics lost seventeen of their first twenty-two games? Hadn't coach Bob Hopkins been fired after only six weeks on the job? Wasn't that J. J. Johnson, who had no future here, starting for them at quick forward?

In another year, this would have been the bugle call for a light-running Boston massacre, an old-time garbage orgy with 140 points on the board and confidence restored on all fronts. But everybody, from Auerbach to the gallery diehard from West Roxbury, is beginning to realize that there has never been a year like this in this city. The final was 111–89, and new coach Lenny Wilkens would say, no, he really hadn't had any time to scout Boston. They just wanted to run and rebound and run again, and apply a little defense in between. By the third quarter, the lead was 28 points, and Sonic guards Gus Williams and Dennis Johnson had become kamikaze sprinters.

"The boos were deserved," Heinsohn would admit. "It's not happening. It's just not happening. Forget the system after tonight. We're back to personnel problems. We've got to find out who can play and who wants to play." Down the hall, J. J. Johnson was grinning. Hugely.

Monday the 5th
BOSTON, MASS.

"We're not announcing lineups now until before the ball game," the Hawk says this morning, as the players head for their post-workout shower at Lexington. "It'll depend on practices, the last ball game, and the competition. It'll go from practice to practice, from game to game."

Only those who've bathed in the blood of the lamb, whose motives are pure and consciences clear will be allowed to start these days. Almost everybody else . . . specifically all of the regulars except for Cowens, who has been Atlas Reborn these last few weeks . . . has been banished to the bench as Heinsohn unwraps Experiment number 7A.

Jo Jo White and Charlie Scott, the backcourt anchors for two years (Belmondo and Delon in *Borsalino*, if you wanted a comparative image) will sit down for the league's only seventy-one-year-old combination, Havlicek and Bing. Curtis Rowe, who's started every game since the opener, will vanish for Saunders, whose unquestioning enthusiasm has always intrigued Heinsohn. And Maxwell, whose defensive flaws are becoming painfully obvious, will be gone for Boswell.

"Is there anybody you're happy with on this team?" I ask him. Heinsohn considers a moment. "Satch Sanders," he replies.

You wanted it cold, without hors d'oeuvres? Tom Heinsohn was serving it to your taste today. He is not happy with his professional basketball players, their attitude . . . or their record (7–14), which is on pace with that of the 1969–1970 transition club that lost forty-eight games and finished twenty-six behind New York.

He hears the same disgusted hoots from paying customers that you do. He sees the same bizarre disparity between the roster and the standings, where only Boe's Jests, down there in Piscataway, New Jersey, have managed fewer victories this fall.

"We had on paper a team that had seven All-Stars," Heinsohn admits. "You would think that seven All-Stars would have gotten it together by now, right? But they just aren't doing it. We have people who are not contributing consistently. Oh, a game here and there they'll do it, but there is not the dedication to concentration that you have to have."

There are not a lot of things. There has not been a willingness to work hard for 48 minutes. There are not enough people who want to do the uncomfortable little things that win games—like banging boards, moving without the ball, playing knuckles-down defense. There are not enough people who care enough for each other or a proud tradition to sit down and discuss their inadequacies, and work toward constructive solutions.

There are too many people with too much to say, and more self-styled leaders than the Five Nations of the Iroquois. There are too many people with too many pointed fingers. And not enough willing to say, "This is a lousy basketball team, and I'm part of the reason."

There are not enough people who are really disturbed by the booing at home, by the horrible losses to the Atlantas and New Jerseys and Seattles, by the postgame tirades from Heinsohn and Red Auerbach. There are not enough real Celtics anymore.

"I think a lot of people have been conditioned to rationalize away losing," Heinsohn said. "Some people are used to losing, maybe, but I'm not. I'm tired of making excuses. There are no excuses left."

On December 6, with a healthy veteran ballclub, there can be none. Any professional who isn't in shape after seven weeks doesn't deserve to be in the league, whether or not he made it to training camp. Any veteran who can't master the variations of an essentially simple system after twenty-one games should be ashamed of himself.

"The system isn't that difficult," said Heinsohn. "It's not that complicated. When we apply ourselves, it produces some great things. And that's what's so frustrating about all this."

Quite simply, the Celtics have been approaching most games with all the zeal of a welder on a Soviet assembly line. Work one full day, ease off two more at lunchtime, and bang in sick on Friday. It is the attitude of a man who has no incentive. It is the attitude of a man who has a lucrative long-term contract, half a dozen years in, and a general manager who is reluctant to trade anybody in haste. In Australia, fat cats say, "Bang the bell, Jack, I'm on the bus." But this bus is going nowhere.

And the sad fact is that not enough Celtics seem to care. They take a humiliating beating at the Omni, shrug, and resume their card games and bitch about the coach. And a season starts sliding into the sewer.

Already you hear the whispers. After the loss at Washington Saturday night, when Heinsohn had made his personnel changes, one benched Celtic laughed them off.

"Hey, man," he'd said. "There's no *W*s and *L*s on the paycheck." Before long, that quote appears in note columns all over America (attributed to Rowe), as evidence of the new Celtic spirit.

Tuesday the 6th
NEW YORK, N.Y.

The ending could have been the finest anti-Gotham fantasy material. You had 17,000 worried people inside Madison Square Garden tonight. You had overtime. You had the Celtics trailing by a point and Joseph Henry White driving the baseline with five seconds to play.

All you needed was the Johnny Most voice overlay, hoarse and urgent. And the winning basket. But in this oddly hollow season, there are no fantasy endings and few victories. And most of the evenings end amid whispered bitterness.

So White's shot was deflected, the Knicks escaped with a 122–119 decision . . . and White let his emotions spill afterwards. He had scored 27 points, but he had been on the bench at the beginning, along with Charlie Scott. If they thought he was valuable enough to

DAVE COWENS "He would run for 48 minutes, the legs pumping hard. sweat pouring, the red hair flopping."

IRV LEVIN "He dropped by every so often, a modish Californian in his fifties with a year-round tan, sculpted dark hair, and a lovely young wife. There were times he reminded me of a Back Bay slumlord."

RED AUERBACH "Ever since Walter Brown had died, it had been Auerbach who had held the thing together, Auerbach who had had to sustain everything with his growl and his reputation and his shrewdness."

JOHN HAVLICEK "He could play forward or guard, shifting back and forth at a moment's notice, running...always running...yet never seeming to break a sweat. He was Hondo, John Wayne in green sneakers, ready for whatever the hell came up."

BOSTON GARDEN, circa 1960. "To us, it was the sporting Louvre, a haunting smoky cockpit that said vertical the moment you walked in, balcony rising upon balcony, seats wedged in everywhere, and all of it overlooking a wooden parquet floor."

TOM BOSWELL "He floated as an unfettered spirit, seemingly unconcerned with trading deadlines, playing time or the waiver wire... sometimes, he was the Wizard of Boz, showing you flashes of brilliance that justified everything they'd said about him."

DAVE BING "At thirty-four, he had no illusions. All he wanted was a chance to finish his career with purpose and dignity, contributing ...somewhere."

KEVIN STACOM "He had more names than anybody in the dressing room. He was the Stakeman, the Snake, Pit (because he sweated freely during a game) but mostly he was the Bird."

DON CHANEY "He was the Duck (what else did you call a kid named Donald?). He was the defensive guard in the role scheme, swatting balls away with oversized arms, rebounding faithfully."

SIDNEY WICKS "He was still a newcomer, and as such, was placed on the same kind of stylistic probation that Charlie Scott had had to endure. He wore the green jersey, but was he a Celtic?"

JO JO WHITE "They said he'd be the next captain, once Havlicek retired, and it made sense, because he was as much of a Celtic symbol as any of them. White was durable and poised, supremely self-confident."

TOM HEINSOHN "He was an Anglo-Saxon type in the best sense—direct, colorful, blunt—and he believed in working where there was no obstructed view."

CHARLIE SCOTT "He was always soaring; it was a combination of his hyperactive nature and springy legs."

CEDRIC MAXWELL "An odd collection of arms and legs who could shoot and dribble and rebound and run."

TOM SANDERS "He was reticent, polished, shadowy, and precise. You could imagine him coming out of the Opera into a foggy Paris night circa 1894 ... the benevolent diabolist."

JOHN HAVLICEK "He went out to midcourt for two deep bows, the noise tumbling down on him, and then, lips trembling, tears brimming, Havlicek ran to the sidelines, waving his hand in a circle above his head."

take the final shot, he reasoned, why wasn't he valuable enough to go out for the tap?

Heinsohn had explained it before the game. White was the quarterback by position and a leader by tenure, but the job was simply not getting done. His shooting had fallen off badly, yet White seemed unwilling or unable to get the ball to teammates who could score. So until further notice . . .

White, humiliated, fell silent, glancing up resentfully when Heinsohn motioned him into the game as a reserve. "I'm human," he would say tonight. "I've got feelings. This is my ninth year and my basketball ability on and off the court has never been questioned. I deserve to be treated like a professional.

"It's tough to deal with what's happening. How the hell should I act? How the hell is someone supposed to perform after he's yelled and screamed at? I did better tonight because I played more, but how are you going to do well when you're on the bench for long periods? When there is pressure on me, I respond to pressure. But I don't respond when I feel that I'm not needed."

In the morning, Auerbach will see White's feelings spread all over the New York *Daily News*—New York writers have a sixth sense for controversy bubbling up in a locker room—and will shake his head. That was Auerbach's Second Commandment (Thou Shalt Not Be Unprofessional was the First)— you didn't go public with private matters. If you were dissatisfied with your playing time, Scott's 30-foot rainbows, or the Hawk's strategies, you hashed it out one-on-one. You didn't go to the papers with it, and certainly not the Manhattan papers. That just produced problems you didn't need, and who the hell out there cared, anyway? Celtics didn't do it. Period.

Wednesday the 7th
BOSTON, MASS.

They say you can sense his presence first by Auerbach, that he becomes abrupt and peevish around the office whenever the owner comes to town to check on his investment. It may be Auerbach's tradition, crafted by his blueprints and his material, but it is Irv Levin's team. And what he's been seeing in the Scoreboard pages recently concern him as much as a plummeting Dow Jones.

He drops by every so often, a modish Californian in his fifties with a year-round tan, sculpted dark hair and a lovely young wife. Levin was a pilot in World War II and he is involved in motion pictures now, partners with Sam Schulman, who owns the Seattle franchise.

"A man of creative talents and staggering achievements," murmurs the team press guide, yet he knows the Boston writers by name, which I find vaguely unsettling. Why would he want to?

"Some people think I'm trying to be the Charlie Finley of basketball," Levin will tell me, "but that's far from the truth. I'm an active owner, but I'm not a basketball expert. I'm a businessman."

And he is talking as a businessman tonight, standing in a corner of the dressing room after a sluggish 113–109 decision over Kansas City, surrounded by microphones and notepads. He was at Madison Square Garden last night for the overtime loss, and read White's complaints this morning.

He had spent the afternoon talking with Auerbach, Levin says. They have been talking for three days, exploring options. They want to make a move, and have been talking to other clubs. "One thing for sure," he says. "We're just not going to lie back and keep losing."

They almost lost again tonight. Again, there were the catcalls from above. Again, there was a double-digit deficit early. Again, there was the Hawk, livid, yelling about defense and rebounding and alertness during timeouts.

It had come down to the last two minutes, before a bad Otis Birdsong shot, an offensive foul on King forward Scott Wedman, a traveling call on giant center Tom Burleson, and two Havlicek free throws finished things—mercifully.

"Boring," was the verdict from Charlie Scott, who, along with White, was restored to the starting five.

"Did it make any difference to you, starting again?" I ask him. "Naw," Scott replies. "Maybe to him," nodding across the room in White's direction. "Could be sitting down tomorrow."

The whole season has taken on all the certainty and structure of a

Looney Tunes picnic, with Daffy Duck stepping in Elmer Fudd's potato salad and Wile E. Coyote chasing Roadrunner over a cliff. Why make plans? Why worry about whether the Hawk is going to use you or whether Levin is going to have you shipped to Denver before lunch? This season is beyond rational analysis already, and we haven't even seen the Coast yet.

Thursday the 8th
BOSTON, MASS.

"You might not want to go in there just yet," says Frankie Challant, emerging from the locker room with armloads of wet practice gear and basketballs. "Hawk is telling Stevie he's been let go."

The room is empty by the time I enter, except for Havlicek, who's stuffing equipment into a bag, and Kuberski, who's sitting on a bench in jeans, shaking his head.

"Sorry," I say. "You got anything you want to say? For the record, I mean."

"Well, I didn't really think I was given much of a shot," he says. "I played only 14 minutes in three games. Just one of those things. A matter of economics, I guess. But here they say they want to make a change, and they make a change with the eleventh man on a team."

Kevin Stacom, the word goes, is the new man. He'll sign his original contract and be back in uniform for tomorrow night's game with Portland. "At least they brought back a buddy," Kuberski says, over lunch.

Which is exactly what Stacom said two weeks ago, when *he'd* been released and they'd brought back Kuberski for a look at his newly healed hand.

The ritual, as it is in the National Football League, is indirect. The Patriots ask you to stop by with your playbook. The Celtics, in the person of the Hawk, advise you to go down to 150 Causeway Street and see Red. This can mean anything, of course, but rarely does.

Auerbach had been sick the last time, and Stacom had gone down to the Parker House for a promotional All-Star game luncheon at which attendance was required. Somehow, promotions director Mike Cole let it slip during the meal, and Stacom, furious, had walked stiff-legged out of the room and towards the elevators.

The whole shuffle was merely a formality, Kuberski guessed. You didn't want to risk a lawsuit by waiving an injured player before he'd had a chance to come back. And it seemed a good gamble that nobody would scoop up Stacom during his two weeks in limbo. But by league rule, anybody on a roster after the end of business today had to be paid for the entire year. It *was* a business, after all.

Still, it chafed at Kuberski to look at the unproductive potpourri of power forwards Boston had on hand, all of them playing with variable degrees of intensity, and then to find himself the most expendable.

"Hell, I can play better than some of *those* bastards," he'd say, laughing. Or play harder, anyway. Although he had a nice straight-arm jumper from 15 feet or so, he wasn't a classic shooting forward by any measure. Kuberski was a banger, a good inside man if you wanted a rebound grabbed or an elbow plunked in somebody's ribs. He would get up on people, defensive mouth twisted into a grimace, arms waving. He would bump and sprint and dive on the floor. Whenever an evening became too placid for Heinsohn's tastes, he'd glance along the bench and nod. Stevie.

He had always been there . . . or almost always. Kuberski had been drafted out of Bradley as a junior, coming in with White, and played regularly until New Orleans plucked him off in the 1974 expansion draft. From there, he had been shuttled to Milwaukee and Buffalo, finally winding up back on Causeway Street for the 1976 championship season.

They loved his style here, and he was a popular endorsement figure. Second best Polish athlete in Boston, you'd tell him. Hell, *you* ought to be doing the kielbasa ads instead of Yastrzemski. How many rings does *he* have?

Kuberski had two. He was a fine playoff player, going out for the tap to set tempo up front ("Designated Starter," he'd chuckle), then coming in later to bump and grind a bit. On a teamful of role players, his fell midway between hired gun and village smithy.

He came with big hands and a mustache ("Stash," they called him), and when he shaved it off one day, Wicks administered the new nickname. Jo Bob, because he looked like a member of the Walton Family.

Actually, with the denims and blue-knitted cap he'd wear to practice, he more resembled R. P. McMurphy, a beer-drinking, good-humored resident of the *Cuckoo's Nest*. Pro basketball was uncertain at best and peripatetic by nature, and Kuberski figured you might as well enjoy the hell out of it. You could become a salesman later.

On the road, he was the one who'd dial your room from a bar somewhere at five o'clock. "This is Kuberski," you'd hear, over the booming of the jukebox, "and we're here having some beers, and . . ."

Around nine, you'd head for dinner, and if there was a hole-in-the-wall somewhere with a pinball machine (the Spot Tavern in Portland was a favorite), Kuberski knew about it. The year before on St. Patrick's Eve, a bunch of us had gone to Butch McGuire's in Chicago. With a choice of Guinness or Irish coffee on the line for stakes, Kuberski organized a pinball tournament with a few of the locals. We never paid for a drink until closing time. At four A.M., we were having steak and eggs somewhere. Hangin' tough, Kuberski would call it, nodding serenely. He was a genuine throwback to a day when the game was played for fun, because you realized it wasn't going to last. Now, at thirty, it's ending for him . . . and he knows it.

"Hell," he shrugs, when I mention Europe as an alternative. "Gotta go to work sometime."

Auerbach, sitting pensively behind his desk amid a swirl of smoke, is denying them abruptly. Flatly. Categorically. Adverbally.

"All the rumors are nothing," he mutters, waving the cigar for emphasis, an hour before the tapoff with Portland. "Absolutely unfounded . . . about Charlie or anybody else. We're still talking, but nobody's come up with anything we're interested in. Everything's the same."

The trade whispers have been growing, ever since Levin came into the dressing room Wednesday and said the club was "definitely inclined to make a move or two." Now, a Boston television station has mentioned Scott for Mark Olberding, San Antonio's bruising young forward. And tonight, word of a three-way deal among the Celtics, Denver, and Houston—again involving Scott—is floating about.

Upstairs, Scott is pulling on his uniform, one eye on the evening news and the fresh speculation. I ask him if *he* feels he's being sized up for trade bait.

"Do I feel that?" he repeats. "Yeah. I don't think Red wants to. At least that's what he told me. I don't think I'm being immature thinking that, just realistic. It's just that everything points to that. It's the general situation. If you're going to get somebody of value, you've got to give something of value. Simple as that."

He could look at a roster as well as you could. Somebody would go if the losing continued, and Scott would tell you, frankly, that he saw no reason for an immediate turnaround.

"We would like to believe so," he says, when optimists stop by with silver linings, "but I'm not a believer in rhetoric, and all we've done so far is talk. As a team, we just don't play well together. We've got talent, sure. And people say, well, why don't you win, then? If we really knew that, we'd win, wouldn't we?"

Scott knew what Levin had said, and he also realized who was marketable and who wasn't. The Celtics weren't going to part with a Cowens or a Havlicek, and who really wanted their tenth or eleventh player? You traded either one of the power forwards or a starting guard. And if it came down to Scott or Jo Jo White, who was going to stay and who would go? No question . . . not in Scott's mind. White was the veteran, with more service stripes than any Celtic except Havlicek. He had been mentioned as the next captain. He had carried the club last year. Scott, comparatively, was the newcomer, having arrived in 1975. What was three years in a city where longevity was measured in decades? They could be diplomatic about it in the front office, but Scott's instincts and experience told him otherwise.

So Scott would shrug, and bounce onto the court for warmups ... and two hours later, a move became inevitable. The result—it could hardly be called a score—was Portland 118, Boston 87, and it was every bit as sorry as it looks. The Celtics were simply never in the same building, falling behind 11–2, then 19–8, on the way to a 20-point deficit five minutes into the second half.

It was a negation of everything the Celtics have ever stood for. They were toyed with from the tapoff and didn't seem to care. They were embarrassed in front of people who have believed in them ever since Auerbach lit his first victory cigar. And Auerbach saw it all. So did his boss.

And when it was done, and the booing came down mocking and cold, Auerbach, Irv Levin, and Heinsohn went into the trainer's room and talked for an hour with the door closed. Still you could hear Heinsohn's voice, strident and angry, in the farthest corner of the dressing room.

When the door opened, Levin and Auerbach said, "No comment," and headed for the team offices. Heinsohn would face the press.

"We had a long discussion," he says. "About everything. We're going to have a long practice tomorrow—a closed practice—and we're gonna practice and we're gonna practice. Because I've tried every conceivable combination that my feeble mind can think of, and nothing's worked.

"I think at this point, these people ... maybe these people don't want to be with us. Attitude? I think attitude has got to be a very definite point now. This team has been in turmoil for one reason or another since opening day. We've got two guys who are like oil and water and another that's a piece of algae eating at them."

Heinsohn is not used to open dissension in the ranks, to half speed, half-hearted efforts, to 31-point losses at home. "I wasn't here for the Chuck Connors era, when they ripped down the baskets," he says, "but this is one of my all-time low points. I was here for the glory days. It used to be on this team that John Havlicek would lead by example. That's why he's been out there so much lately ... to try to recapture some of that. But it's an awful job for somebody thirty-seven years old. He's doing all he humanly can do. I wish some of my other people would do that."

One man did tonight—Dave Cowens. While his teammates were bagging it all around him, he fought a splendid personal duel with Bill Walton, winding up with 27 points and nine rebounds to Walton's 21 and 15. But the battle was decided elsewhere, and it was decided early. The statistics, from end to end of the box score, reflected total Portland domination. "I couldn't believe how mixed up the Celtics looked on the court," Blazer forward Bob Gross would say. Neither could 15,000 other people . . . including the man who signs the checks.

Thursday the 15th
BOSTON, MASS.

And then there was the one about how the Big Guy comes to play this year and everybody else takes a sabbatical. Dave Cowens has heard it before.

"The idea is that I'm doing my job," he nods, when I mention it to him after practice, "and implying that the other guys aren't. And that's not the truth. I'm inclined to say that when a team's losing, nobody's doing enough. Like Pete Maravich. Maybe he does his job scoring all those points, but his teams never win. Doesn't mean a damn."

But now that the Celtics are losing and paying customers are heading for the subway with eight minutes to play on Friday nights, it has become fashionable to regard Cowens as a red-haired Horatius, holding off the Etruscans while his mates scramble back across the bridge. Which Cowens thinks is absurd, and he's a little worried about my doing a feature story along that line.

"Some of the fellas read the papers pretty closely, as you know," he tells me. "I wouldn't want them to get the wrong idea. Besides, when you lose, you lose as a squad and the singling out of individuals is ridiculous, either in a winning situation or a losing one."

More than any of them, Cowens had relished the professional

camaraderie of the early seventies, when you glanced up from your dressing stall and saw a man you admired and trusted in every corner of the room. You didn't need scouting reports, Gipper speeches, or est sessions. You knew Silas was going to get you the rebound, that Sanders was going to force his man baseline, that Nelson was going to set the pick.

Played that way, with intelligence and selflessness, basketball was a joy, and Cowens had looked forward eagerly to game days. Now, the faces had changed, the play was frequently self-centered and careless, and victories were greeted with relief. Watching Cowens come into the dressing room before a game reminded you of a child who arose on December 26 to find the living room strewn with torn paper, the stocking empty, the toys familiar. Just once, I thought, he'd like to come in here and see Silas and Nellie and Havlicek tying their shoelaces, wisecracking.

Instead, Cowens finds himself the focal point. Silas is in Seattle, Nelson is coaching the Bucks, Havlicek is thirty-seven years old. White is hurting and disillusioned. The brotherhood is disintegrating around him, and every night, the demands are heavier. Cowens is playing 42 minutes a night now, more than anybody but Truck Robinson in New Orleans and Bernard King at New Jersey. He leads the Celtics in every important category—scoring, free-throw percentage, assists, rebounding. He has outplayed Moses Malone, Wes Unseld, Dan Issel, and dueled Bill Walton to a standoff. And Cowens has done that for twenty-five nights, banging and crashing and daring a man to run with him for two hours.

He has been a glowing show-and-tell example to a club that badly needs one, a club that all too often has favored rhetoric over rebounding. Cowens has always found that distasteful.

"No sense in talking," he tells me. "I'm not a guy who talks. My contribution is to go out and be rough-and-tumble and exude enthusiasm and all those nice words they use to say you're playing crazy."

Some people had begun to think that period was over—the wild hair flopping, the sweat dripping, elbows flaring, eyes flashing. That his leave-taking last November hinted at a disaffection with the team or the game or both. Cowens knew better, and when the season had ended at the Spectrum last May, he'd changed a few things.

He spent more time in Kentucky, messin' with friends. He

delegated much of the busy work at his summer camp to others. He bought a basementful of Nautilus machines and worked on them. "Life was just a whole lot more relaxing," he decided. And when he came to camp in September, he came trim and rested and eager, the way he wanted to. Now, he is giving what Dave Cowens has always given—42 minutes of gravel and spit a night with the enthusiasm of a high-school sophomore dressing for his first varsity game. Yet he has found himself in the middle of a season and a feeling he's never known before.

"The *most* frustrating," he nods. "Yeah. And it's still going on. It's like everything is going so badly, sometimes you want to say, hell, it's not worth it. But then, you sit down and say, well, if you wanted a challenge . . .

"Instead of giving up, you say, well, I've never been involved with this situation before. How do you deal with this one? You sit back and evaluate your own attitudes and performance, instead of saying, well, I'll make this excuse or that excuse or it's this guy or that guy. I think if everybody does that, you can come out of it all right."

Cowens looks at the schedule, at ten straight games away from the Garden, and he sees winnable ones. He looks around the dressing room and sees talented people who should win them. He sees playoffs that should be made, and a title that could be won.

"It's really like a mind battle, you know? Like those kids involved in the school busing. They can say, hey, there's no way we can learn anything under those circumstances. They can give up, and that's a legitimate, reasonable out. They've really got to work hard to learn something in a situation that's not really their fault. But if they want to make the sacrifice, they can do it."

Cowens pulls on his work shirt and raises his eyebrows, heading for the door. "And there's no reason why we can't look at it the same way."

Since this is the last free day the Celtics will have in Boston before Christmas, they've scheduled the annual team party for the Garden this afternoon.

Over the years, Bostonians had become used to seeing the ritual pictures in the papers the next morning—toddlers bouncing basketballs, the presents clustered around a tree in the background, and Auerbach off to the side, beaming.

You have your family, it said, and we have ours, too. We have a

Russell and a Heinsohn and a bunch of Joneses, blacks and whites together, and we were here when you were a child and we'll be around for your children.

It was good public relations, all of it, yet the hype seemed minimal. The players, their wives and children, really *did* like each other, you felt. You'd see Estelle White and Beth Havlicek chatting in the stands between halves, and you knew, somehow, that if a bachelor forward had nowhere to go for his holiday dinner, he would have half-a-dozen invitations to choose from. And you sensed that Auerbach, the patriarch, wanted to believe it more than anybody.

There are fewer families now—Kevin Stacom, Dave Cowens, Cedric Maxwell, Fred Saunders, Charlie Scott, and Tom Boswell are all unmarried, and Dave Bing's family has remained in Detroit—but Auerbach still makes sure the gifts are bought and wrapped, the players invited and the newspapers and TV people informed.

But today, only Havlicek and White and their families bother to show up. The office staff says you wouldn't believe how sad and hollow the atmosphere was, once it became obvious that there just wouldn't be anybody else.

But the most painful moment of all, they said, was watching Auerbach going around, silently, gathering up the gifts. A little bit of him died this afternoon.

Friday the 16th
BOSTON, MASS.

The call comes from Dave Smith, my sports editor, at ten minutes past nine, as I'm sipping coffee and contemplating a lazy pregame day. *The New York Times* says that Levin has offered the coaching job to Auerbach, he says. Could I check it out?

For a moment, I have the same reaction John Mitchell had when Carl Bernstein called him about the slush fund—JEE-zus. Burned by the goddam *Times,* who happened to have a correspondent at the party and got Levin to let it slip.

I call Heinsohn, who says, really, he can't comment. But later, sitting with friends in his office, Auerbach admits it all. Yes, in the middle of a number of wide-ranging conversations, Levin brought up the possibility, but Auerbach said no. That part of his life is over.

But word was that Auerbach did take over one of the closed practices and laid down some old-time dogma and discipline.

"Did you coach a practice?" I ask him.

He nods solemnly. "Two."

It is beginning to unravel, day by day now, with trade winds blowing stronger, Heinsohn's status shakier, Levin's influence seemingly heavier. He will be on the Coast all next week with Auerbach, moving from Los Angeles to Portland to Oakland, watching from the loge seats, making up his mind.

And yet, the team has been improving, ever so slightly. Tonight, in what will be the final Garden appearance until January 11, they shred Golden State, 118–113, coming from five points down to rip the game away in the final seven minutes.

It was the third victory in four games, the best stretch since mid-November, and it ended with Scott dribbling away the final seconds in the backcourt, a a shrill, joyous boom from 12,000 throats washed over everybody. Rarely has one December victory meant so much in this town—especially to Heinsohn, who can hear the bough cracking under him and see the crocodiles below.

"I coached the game tonight," he shrugs afterwards, when they ask him about the future. "So what can I say?" Now that "the newspaper of record" has said it all.

Saturday the 17th
EN ROUTE TO LOS ANGELES, CALIF.

Henry Kissinger couldn't go back-door on his best day, but he knew about this stuff, about six A.M. wakeup calls, plastic eggs, and a weak feeling behind the knees. And he realized that a bad road trip might touch off a war or two.

The Celtics have only a season at stake out West. All they have to do is play five games in six days with no sleep, their jobs on the line, and Levin and Auerbach peering over their shoulders.

"It certainly is a challenge to all concerned," says Heinsohn, in a fake British accent, as we get ready to board an evening jet. He'll be feeling the heat more than anybody, though, and he knows it. As they make the final boarding call, Heinsohn lumbers toward the ramp . . . then stops short, in mock alarm, fishing through his jacket pockets for the thick sheaf of tickets, stapled together and stuffed in an envelope.

He riffles through them quickly, then exhales, audibly relieved. "Well," he laughs, "at least they gave me a round trip." At this point, he is beyond paranoia. A Coast trip is a dice-roll anytime, Heinsohn figures. The ice show moves into the Garden (one in December, another in February) and the schedule maker (old Eddie Gottlieb, specifically) finds you a succession of one-night foster homes. If you happen to be playing well, maybe you come back with a sweep. If not, you drop five games off the pace, and wait for time and tide.

The whole disorienting business will begin with the Lakers at the Forum tomorrow night and end in Phoenix Friday, two days before Christmas. There will be a plane trip or a game—frequently both—every day, with the chances for a victory diminishing sharply as the week grinds on.

"Five would be maybe more than we could expect," says Havlicek, who's been through this pilgrimage maybe three dozen times. "Four would be great. Three is what we really have to think about, though. Anything less than that, and what have we accomplished?"

Before leaving for the airport, I'd typed out a crystal-ball preview for the Sunday edition, forecasting three victories . . . maybe. The Lakers have been riddled with injuries, and their superb rebounder, Kermit Washington, has been suspended for sixty days for punching out Houston's Rudy Tomjanovich two weeks ago.

Golden State, rubbed out so effectively last night, is a tougher proposition in Oakland, but still beatable with good defense. And the Celtics came from 22 points behind to steal one in Phoenix last year, didn't they?

Those are the best possibilities. Portland and Seattle, who become guerrilla saboteurs when cornered in their own buildings, seem beyond reach.

Still, for all the modest prospects, there is abundant optimism all around. The mere sight of a California-bound jet will do that for you.

A smiling stewardess takes your coat and shows you to your first-class seat. Somewhere over Cleveland, she feeds you chateaubriand, champagne, and hot-fudge sundaes, smuggles you half a dozen nips of scotch (Havlicek has an awesome collection), and hints that she has nothing to do Monday night. They've set aside four of those revolving seats with a table in the middle so Wicks, Rowe, White, and Scott can play cards. And when you land, it will be 70 degrees in L.A. and still only nine o'clock, and somebody will have a rented car and directions to an Italian restaurant in Brentwood.

So who's worrying about how they'll feel five days from now, after Gottlieb (and a few Lakers and SuperSonics) have bounced them around?

Right now, Boston and 20-degree weather are 10,000 feet below and receding fast, and they're announcing the movie—*The Island of Dr. Moreau.*

"Hey, that's a good one," Scott says, genuinely excited. "That's the one where the guy ends up hanging from the palm tree with everything in flames."

"Hey, 'Bread." Cowens calls. "You can't watch this one. It costs $2.50."

"Naw, man," Maxwell replies, grinning. "I'm in the *big time* now." *Cornbread, Earl and Me* was *last* year. Carolina was *last* year. That's Hollywood up ahead, and Hondo himself, sitting across the aisle, checking out the Coast restaurants in a thick yellow book.

Sunday the 18th
INGLEWOOD, CALIF.

Late morning, with the sun up high over the San Diego Freeway and a light breeze coming off the ocean. The L.A. *Times* is Sunday-bulky, and the Hawk is sitting in a booth at the coffee shop, signaling for another cup.

We chat briefly about the Lakers, about matchups, and the importance of getting a jump on the week with something tonight. As always, Heinsohn is frank, expansive, philosophical; he does not talk like a man with his neck on the chopping block. By now, he has passed from anger through frustration to resignation. He knows several of the players have been going to Levin and Auerbach with their complaints. And it's public knowledge now that Auerbach can have his job simply by nodding his head.

Levin didn't want to rehire him in the first place, Heinsohn feels. It was Auerbach who'd argued for him last spring, when a new contract was being discussed. And it had to be multiyear . . . at least two seasons, with an option for a third. Despite the recent taste of a championship and the seven All-Stars, there was rebuilding to be done, Heinsohn thought, and both he and Auerbach knew it was far from cosmetic.

It was an aging club, when you looked at it, the oldest in the league. Your best shooting forward was thirty-seven. Your three best guards were thirty-one, twenty-nine, and thirty-four. Dave Cowens had been wearing himself down dueling seven-footers night after night with no dependable replacement. And the draft, the source of the dynasty, had produced only one legitimate starter since 1970. The nontraining camp in September had merely compounded the uncertainties.

Heinsohn wondered how much Levin understood, really. He was not a basketball man . . . wouldn't he be the first to admit that? When the season had reached the midway point and the losing still hadn't stopped, wouldn't he choose the obvious solution?

"It's the owner's ballclub," Heinsohn would shrug, finally. "But if he thinks he can turn it around by getting rid of me . . . ahh, fuck it."

The game is close until the final half dozen minutes, because Cowens is playing a monstrous game against Kareem Abdul-Jabbar in the pivot. When he first came into the league, teammates said, Cowens would plunge himself into a serious psychic and emotional ritual before games with Jabbar. Frequently, it took him hours to unwind afterwards. But he also played Jabbar (who had six official inches over him, and as many as nine by player word-of-mouth) better than almost anybody.

Jabbar could dominate a game like the Jolly Green Giant if you let him work inside or sweep in the "sky-hook" from the corner. But he didn't like to run for 48 minutes or dive for loose balls or play pit-bull with you. Cowens didn't mind any of that.

You dealt best with the Big Guy by making him move, Cowens figured. You bumped him when he got the ball out high, and you forced him to leave his *querencia* down low to come out and defend against you. If he didn't, you simply flicked in jumper after soft left-handed jumper from the top of the key and neutralized him that way.

Tonight, Cowens matches him point for point—32 in all—outrebounds him, and makes him work. He finishes the evening vacant-eyed and exhausted, but the Celtics are only four points behind halfway into the final quarter.

"I thought we were going to win the game," Havlicek would say later. "I really did." But the late charge that had beaten the Warriors Friday never materialized. Within 85 seconds, Laker forwards Adrian Dantley and Jamaal Wilkes and rookie playmaker Norm Nixon ran off six unanswered points, and Boston was finished, 104–97. Cowens couldn't play Atlas for everybody.

Later, Levin comes into the locker room, dressed in a blue corduroy suit and flanked by Harold Lipton, his executive vice-president, and the focus of attention immediately shifts away from Heinsohn, who is left sitting, sprawled, in a folding chair, in the opposite corner.

This is Levin's town, after all, and his team . . . and, presumably, his opinion is the one that matters now. The first question, from the *Herald-Examiner,* concerns the offer to Auerbach.

"Tom Heinsohn is the coach," Levin is saying. "He has a two-year contract, and we have every hope that he will be able to complete it."

Again, Auerbach's name is mentioned.

"As far as I'm concerned," says Levin, evenly, "Tom Heinsohn is the coach."

He is encouraged by what he saw tonight, he continues. "I think there were spurts of good play . . . a hell of a lot better than what I saw against Portland last week. Obviously, their game is looking better than it did for the last few weeks, but I'd rather they didn't look so good and won."

Levin glances across the room and sees Cowens, drained, sitting at his stall, talking softly to Auerbach. "Dave played fabulously tonight," he says, "but he can't do it all himself. Every guy out on the floor isn't giving it 100 percent every minute he's out there. I've got eyes, I can see."

And what, I ask him, if you don't win any games out here?

"If, God forbid, we don't win any games out here," Irv Levin says, calmly, "there are gonna be a l-o-t of changes made."

Tuesday the 20th
PORTLAND, OREG.

Telefon, the Charles Bronson–Lee Remick combo about USA/USSR double agentry, is showing across the street at noon, Havlicek says. Maybe we should see if Tom Sanders, a *cineaste* from way back (and another former Havlicek roommate), is interested.

Certainly—and we head across to a marvelous old theater in the Fox-Orpheum-Paramount style, with winding flights of stairs, a massive balcony, and attar of popcorn everywhere. Portland is one of the last great matinee towns, with a first-run house every hundred yards or so along S.W. 6th Street. You could always find one to suit your needs.

Last winter, when Havlicek was having trouble with a knee and his shooting had fallen off badly, he'd hobbled across to watch *King Kong* and came away feeling better about the whole thing.

He was always up for an off-day excursion, noon or evening, and could recall seemingly minor details from hazy plot lines. Once, after a bunch of us had emerged from an evening show in Seattle, heading for the car and a late dinner, Havlicek had been hung up in the crowd at the exit, and been left several hundred yards behind.

Hearing our shout, he had broken into a full Ratso Rizzo, with clubfoot and shimmying shoulders, gimping down the center of the street in pursuit of the Midnight Cowboy.

Maybe it was the long afternoon hours, or the vacant evenings in big cities when there was no game, but the Celtics were nearly all film addicts.

Sidney Wicks, they said, could give you Butch Cassidy and the Sundance Kid line for line—*If he asks us to stay, we'll go. He's gotta ask us to stick around*—with the appropriate quick-draw gestures.

Stacom loved Woody Allen and the whole New York genre. A week after *Annie Hall* came out, he had it memorized. He'd daydream about having Marshall McLuhan come around the popcorn machine to settle an argument about media and messages. And Allen was right—turning right on a red light *was* the only cultural advantage California had over Manhattan.

In a league whose superstars imagined themselves in the Hollywood image more often than not, Stacom was DeNiro, walking down 42nd Street in the winter wind. You wanted reality? How about *Taxi Driver?*

"You talkin' to me?" he'd called over, as I'd wandered into the Lexington gym after practice to find him shooting, alone. "You talkin' to *me*? Well, I'm the only one here."

Once, on a bus ride from Chicago to Milwaukee, we'd gotten into a critical discussion about New York films, amateur Vincent Canbys at work. Suddenly, Tom Boswell and Fred Saunders were talking, with great animation, about Oriental martial arts movies they admired.

"There's this one-armed Samurai mo'fuh," Saunders would swear. "With balance, man. You knock him down, and he lands on one finger, levitates, and comes back up."

Stacom rolled his eyes, hopelessly.

"And he can jump, man. He flexes the knees, just a little bit, and jumps over everybody. Winds up on the roof."

Cowens, laughing, turns around in mock disbelief. "Man, not even David *Thompson* jumps like that," he said.

"It's there," Saunders said, convinced. "You don't believe me? The one-armed Samurai mo'fuh."

There are none such in Portland. Not this week, anyway.

Less than nine hours after another semirespectable miss ... Portland 104, Boston 99 ... the wakeup call comes and we're on the bus again ... blearier ... as holiday bells tinkle in the cold downtown air.

As the engine belches and we pull out, a soft Southern voice floats up from behind me.

"Doesn't the Christmas spirit overcome you?" Cowens wonders. "Overwhelm you? You know, carols, trees. Anywhere I am, I feel it. Don't you wish it could be that way all year round?"

Sanders, stroking the chin, leans forward, intrigued. "Yeah," he says. "People reaching out in warmth and tenderness. Those heavenly expressions ..."

"Halos," Cowens nods.

"I don't know if I could handle that all year," Sanders muses. "Five days, maybe. Then, I think people might return to their natural, comfortable state. Animals."

Sanders leans forward again, the gentle inquisitor. "You really believe in the Christmas spirit, though?" he asks Cowens. Cowens scowls, in his best Kentucky Scrooge imitation.

"Hell no," he says. "Phony bastards."

The flight to Oakland consumes 90 minutes, arriving before noon and leaving the tourist-explorers with a dilemma. Do you cross over to the City and spend the afternoon shopping for leather and jade and wolfing down Italian food around North Beach? Or do you dive into bed for six hours and stockpile sleep for the next three days? If you're a writer, you ask where the BART station is. Levin's pronouncements do not extend to you.

But then, the Celtics go out and play as though they're immune, too. At halftime, with the Warrior fans whooping in surprise and delight, Golden State has an incredible 67–44 lead and Heinsohn stomps off to the dressing room, steam rising overhead.

When the second half begins, he sits down Wicks for the rest of the night. He lets Scott, who was two-for-eleven in the first 24 minutes, gather dust until the final eight minutes. And he never looks at Curtis Rowe, who spends the entire evening in his sweats.

Instead, he sends out Stacom, Saunders, and Boswell to work with

Cowens and Jo Jo White . . . and they nearly produce the most startling resurrection of the decade.

Catching Warrior coach Al Attles with three starters on the bench, including ace Rick Barry and center Clifford Ray, they outscore Golden State, 19–3, towards the end of the quarter, to get it back down to routine rout proportions. Down the stretch, Heinsohn sends in Havlicek for a quick dozen, and with 40 seconds to play it is down to 109–106, and Attles, feeling sick, is at midcourt, shouting instructions.

Finally, Barry drives in for the crowning basket that ends it, 111–106, but the Celtics leave the floor with heads high. Some of them, anyway.

It is nothing less than a personal triumph for Stacom and Saunders, who cherish playing time as one would a rare spice. "And you know, you put in Stacom and Saunders, the guys who are hungry and want to run," Levin observes later, "and Jo Jo is a whole different guy with that group."

"It was an effort of some positivity," Heinsohn decides, even if it was a loss, the eighth straight and thirteenth of fourteen on the road. "I think we've exhausted all the ways there are to lose a ball game," Cowens says, glumly. "First quarter, second quarter, third quarter, the whole ball game. Bad shooting night, bad defensive night . . ."

I mention the Rise of the Reserves to him, though, and he brightens. "Some guys came in and busted their ass," he says, "and it was fun. I was tired most of the first half . . . but I wasn't tired at all in the second."

Thursday the 22nd
SEATTLE, WASH.

"Well," Charlie Scott says, sitting down beside me to kibitz on the card game en route to Seattle, "when am I going?"

"Wha'?" I say, as my eyes jolt open. "You're serious, aren't you?"

He nods, smiling sadly. "I don't think it's speculation anymore. I think I'm going in the next few days—I don't think I'll be going back to Boston. Just caught in the middle, that's all. That's the way the situation is. It's no secret that Jo and I are getting along like shit and toilet paper for some reason, and I don't think they'd want to trade Jo."

So Scott has run his finger down an imaginary roster, just as all of us have been doing for two weeks, and found that he is the logical sacrificial lamb.

"They've got to make some changes, they feel, and it has to involve a player. And I don't think there's any question that I'm the man. I'm a marketable commodity, which is ironic, because that's what I tried to become when I came here, overcoming the bad attitude thing and all."

He is not bitter about it, Scott says. Just disappointed. For three years, he has tried to do what they wanted. He came from Phoenix with a shooter's reputation—you didn't expect to get the ball back from him, they'd tell you down there—and had worked on his defense, and gone about his new role, his team role, with enthusiasm.

And in an era when training camp had become a nuisance to be avoided, especially if you were a tenured veteran, Scott had been there, in shape and ready to scrimmage, ever since he'd been a Celtic.

It would be four o'clock in the afternoon at Buzzards Bay, with people sitting out with bad ankles and hamstrings and Heinsohn whistling for another one, five-on-five for ten baskets. And Scott would come bouncing upcourt, the ball waist high—"Let's *crush* these suckers."

He would take losses hard—last year, when Burleson had fouled White in the backcourt, had pirouetted his way to the hoop without a dribble and had stuffed one to beat Boston at the buzzer in Seattle, Scott had been the one who stalked over to the press table in frustration and rage and lashed his foot against the metal support.

But Scott also knew he had the label of a man who talked, and who would take the rainbow jumper from 25 feet when somebody else was loose underneath. He might have played on a championship team, but he was still untenured in Boston by some estimates.

Hadn't outsiders snickered when word got around about a team meeting on the Coast last year, where Scott had supposedly stood up and pointed at Wicks—he's the reason we're losing, he's not a Celtic. Nobody had ever confirmed that story—or even the meeting—but you still heard the anecdote. It was too juicily ironic to die.

Now Boswell, dealing the cards, looks over his shoulder and nods his head. Yeah. "Hey, John P., put in there that we won't do nuthin' until they trade his troublemakin' ass out."

Isn't that what they really believed out there? Scott wondered. "People have come to expect it, you know? Word of a trade slips out and a name gets mentioned, and the attitude is, hey, you're still here? Aren't you going?

Denver is what I've heard, I tell him. The coach there, Larry Brown, had been Scott's freshman coach at North Carolina a decade ago, and still liked him. And Carl Scheer, the president of the club, wanted him, too. We'd love Charlie, Scheer had told me over the phone. Always have.

I'd called Scheer two weeks before when the trade rumors had first surfaced, and he'd confirmed them readily, where Auerbach had balked. If players heard they were on the block, Auerbach reasoned, it damaged their loyalty and incentive, even if you wound up not dealing them. So he always talked in generalities . . . yeah, we're talking to people, but they don't have what we want.

"Well," Scott says, "Red told me he wouldn't send me someplace like Houston or Chicago."

I reach for my traveling bag, pull out the fat NBA guide, and flip to the Denver section. Scott shakes his head, grinning. "You're pretty sure it's Denver, aren't you?"

"It's not bad," I say, glancing at the upcoming schedule. "You'd play Phoenix the day after Christmas, then Atlanta . . . at Charlotte . . . two days before the New Year."

"Yeah?" he says, interested. "Let me see that book. I want to check out *all* the potentials." He turns to Los Angeles, which he thinks is a more likely possibility. Wouldn't be bad there. Kareem and Wilkes are both Muslims, just as Scott is. Shaheed Abdul-Aleem is his other name, and he wears the crescent and star on a necklace.

Scott had been to law school, and if the Muslims ever came to power, the joking went, he'd be their attorney general. Certainly, nobody on the club talked better . . . or faster.

Get him in a debate, and the words would come out in a torrent, a logical, intelligible torrent, granted, but a torrent nonetheless. It would be dizzying, fascinating, and you would forget what it was that your rebuttal was going to be.

He read widely, and had an opinion on all of it, and when his detractors listed what it was they disliked about him, that was it. Scott always thinks he's right.

Once, Bob Ryan had told me, there had been a dressing-room bull session that had arrived at the Pillsbury National Bake-Off. Scott had volunteered that he might just be able to win it sometime. "Man, you gotta do some serious cuisine to win that," Boswell had frowned. "You can't just come up with those eggs 'n shit."

Still, Scott had remained unbowed. And if he had tried to stamp his personal imprint on the Celtics system this year, which some of his teammates had grumbled, hadn't the opportunity—and the need—been there?

Havlicek hadn't signed yet. Bing hadn't been picked up yet. White's heels had him on the sidelines as often as not. Who was going to provide backcourt leadership in camp?

Now that the season was a shambles and the backcourt a mess, though, Scott would go. "I understand the situation," Scott would say, again and again. "I may not be the entire problem, but I'm the solution."

He sits resigned now, shaking the head. "Bad time to get traded," he murmurs. "Christmas. Just time to go back to Boston, get some clothes, and leave again. Well, let's write my epitaph. Every man should have an epitaph. We all should."

Scott's, when it comes, will be variable, depending on the author. Some people had viewed him as a permanently bad apple, the caustic element in any compound he came to. Charlie polarizes teams, Phoenix people told me, entirely serious.

He's the reason it isn't what it was here, Boston people told me, equally sincerely. Yet somehow, that thesis seems too simplistic now. Whatever success the Celtics had together came from a complicated chemistry, and their dissolution is complicated, too. Too complicated to be corrected by the exile of one scapegoat . . . real or imagined.

Whatever else he was, Scott has always seemed to be sincere. He would work hard and he cared about winning. And in a season when too many people were inspecting chicken entrails for the answer to all the losing, Scott would drag out the ugly truth. We are a bad ballclub . . . and we still aren't quite sure why.

The memory lingers of one particularly dismal evening in Los Angeles last year . . . so bad, in fact, that some Celtics were laughing about it afterwards.

"Well," I said tentatively, approaching Scott's locker.

"This was what you call your basic . . . country . . . ass-whippin'," Scott said. Couldn't improve on that.

Later, as we're waiting for the luggage at Seattle, Cowens comes over, feeling puckish.

"You ought to print something really crazy," he suggests. "You've got a good imagination."

"How about, 'The Celtics led from start to finish last night,' I begin, 'on the way to a 130–105 victory over the SuperSonics . . .' " He laughs . . . and nods.

Over in a corner, Ed Gillooly comes up to Heinsohn. "And what do *you* want for Christmas, Tommy?"

Heinsohn looks up, mischief in his eyes, and begins to sing, the bass voice carrying.

On the third day of Christmas, my true love gave to me,
A forward with hands,
A center 7–3,
Two h-a-a-ppy guards.

Outside, before boarding the bus, Cowens breathes deeply, savoring the crisp Pacific Northwest climate. "Fresh air," he proclaims, looking over at Auerbach, who has existed five dozen years on Havana tobacco and Chinese food, nicotine and monosodium glutamate.

Auerbach smirks. "That clean livin'," he mutters, waving a cigar. "It'll kill you every time."

Dusk is already falling by the time we check into the Washington Plaza downtown—from the hotel room you can see the ferries with their lights switched on, heading across Puget Sound to the islands, and the bus leaves in two hours for the Coliseum and the rematch with the Sonics.

"After what they did to us at the Garden, we should go out there and kick their ass," Cowens had said, but he is sick now. He could feel it coming on when we checked in—heavy flu. Wicks will play the pivot, knocking heads with the Eraser, 7–1 Marvin Webster.

Upstairs in the press room, a local camera crew shoots footage of Auerbach igniting a cigar. "Lighting up *before* the game now, Red?" they tease. Auerbach grunts.

Since that Garden whipsong, Seattle has been riding high, with ten victories in eleven games, the hottest team in basketball. Tonight is something like Dr. Frankenstein confronting his own monster three weeks later . . . tell *them* they don't know their place.

For a quarter, everything is fine, as Wicks handles Webster easily, forcing Lenny Wilkens to go to rookie Jack Sikma, a blond banger who looks like he stepped out of a Jack-and-Jill tale and pumped up on steroids.

And as the Celtics forget each other's names before halftime—just more of that old Coast amnesia—Seattle gains control.

Still, Havlicek and Boswell get hot in the third quarter, Boston crawls back to within three points, and Heinsohn is talking optimism in the huddle. "C'mon, it's our ball game," he shouts urgently. "They don't want it. Take it to 'em."

And so Boston died. Peacefully. Seattle looked for Sikma inside and quicksilver guard Gus Williams outside, ran it to 85–74 after three quarters, then socked it to Boston with relish down the stretch. Within four minutes, it was 98–76, and it grew worse, a lot worse. Wilkens cleaned the bench, bringing in his bombers, including Joey "Sonar" Hassett, who'd grown up in Providence, played with Stacom in college, and had always idolized the Celtics. "Hondo," he would marvel, eating with Havlicek after the game. "I can't believe I'm having dinner with Hondo."

Hassett went six-for-six, letting the ball fly almost as soon as he passed midcourt, and before long, the margin was a full 30 points. I hoped Cowens had fallen asleep back at the hotel. This would send him into delirium.

The final is 132–99, the worst beating of the season, and one of the worst in franchise history. Auerbach and Levin, who sat through all of it, stop by the locker room just long enough to retrieve their overcoats. And Heinsohn, hunched by himself in a chair, can barely whisper.

"Haven't got much to say tonight, fellas."

Friday the 23rd
PHOENIX, ARIZ.

The Marines used to call it the 2,000-yard stare, the hollow, distant cast that would come over a man's eyes after six months on the line, after he'd seen so much—the mud, the ruined jungle, the dying buddies—that nothing was registering anymore.

They sent you to a field hospital when they saw The Stare. In this league, they send you to Phoenix on the earliest available flight. NBA policy.

So the hotel operator rang the rooms at 5:45 A.M., and within 45 minutes, the Boston Zombies are staggering out onto the sidewalk, glancing up at the ink-black sky and watching their breath turn to white smoke in front of them. The bus battery is dead, and the driver is phoning for a push.

"This," Frankie Challant says, definitively, "is 0-Dark-30."

0-Dark-30. Jo Jo White conceived the term last year, after a Seattle-to-Phoenix-to-Denver lurch within forty-three hours had turned legs to rubber and minds to mush.

"It's hard, man," he'd sighed then, after the buzzer had mercifully concluded a Sunday afternoon loss in the Rockies. "Gettin' on planes, playin' every day, getting' up at 0-Dark-30 . . ." You didn't have to ask for elaboration.

It was the sensation of staring out your hotel window and seeing the mercury vapor lights still burning, the streets still wet from the sweepers and dawn half an hour off.

It was a burned-out feeling behind the eyeballs, a tightness in the thighs, an overall emptiness that you associated with walking basket cases. And it hit harder when one loss was barely eight hours old . . . and another was waiting after supper.

Cruising along Interstate 5, on the way to the Sea-Tac Airport, there is still no sign of dawn, and the traveling party has been reduced.

Levin and Auerbach, who've seen more than they wanted to last night, have departed, Levin for L.A., Auerbach for Boston, where he'll presumably begin dialing for deals.

Cowens, sitting across the aisle, looks deathly ill, a blue knitted cap pulled down over his ears. Heinsohn is sending him home to Kentucky and Christmas. Wicks can deal with Alvan Adams tonight . . . what the hell difference does it make at this point?

At the airport, the headline in the *Post-Intelligencer*'s "Sporting Green" tells it starkly: SONIC BOOM BOMBS BEANTOWN BUMS. Havlicek, seeing it, shrugs. What can you say? He is chewing on an enormously fat hot dog, reeking of garlic, that he picked up at the self-serve cafeteria. "Everything else they had was what I usually have for breakfast," he figures.

The flight to Phoenix is endless and uncomfortable, four hours in all, including the layover in L.A., and when we arrive in Arizona just before one, it's overcast and chilly. At the baggage area, a TV cameraman is running around urgently, looking for quotes.

"John, John, could we get something on film?"

"Sure," Havlicek says . . . then, on second thought, shakes his head. "I don't think I want to. There are a lot of things that don't really need to be commented on at this point."

The cameraman is desperate. "Aw, c'mon, John, you're the captain. Everybody else is saying no."

"Well, all right."

So Havlicek stands there, in the spotlight glare, giving out The Litany as the carousel revolves behind him and his teammates grab for their bags. The training camp problems, role confusion, all of it.

In a cab, on the way to Del Webb's Towne House, Heinsohn begins to laugh, a little sardonically. "Can you believe this game was originally scheduled for Christmas Day?" he says. "That would have been the end-all, man. I mean, I would have stopped believing in Santa Claus."

There is time for maybe a four-hour nap before it's time to go to the Coliseum, but I want to call Scheer first, and ask him about the Scott rumors again.

"We want Charlie badly," he tells me . . . again. "We begged Red to take Tommy LaGarde and Brian Taylor, but he wants more. I told him, look Red, this isn't 1962. You can't put the squeeze on people anymore. You can break into that David Thompson–Dan Issel–Bobby Jones group, but then I'll be talking Cowens or White."

By dusk, nothing has happened, and it seems likely nothing will until after Christmas. The NBA might be more business than playground pastime, but they don't like dealing on a holiday eve. Even Scrooge gave Cratchit time to buy a goose.

Meanwhile, the Celtics are as much in the mood for a basketball game against a running, pressing team tonight as they are for a Ralph Nader symposium on fan exploitation. But they give it a shot for 30 minutes or so before melting before the Suns in the third period.

Towards the end, it becomes a relay carnival, as the weary Celtic guards make mistake after mistake, and Boston winds up giving the ball away thirty-five times, twenty-two of them on steals, which Phoenix converts into a bushel of fast-break layups and rim-swinging dunks. The final is 129–110—the tenth straight loss on the road, and fifteenth in sixteen games. And the Coast trip ends up with the 0–5 cipher that Levin had promised would bring the changes.

The only question now is which flight back. The squad is booked on a nonstop at ten in the morning, which would get everybody back to Boston just in time to buy egg nog and tinsel and spend twenty-four hours at home before leaving for Detroit and a six-day Midwestern swing.

But there are three red-eye specials leaving around two or three o'clock tonight, and a number of people have already reserved seats on their own.

"Do I stay over and prolong it?" wonders Stacom, over enchiladas and Coors around midnight. "Or do I take the red-eye and get home feeling like a bag of shit?"

He decides to stay over, but a bunch of us head back to the hotel to pack and find a cab. How could you possibly feel worse than you do now, the eyes itching, the knees weak, the mind scrambled?

In the elevator, Ed Gillooly asks Dave Bing if it's possible to turn things around with the people on hand. Bing shakes his head, sadly.

"Naw," he says, softly. "I've been in this kind of situation before. I hear guys sitting around talking, and where their heads are at, and I can see it's just not right."

After eleven years of playing for losers in Detroit and under-achievers in Washington, Bing could have written the Encyclopedia Americana on losing locker rooms, I guessed. Coming here, hearing the snickering from the stands and Heinsohn's bellowing on the sidelines must be like sleepwalking through an endless bad dream.

He could have retired . . . did retire, in fact, once Dick Motta had made it clear there was no meaningful role for him with the Bullets. Bing didn't need the money, friends told you. He was one man who could fare nicely for himself in the real world. Hell, he already looked like an economics professor at Michigan.

And he certainly didn't need any more individual blue ribbons. In his prime, before he'd had the eye injury that nearly ended his career, Bing had been the finest guard in the league, a lovely pure shooter who could also sense if you were getting open—anywhere— and get you the ball.

"Playing with the guy is a pleasure," Stacom would tell you. "All you have to do is move." Bing had been Rookie-of-the-Year in 1967, coming to the Pistons out of Syracuse, and had won the league scoring title the next year, beating out Elgin Baylor and Wilt Chamberlain. He had played in seven All-Star games, and won the MVP award as a Bullet two years ago.

The only thing missing was a ring. Maybe, just maybe, he could get one in Boston. Instead, Bing found what he had left in Detroit, a promising team that had split in half a dozen directions, that bitched about the coach and about each other, losing amid a cloud of illusions.

At thirty-four, Bing had no illusions, about himself or anything else. He knew Auerbach had brought him in as a reserve, marking time for White and Scott, and he'd accepted that. All he wanted was a chance to finish his career with purpose and dignity, contributing . . . somewhere. If he helped produce a championship, that was Xanadu. But Dave Bing wanted no garbage minutes, sprinkled in three- and four-minute bunches as a bouquet to a fading star. A man has his pride.

Instead, Bing had become a positive moral force here, talking rationally, calmly, building bridges wherever he saw natural sites. He would play poker with the Rowes and Whites on the road trips, but he dressed next to a Havlicek, joking softly after games, tandem members of the Golden Era backcourt.

" 'Cek and I, we've been around so long . . ." he'd begin, and Havlicek, brushing his hair, would giggle. Writers warmed to Bing quickly, and always stopped by his stall after games. He would tell you the truth with some wit to it, pondering a question, then nodding, the lips pursed. Ten-point win or 30-point loss, Dave Bing was the same. The black John Havlicek, you heard them say in the press room, meaning it as the highest compliment. Before long, you heard his name mentioned along with White's as the next captain (Cowens, the word went, didn't seem to want it, though nobody ever asked him), and it made sense.

You could imagine him going out to shake hands before the tap, reminiscing with a Monroe or a Lanier, or coming over to debate a point with Richie Powers during a timeout, the hands gesturing like a lawyer's, the voice even. Bing had been a Celtic for a decade, the press guide had insisted. Just wore the wrong uniform until now.

Maybe, I wondered, he's still wearing the wrong one. At least this year. After eleven years, four of them spent with the worst team in a division, Bing deserved something better. He didn't need another 32–50 season . . . and tonight, the record stands at 10–21, second worst in the league.

"It's discouraging," Heinsohn says later, drinking his three-thousandth cup of coffee of the week at the airport, with our red-eye to Boston now delayed 90 minutes. "This is all so confusing. I don't know what way we're going. I don't even know if *I'm* going."

Tuesday the 27th
MILWAUKEE, WIS.

After two seasons and two months, he is allowed to keep his socks—basic white with two green stripes at the top. The Celtics, in the person of Frank Challant, would like everything else back before Charlie Scott walks down the corridor and takes the plane for the Coast.

So Scott opened his equipment bag in the lobby of the airport here this morning and handed them over—the green number 11 jersey, shorts, warmups. If he'd had a sword, Challant might have broken it over his knee.

Nothing personal, but maybe that's the way it's going to be done now, whenever they're going to drum a Celtic out of the corps. The phone call will come from Red Auerbach in Chicago or Hartford or Philadelphia, the bugle will sound, and it will be the opening scene from "Branded" all over again, with Chuck Connors (a former Celtic himself) shuffling through the garrison gates as a sudden civilian.

They were paging Scott as soon as the plane arrived here from Detroit and another sorry evening. It was Auerbach, telling him not to worry about getting on the bus. You're a Laker now, traded for Don Chaney, Kermit Washington, and future considerations. Tapoff at Oakland is at 7:30 tonight, and Jerry West is expecting you. Good luck.

Scott takes it graciously. His years in Boston were good ones, he says, and he thinks his game took on a new dimension there. Nothing wrong with L.A., and the trade looks like a good one for the Celtics. I understand the circumstances. They told me I wasn't the problem . . . and I accept that.

Minutes later, the Celtic bus leaves for downtown, and Scott boards another flight and arrives in Oakland by nightfall. In the morning, his ex-teammates will pick up the Milwaukee *Journal* and see that Scott, starting at guard, scored a dozen points and handed out nine assists, and that the Lakers dealt Golden State a 41-point beating, the most decisive of the year in the NBA.

The returns will be less immediate for Boston. Chaney, who spent seven years on Causeway Street before going over to the ABA, is a known quantity, a hard-working defensive guard who can also play the corner for you. He can report for duty immediately.

But Washington, a model power forward who'll leave his skin on the floor, won't be available until February 10, if then. He'll have to petition the Commissioner to end his sixty-day suspension, and the whispers are that Larry O'Brien, for want of a precedent, will invoke the Hammurabic Code. Washington won't play until Tomjanovich can. And doctors have said that the damage from Washington's single punch—fractured skull, broken jaw, torn lip, loosened teeth—will keep Tomjanovich out for the season.

The future considerations can be anything—money, draft choices, another player—but the gossip from the Coast says that the Lakers have offered a first-round draft choice.

At the moment, though, the fruit of the trade seems secondary to its symbolic impact. The Celtics will trade a starter in midseason—by phone, if they have to. They've never done that before—or needed to.

JANUARY

Year of the Hoss

Tuesday the 3rd
BOSTON, MASS.

He never heard a word from Irv Levin, who paid his salary. There were no final discussions, no hints that something was imminent. Tom Heinsohn just went out to practice at Lexington this morning, as he has for the better part of nine basketball seasons, and saw that Red Auerbach had taken over. Period. There had been a handshake, and Auerbach had introduced Tom Sanders to the team as their new coach, and Heinsohn had taken off his green and white jersey and gone home to Natick.

"That's life, man," he tells me over the phone an hour later. "I think the pressures were brought to bear even before the road trip. The last two games probably didn't mean much. I think Red just waited until after the holidays."

I thought back to Logan Airport, how Heinsohn had studied his travel envelope to make sure it was round trip. When the last ticket—Chicago to Boston—had been used up, so had Heinsohn's Celtic coaching career, which had produced five division titles and two league championships.

And the irony was that the last two games had been good ones, a

124–115 victory at Milwaukee (where else?) and a near miss in Chicago. "The most enjoyable I coached all year," Heinsohn is saying. "I thought we'd begun to turn this thing around, but I guess they thought it was the best time to make the change. I wish Satch the best. He's the best man to do something with this crew at the moment.

"And I have a tremendous feeling of loyalty to Red. I think he did everything he could to make it a livable situation. I think he understood what was going on—even if other people didn't."

Through it all, amid the unrest from the veterans, the presence of the owner in locker rooms from Causeway Street to Seattle, the worst Celtic start ever, and public speculation about his future, Heinsohn had operated with grace and wit. And now that the end has come, he is taking the philosophical approach.

"I did the best I know how to do," he says, finally, "but I'm not the one to evaluate it. If somebody's paying my salary, he's the boss, and it's his ballclub. Irv pays the freight and I wish him all the best. I have other careers. I'm still in the insurance business, as I have been for twenty years. There's broadcasting, painting, a number of things. I'm not afraid of the world."

I wish him well, and make arrangements to drop by his house tomorrow for a rambling postmortem. The official announcement comes at the Garden in the afternoon, with an ashen Auerbach sitting down with Sanders before a mob of writers and broadcasters.

"You know what happened today," Auerbach begins. He looks terribly fatigued and melancholy. "We gave out a release I think you all have. We've relieved Tommy Heinsohn of his coaching duties. I felt that at the present time, the situation could not be turned around, given the direction we were going in. We needed a new slant on this thing, a new direction, a new motivation."

It was *his* decision, Auerbach continues, and in his thirty-two years in professional basketball, it was the toughest of all. "I procrastinated," he says. "I didn't have the guts to do it. I love the guy. I was hoping I could stretch the thing out as long as I could, because I was hoping and hoping these monkeys would turn it around.

"I gave Tommy a vote of confidence in every conversation I had with him. I backed him a thousand times. And when I made the decision, I didn't want to call him. I wanted to face him, to look him in the eye and tell him just how I felt."

The players liked Tommy personally, Auerbach felt. Hell, everybody liked him. But he had been here so long, the voice had been booming so often, that maybe his people had tuned him out. "Familiarity breeds contempt," Auerbach figured.

It was a different era now, with the long-term, no-cut contracts, and Tommy Heinsohn belonged to another generation. There had been all the talk about bringing back Auerbach for a little fire and brimstone, as though he had an Elmer Gantry magic that was timeless and universal. "But I don't know whether I could do any better," Auerbach says.

Sanders was the obvious solution. He had played with these people, and had coached them as Heinsohn's assistant. He had put in time across the river, banging his head against all that Harvard apathy for four years. Could there have been a better preparatory course in modern motivational techniques? And Satch spoke softly. Maybe that was the only answer at this point. If all the fine tuning had failed, you reached for the volume knob.

Wednesday the 4th
BOSTON, MASS.

"Indian Ridge Road?" I ask the man at the Natick toll booth, eyebrows raised.

"Goin' out to see Tommy Heinsohn, huh?" he says, giving directions. "Hell of a guy. A shame."

Maybe, after eight and one-half seasons and two championships, that should be the epitaph—that even the toll collector knew where he lived.

His phone number has always been listed plainly in the Boston book—HEINSOHN THOS W—and he is at home this morning—why not?—perfectly willing to talk.

After twenty years in this city, the man hides from nobody. Tommy Heinsohn worked out in the open, where you could see his passion and his creativity and his warts, and he made no apologies for any of it.

"One thing I learned a long time ago is that that there's no control over what people think of you," he is saying this morning. "Some people said of me, 'Hey, it's great to see somebody with enthusiasm!' Others said I was a screaming ass. And all I can say is, 'That's me, pal.' I'm involved, and when I'm involved, I let it all hang out. I don't worry about my image."

You either bought the whole Tom Heinsohn package or you didn't, and when the Celtics decided yesterday that they'd seen enough, Heinsohn shrugged, shook hands, and went home to answer his phone.

And if you wanted two hours' worth of answers today, in person with coffee, black, he gave you two hours' worth of answers. Light on the sugar.

We'd agreed that I could come out this morning for a lengthy chat. An hour or so, I'd suggested, and I'd like to use a tape recorder, "if you don't mind." Once the Hawk was in full verbal flight, I'd figured, a mere notepad wasn't enough. You lost the rhythm, which was his essence. No problem, Heinsohn said, and had given me directions.

He lived in an upper-middle-class suburb in a modern home in a cul-de-sac at the end of a street. Heinsohn was wearing jeans and a knit shirt when he answered the door, and he was ready with a handshake, hot coffee, and frank answers—as always. We could talk in the recreation room, where plaques, pictures—and the CRANK CORNER—lined the walls, and scrapbooks were stacked on a table.

No, Irv Levin hadn't really wanted him, he begins, not even last spring, when the contract had been signed. Yes, he could see the problems coming, despite the seven All-Stars and the high draft choice. Yes, there had been a breakdown in communications between him and his ballclub. And, yes, he had been hurt and disappointed when Levin admitted publicly that he'd asked Auerbach to become coach.

"I kept waiting after that announcement came out for somebody to say, 'He's our coach and we're gonna back him.' Instead, the man came out and ran the practice. I mean, that was it. It took the heart out of me."

He'd known he was through even before he boarded the flight for Los Angeles in December, even before Levin had come to the Forum dressing room and given out the postgame quotes.

That was the starkest symbol of all. In spite of the 427 career victories, the five division titles, the world championships in 1974 and 1976, Tom Heinsohn had been deprived of the mantle of authority in his own locker room.

Actually, he had been losing it, thread by thread, ever since he took over a rebuilding club from Bill Russell in 1969. Veterans soon learned that you didn't have to iron out your differences with Heinsohn face to face.

"The main charge against me was lack of communication," Heinsohn felt, "but none of these players ever thought they *had* to communicate with me. They never had to bring anything to me. They would bring it to Red.

"Or Levin would pick up the phone and call them. So why would they have to bring anything to me? In fact, they could solidify their position by running to these people rather than to me.

"And that really became the biggest obstacle to surmount, although Red was smart. He handled it adroitly. He needed communication with these players, too, for tradition and signing 'em and everything else.

"But it was a tremendous problem for me to handle. And after eight-and-one-half years it finally whittled away and chopped me down to where I just fell off the tree. Perhaps it was my failing, too, because I'd given carte blanche to my veterans. A guy like a Havlicek or a Silas or a Nelson felt that they could bitch to anybody they wanted to anytime they wanted to. And I gave them carte blanche because they were Celtics and they were entitled to blow off steam, too, and I asked them to.

"This was part of my undoing ... but it was a double-edged sword, anyway, because I got the benefit of a lot of good things, too, and it worked to my betterment."

The coffee cups were empty now, and Heinsohn called for Donna, his tall, striking teen-aged daughter, and a refill.

"Levin always talked about the talent," I continued, "how much there was and about the bottom line ultimately being victories. Did *you* think the team was that good going in?" Heinsohn winced, shaking his head.

"The feeling among a lot of people was that we had come close in Philadelphia last spring and now we had the whole team together and all . . . but it wasn't. It wasn't together, and it hadn't been. If Irv thought this was a stand-pat ballclub, it wasn't. It's not the seven best players, the so-called All-Stars. It's the seven who play best together. And it ain't easy, McGee. Irv felt we had a better team than Portland on paper, and he has a right to feel the way he did. But I didn't think so."

Heinsohn felt he had a team in transition, built around a core of Jo Jo White, Dave Cowens, Charlie Scott, and, to a diminishing degree, John Havlicek. Entering the season, he had three men who'd never been to a Boston training camp, plus a rookie. In terms of molding a team and teaching a philosophy, Heinsohn thought he'd be starting from scratch.

"What I think Irv Levin never really understood was that we were teaching these people basketball, and not just how to run a play. And it was built around creativity—that a ballplayer could make a decision on the floor, that two or three different options would present themselves and that he would have judgment as to what to do with them.

"I fostered this over the years, to make it more interesting for the players, and it became a very successful thing. But it's not an easy thing to teach. The ballplayer has to fit into it, grow into it. He makes mistakes, and yet you can't nail him to the cross, you can't frustrate him.

"And what we tried to do all along was to get the guys involved in that way of thinking, but the man didn't understand that that's the way we played basketball, and that's the way I taught basketball. And once you'd taught a guy to play that kind of basketball, there was no way to defense that system, 'cause the ballplayer was out there doing the thinking. It's always been said that we were the smartest team, but that's how you teach them to be the smartest team . . . and yet you don't want a robot out there. That, again, is why this training camp was so important."

I nodded. Heinsohn had been saying that from the first day at Buzzards Bay, when he looked out on the floor and saw half a team. And in the airport at Phoenix two weeks ago, when the Coast trip had ended in disaster, he'd mentioned it again. It all began going sour at camp. Heinsohn sipped from his coffee, and leaned forward, the hands describing circles again.

"When we got there, I needed certain players to transfer the tradition on to the new players. I can remember rookies who'd come walking in and say, hey, look at Havlicek running and playing tough like that. I guess I've got to do that, too, if he's going to.

"Instead, we had guys sitting on the sidelines and other guys not even showing up. My key players were Jo Jo and Cowens for tradition purposes, but Jo Jo didn't participate in the drills and Cowens was gone every other day lifting weights. Other guys had done this for them. The Havliceks and Nelsons and Sanderses had paid that kind of price while *they* were learning, but the Cowenses and the Jo Jos didn't want to be involved in the learning process, so they backed off a little bit and weren't total contributors. It was, like, 'Man, we gotta do this again and again?' It might have been again and again for them, but for the other guys it wasn't. Hey, you gotta teach somebody for the first time, and you gotta do it with everybody. I think they really felt they had a hell of a ballclub and that all they had to do was show up. And the veterans didn't want to work until they found out they had to."

So the training camp had been meaningless in any team sense, and the exhibition season a disaster. And Heinsohn was less than enchanted to have Wicks show up five hours before the opener at San Antonio.

"If you'd had your druthers," I wondered, "would you have wanted Wicks back, given the fact he'd missed two training camps and wanted the money and the long-term contract?" Heinsohn shook his head.

"There were other people that I would have much preferred that could have fulfilled the role of power forward better. A guy like Kermit Washington, whom we couldn't have pried loose at the time. A guy like Harvey Catchings at Philadelphia. I put any number of names to them, to try and get them, but they couldn't be pried loose.

"And the only thing left after we went through the exhibition games and we all looked at the team was the hope of Wicks coming back and assimilating him into the program. This year, we were going to try to teach him to be a pure power forward, but we never had a chance to do that. We wanted him to play in a complementary way with Cowens, which wasn't really possible last year. That's why it was necessary for Sidney to be at training camp, and when he wasn't there, I began losing interest in him each day, and I said that." Heinsohn slumped back into the couch, and sighed.

"The tragedy of the thing was that we didn't have time to rehearse Romeos in the part of Macbeths, and we had a producer that wanted a sellout the first night."

The San Antonio game began the unraveling process. "And when we began losing games, people began pointing fingers at each other," Heinsohn continued, "and it created an insecure atmosphere among the ballplayers, who then also found out that my job was on the line, that I wasn't considered worthy of conducting this thing . . . and why do they want to listen to me at that point?

"I've been a fighter all my life, in everything I've been involved in, but they took the guts out of me at that point. Because, man, I hated to lose, and I still hate it. And those bastards, they just chewed me up and took all out of me that I could give to a ballclub. I couldn't go this way, I couldn't go that way, I couldn't go in any direction. And I felt frustrated."

And his players, caught up in a swirl of trade rumors, felt threatened and defensive. "When they threatened these players, I think it produced a backlash. I don't think you can threaten these guys anymore. How do you do it? With what? You can't just come up and say, hey, you play or you're gone, which used to be the ultimate. Now the attitude is, I've-lost-before-and-you've-got-to-pay-me. I think every one of those players reacted to that, especially Charlie Scott.

"When he found out he was being traded, it just tore his guts out, because he had tried harder for this ballclub to be something than any other place he's played. Once he lost his trust and enthusiasm for me, it was all over . . . not only his trust for me but for Red and the ballclub. Because Charlie thought he churned up his guts for the ballclub, and I can't sit here and say he didn't.

"He was as big a part of our winning the Phoenix championship as anybody that ever won a title for the Boston Celtics. The guy fit in with us. He became a team player. And when he felt they were disloyal to him, he really didn't perform in those last five or six games. And why nobody saw that and recognized it is beyond me.

"He'd played on other ballclubs, but we got him to play a role that was completely unlike anything Charlie Scott had ever done before. I fit him into a tight shoe and kept him there for two years, and he did it willingly. And I didn't let him out of that mold. What happened was that Jo Jo White didn't really get to camp. And Charlie, an emotional, competitive guy—he wanted to do more—grew out of the thing and because the other guy wasn't doing the job, he assumed more control. His erratic emotions influenced the ballclub and you could never get him back into that mold. And it wasn't because Charlie is a bad ballplayer, but because he's a hell of a competitor that this happened.

"There was money involved in his conflict with Jo Jo, prestige, a whole bunch of things. It became a very difficult thing for both Charlie and Jo Jo, not an issue of winning, but a macho thing."

When Scott was sent to Los Angeles, Heinsohn sensed a different atmosphere, possibly because there was less tension in the backcourt. Or possibly because the players thought Heinsohn was through.

I heard the door open upstairs, and a splay-legged greyhound came bounding down, heading for Heinsohn's lap. A racetrack had given him the dog, which he promptly named "Babe." He called everybody that. "Easy, girl," he said, removing paws from his shoulders. Diane Heinsohn, whom the Hawk had met back in his Catholic school days in New Jersey, appeared presently. She looked flushed. "Running the dog," she explained, leading Babe away. "The dog walks, I run."

"Where were we?" Heinsohn says.

"Last week," I say, "the Midwestern trip."

"I know the last two ball games were played with enthusiasm and heart," he said, "and I was there. I was part of that. It wasn't still going downhill.

"Maybe that's why they waited. Maybe they said, 'Hey, the thing's ready to go.' They've reached the bottom, here's the upturn, and here's the new face that's going to guide them. And that's fine. They're entitled to that. My association with the ballclub over the years had produced a whittling down of me in the eyes of the ballplayers. There's no way that you can communicate with somebody if they don't want to listen to you. I think they just want a new face, and they're entitled to have it . . . and Satch is the perfect guy.

"Maybe at this point it makes no difference who coaches the club, because the players now understand that they've been taken to task in every conceivable way. They have been deemed losers and they've gotta do something about that. If they're superconcerned about the playoffs, maybe this was the best move."

Heinsohn shrugs. He is not talking for sympathy now, because he wants none. Heinsohn understands the game and the era and the demand for instant success, and he is grateful that Auerbach, the man who hired him, backed him for so long.

"I think Red fought tooth and nail for me. He's tremendously loyal to his people and always has been. And, hey, I understand how owners feel these days. They're paying heavy bread and they want the rainbow, man, the pot of gold. They're not basketball people, for the most part, and they don't know what it takes to put a club together.

"With Irv, I think, the philosophy of what we were trying to do passed in the night. You've got to win, they say. Well, I know how to win, and how to build a ballclub. But it's one or the other. You win . . . or you build a ballclub. If Irv thought this was a stand-pat ballclub, it wasn't. You've got to walk the mileage for the pot of gold. You can't take a jet."

And Heinsohn, charged with sustaining a dynasty in a new age, found himself hamstrung. It can never be 1964 again, and both he and Auerbach knew that. If people thought that Red could just walk in again and spin gold . . . hell, even Auerbach would tell you that a basketball generation only spans half a dozen years or so. You're forced to adapt to survive . . . and maybe you can't survive anyway.

"You can't be a dictator now," Heinsohn is saying, over fresh coffee. "The Knute Rockne era, the Vince Lombardi era, the Red Auerbach era are all dead now. You're the Henry Clays now, the Great Compromisers. You can't yell at these ballplayers. You can't stand up and scream like Red used to. There's nobody who walks in as a dictator. You are trying to find a way to have a workable relationship and a workable system. You devise a program, and then you present it. But sometimes it comes in conflict with what other people think ought to be done."

In the end, Heinsohn found compromise difficult, although he worked sincerely at it. But he has no regrets now. "I think perhaps my time had just come. I coached in a certain way and had expectations for excellence. I drove myself towards that, and I had patience if people were willing to work for it, too. I knew there was no such thing as a perfect player. I tried to fit people in, people who'd help you win a title, like Glenn McDonald, but who'd never make other clubs after we'd let them go."

He'd come during the Reconstruction, when Russell had gone and Cowens had arrived, a fiery, untutored rookie, and he'd reformed the offense—hadn't Heinsohn been an offensive force himself?— and watched the fast break come back to life, and the record improve.

"I had a sense of watching something I'd created work," Heinsohn says, "and I did it for the pleasure it gave me to do it. I can remember during that second season, remember playing five games in a row on the road and winning three of them after coming from as many as 22 points down at halftime. And I called Red and said, 'Hey, we got a ball team.' And that was one of my kicks, because I knew we had a team, and I knew it before anybody else.

"From that, the championships necessarily followed, because it was a team. And it went from that to the low point of walking in yesterday and finding that it was all over. So I've had the roller coaster ride. I've been in Playland and went up and down and I've looked in all the mirrors. I've done all of that. And I've never looked back on anything. And if I was gonna go, I think this is probably the best time for me to go. Right now."

Both sides of the tape reel had been exhausted now. I had taken notes for 20 minutes or so beyond that, then put the notebook away, too. We had talked for two hours, most of which I would use for a massive piece in the morning edition. HEINSOHN SPEAKS, the headline would read.

He had always spoken to me, and I'd appreciated that. "I don't care what you write about me," he'd said, when I'd inherited the beat. "All I ask is that you give me a fair shot to respond." If he'd been misquoted over two years, he never said so.

The phone rang upstairs. Another writer, Donna called down, looking for you. They'd been calling for two days, and Heinsohn had stayed home to answer them all. The press had been fair to him, he felt. He should be accessible to the press.

We shook hands, and I headed for the door. "Thanks for

everything," I said. Heinsohn winked. "Catch ya later, Babe." I was back at the office by midafternoon. The Hawk transcribed easily.

Thursday the 5th
HARTFORD, CONN.

They were expecting maybe a blinding light and a heavenly choir and something out of Cecil B. DeMille? They thought—like some people did—that one coaching change would change tap water to pure Chablis? Or produce a 20-point laugher in the first "home" game since December 16?

They've been watching too many soap operas out of Philadelphia and Seattle recently. The Sanders Era may have begun tonight—in Connecticut, of course, where they always try out new productions—but it was still Phoenix 121, Boston 111, at the Civic Center. That's two losses in a row and eight in the last nine games.

"I didn't expect an immediate turnaround," Sanders would say afterwards, surrounded by more microphones and notepads than he'd ever seen at Harvard. "But I'd hoped for it. That's been happening recently when there's been a coaching change. I think the effort was there . . . but the idea is that the job just didn't get done."

That was the primary axiom in the Sanders philosophy—the ruffles and flourishes were fine, but what did the scoreboard say, Hoss? So there may have been all those nice, positive signs, the sincere hustle and scrap, a minimum of errors, the good-ball movement.

But there were also 43 points from ex-Celtic Paul Westphal and 40 more from rookie Walter Davis, and the Celtics quickly found themselves grabbing at shadows.

There was an immediate 10–2 deficit that evolved into 18–10 and 49–41, and in spite of a second-quarter rally, you could chalk up the evening as an experiment and read the box score as you would a Chinese wall poster . . . for evidence of who was in favor and who wasn't.

Sanders used the same starters Heinsohn had in his final two games—Cowens, Boswell, Havlicek, White, and Bing—but he introduced newer bench faces earlier.

Kevin Stacom came in for 25 minutes, spread across both halves. Curtis Rowe found himself with 20. And Cedric Maxwell, a forgotten man amid the turmoil of the past two weeks, played 13 important minutes in the second half.

Meanwhile, Boswell rode the bench for the second half, Wicks played only 16 minutes, Don Chaney five, and Fred Saunders not at all. Still, Sanders, ever the diplomat, warned everybody about peering too deeply between the lines.

"I'd rather not have anyone drawing real conclusions from this," he would say. "I'm trying different combinations . . . and I'm looking for gentlemen who can give us consistency. Every night."

Sunday the 8th
PHILADELPHIA, PA.

The man with the six-sided glasses walks quietly across the visitors' dressing room here at the Spectrum and draws two chalk lines on the blackboard. He studies one of them for a moment, stroking his goatee, then retraces his steps, finds a towel, rubs out one of the lines, and redraws it.

"Wasn't straight enough," Satch Sanders murmurs.

Hadn't they gone the other way . . . and hadn't the season still been an incipient disaster? Hadn't they tried the postgame tirades from Auerbach? Hadn't they tried humiliation, sitting down regulars for reserves? Hadn't they given them the owner, looking over their shoulders from Oakland to Seattle? Hadn't they traded a starter? How much of it had worked?

So they've changed the Voice. They've changed the Style. That's what the departure of Heinsohn and the arrival of Sanders is all about, really.

Tom Heinsohn knew basketball. Tom Sanders knew basketball. They had been Celtics together, playing in the same frontcourt, earning the same title rings. They had stood next to each other in the second row of the championship team photographs, had retired on bad knees, worn consecutive numbers (15 and 16) and watched them raised to the Garden rafters.

But they were not the same. Heinsohn had been Offense and Sanders Defense. Heinsohn had been fuming, raw, earthy. Sanders was reticent, polished, precise.

John Havlicek, who'd roomed with Sanders when they were teammates, remembers the involved security ritual the man would go through on the road when it was time to turn in for the night.

"He'd shut the door, bolt it, and pull the chain across," the Captain says. "Then he'd hang wire coathangers through each link, prop a wastecan against the door, and lean an ashtray on top. Then, he'd tape empty cans across the top, so if you opened the door, it would bump against them, like chimes. Satch did that every time we went on the road."

I asked Sanders about it, and he'd chuckled. Sure.

"What I wanted was an early warning system. You have to realize that some of the hotels we stayed at had only self-locking doorknobs. And I'd seen players leaving keys with bellhops, cabbies anybody. 'Hey, take care of this, would you?' they'd say. So it made me aware of the possibilities."

It seemed logical, practical, precise to rig a Rube Goldberg Defense System, no matter how primitive. And in thirteen years as a Celtic, sleeping in hotels from Manhattan to Seattle, Thomas Ernest Sanders never had a thing stolen.

He has always been that way. Go back nineteen years to when he was a senior at New York University and you will find Sanders telling a *Times* reporter that the Violets "may go nearly all the way" to the NCAA title.

Nearly?

"Well," he'd figured. "I more or less appreciate the talents of Oscar and his friends." If you check the records, you'll find that Ohio State was the national champion that year. Cincinnati, behind Oscar Robertson, defeated NYU for third place.

Sanders is thirty-nine now, and NYU no longer has a basketball varsity, but the man still believes in telling the truth, garnishing it with a sprig of understated wit.

He could come to the job waving title flags and preaching a

revival . . . but be serious, Hoss. No miracles at this address. Tom Sanders is not going to weave a spell with long, nimble fingers and make it 1965 again.

He knows that it is already half-past January, and that he is probably going to have to live with most, if not all, of the men he has on hand.

He sees that Philadelphia is virtually out of reach already, that four clubs stand between the Celtics and a playoff berth, that it will take better than .600 basketball to qualify.

"An uphill climb," he admits today. "No question about it."

Tom Sanders has no illusions. He has played alongside four of the men he will have to coach. He guarded Sidney Wicks seven years ago. He spent three months scouting the teams he will coach against, and he knows every ripple in the upcoming college draft pool.

If, as Auerbach says, a basketball generation lasts five or six years, Sanders has been here for nearly four of them. He goes back a long way, to the days when you used to sit down personally with Auerbach and haggle for a raise. If you had a misconception about your true value, it vanished quickly.

Sanders was the best defensive forward of his time, matched nightly with the Baylors and Lucases and Arizins, yet he scored in double figures for nine straight years. But because he played the most unselfish role on the finest role teams of all time, he never made a league All-Star squad.

View the man in the perspective of his era, and you will see what he expects of this Celtic team, where one man pounds the ball, one moves through the lane . . . and three stand and watch.

He wants flexible role players, who realize that 20 points or 10 rebounds or five blocked shots don't necessarily constitute a night's work.

"When I was a player, my game was always defense, they said. Toughest man, all that kind of thing. But if Lucas had a bad back or Arizin was on me at 6-5, they said, Hey, Satch, post up. What was I going to say? Hey, I only play defense? Doesn't happen that way, Hoss."

The assumption now will be that a man will do whatever is necessary to win games. And the implication is simple. If a man is not doing his job, he will not be screamed at or coaxed like a wayward high school sophomore. He will merely be invited—in soft, professorial tones—to become a spectator for the balance of the evening.

It will be a matter of style, after all. The hexagonal, gold-rimmed spectacles, the long black coat, the scarf, the slouch hat are the externals. If you could imagine Tommy Heinsohn roaring with laughter in an Elizabethan tavern, you can see Sanders coming out of the Opera into a foggy Paris night, circa 1894 . . . the benevolent diabolist.

Where Heinsohn was blunt, brash, and direct, Sanders will be subtle, understated . . . and direct.

"Tommy was a volatile individual," Sanders muses. "Controlled, but volatile, If he had something to say, he said it loud, strong, at the moment and emphatically. If he disagreed with a call, he'd say—loudly, and with appropriate gestures—'Ref, that was an awful call.'

"Now, I would say, 'Ref, that was an awful call' . . . maybe without the loudness or the gestures.

"Or, if I want to remove a player from the game, I might say, 'You can't be playing if you're going to be doing this or that on the floor. Why not have a seat on the bench?'

"Hey, the result's the same, isn't it? The man won't play. Or the ref will know it was an awful call."

A different tone, essentially. If Heinsohn was the sound of AM rock, 50,000 watts of blaring, undiluted volume, Sanders was FM stereo, easy-listening, waking you gradually over four cups of coffee. The hammer would be shrouded in velvet, but it would still raise the desired lump.

The assumption—unvoiced, of course—is that a man is a skilled, intelligent, and well-paid professional. He will be expected to turn up on time. If you were late for a practice or a bus last month, it cost you a dollar a minute. Now, the Sanders price is $25 for the first minute and $5 a minute thereafter. Late naps, long showers, or leisurely breakfasts are going to become luxuries.

"We won't make it difficult for them to live the way they want to," Sanders assures me. "But we may make it a bit more expensive." He is not coming in like a Chilean dictator with sweeping reforms and a proscription list. He is not going to install a 96-point offense to produce a 95-point defense. He knows that time and circumstances are working against him, at least this year.

So the basics—the fast-break offense, the pressing defense—will remain, with slight alterations. Sanders will want more people touching the ball on offense, and more of them helping on defense.

He is not unrealistic about this. Tom Sanders knows he has no Russell underneath, no Cousy flinging the ball upcourt, no Ramsey on the bench. But he has a nucleus that matches anybody's and sufficient talent around it to create a contender.

And he is going to want to see improvement.

"When Dave Cowens first came into the league, I said to him, 'Hey, maybe you should learn to shoot with your right hand as well as your left. You know, learn a few new moves.' Of course, he has since then.

"But at the time, he looked at me and said, 'You don't want much . . . you only want a man to be perfect.' You know, I think about that once in a while. What's wrong with looking for perfection?"

Or a straighter chalk line in Philadelphia.

Sunday the 15th
BOSTON, MASS.

They'd blacked the game out of every living room in eastern Massachusetts because there was no sellout, but it didn't matter. Not really.

You could've seen it on one of the double-digit stations where they show flickering battle footage from France and 1917, and a deep voice talks about mounting casualties and a War of Attrition on Sunday afternoons.

Because that's what we had at the Garden this afternoon, where enough Boston and Portland players were hurt, fouled out, or on parental leave to fill two Yellow Cabs.

The Celtics began without Tom Boswell (sprained ankle) and

Kevin Stacom (hyperextended knee), lost Sidney Wicks and Jo Jo White on personals along the way, watched Dave Bing limp to the sidelines with a pulled groin muscle, and had both Dave Cowens and John Havlicek working with five fouls at the end.

Meanwhile, over at the other field hospital, the Trail Blazers were missing Bill Walton, who was visiting his wife and newborn son in Oregon, and Larry Steele, who had foot tendonitis. They also lost two starters to fouls, and had two others working with five when the buzzer sounded. Finally.

So what we had was the fifteenth round from *Rocky,* with both principals gasping and glancing at the clock. And Lloyd Neal— who'll be trivialized for generations yet unborn as the center before Walton—hitting two jumpers in the last 71 seconds of overtime to end it, 107–103.

It was enough to make the balcony faithful chew their forearms in frustration. How often could you catch Portland with Walton out? How often could you roll up a 17-point lead one minute into the second half?

Cowens had been responsible for most of that, working out nicely on Tom Owens, Walton's lanky substitute, throwing in left-handers every time he saw the ball. All Owens wanted to do was keep Cowens from running amok, he would say. Under 20 points and 30 rebounds, hopefully. As it was, Cowens's own teammates did it for him.

After making five of six shots in the first half, Cowens, who never left the floor all afternoon, saw the ball exactly six times the rest of the game.

"They just surrounded Dave every time he went in," Havlicek told me afterwards. "They just total-zoned him. We couldn't get him the ball. I told him, 'I don't know what we can do.' "

Cowens, who'd been averaging better than 23 points during the past fourteen games, scowled at that. "I was hitting," he said. "And then, I wasn't getting the ball."

And Portland, who've now beaten Boston six—count 'em— straight times, just ran what they always run, as Jack Ramsay simply shuttled new faces back and forth. They are used to doing without people.

"All our people play," Ramsay said, matter-of-factly, after his men had whittled the Celtics down point by point. "Every game. And they know what to do. We have a game plan that applies to everybody on the squad. . . ."

And which allows for paternity leave—even on the road.

He sent the reinstatement request to New York this morning, Kermit Washington says when I call him on the Coast for a progress report, and it will all be in Larry O'Brien's hands now. All he can do is sit in Palos Verdes with his daughter and his pregnant wife, take off for conditioning runs in the California sunlight, and check the mail gingerly for razor blades and hate.

It comes from everywhere, he says—from Houston and Denver, and, yes, Boston—and most of it is unsigned. Dear Nigger, some of it begins, and Washington shakes his head and thinks of how it's going to be when O'Brien lifts the suspension and he goes out on the floor again.

"It hasn't been easy," he says. "And it won't be easy. There'll be people, as you know, who've never seen me but already have their minds made up. I guess I'll have to approach it as just another challenge to turn around. And the only way I can do it is to play well when I do come back."

It bothers him that judgment has already been passed, he says. "I'm really very conservative and quiet. Ask anybody who knows me. But because you're big, because you play aggressively, they think you're a big bully. But that's the only way I can stay in this league."

He thinks back to the picture in *Sports Illustrated,* to the preseason preview issue that had "The Enforcers" as its theme, and Portland's bruising Maurice Lucas on the cover, boxing out Seattle's Dennis Johnson.

"You know," I tell him, "the people there asked me to get some opinions from the Celtics as background, whom they considered the enforcers around the league. And the Celtics said there weren't any, really. Not these days."

Sports Illustrated had gone ahead with the concept, anyway, and Washington had been one of the six men they'd tapped as models.

"I didn't want that label on me," Washington says now. "But the Lakers thought it would be good publicity... and management pays my living."

So they had taken his picture, and it had run as part of a montage, with Washington, bare-chested, glaring over one shoulder, his jersey draped over the other. "L.A.'s 6-8, 230-pound Kermit Washington believes in fresh air, weights, and letting no one push him around," the caption read, even though the accompanying story had Washington downplaying the image. "I'm not a policeman," he'd said. "I'm not a fighter."

But Washington had guessed how it would be presented. "When they asked me to take off my shirt," he said, "I knew then . . ."

He doesn't want to talk about the punching incident, about the fist that had caught Tomjanovich flush and knocked him to the floor. It is a matter for lawyers, now.

But everyone knew—at least anyone close to the league—that Washington had been jumped from behind last year. This time, he'd tussled briefly with Houston center Kevin Kunnert, and coming back up the floor, could see a large figure in a Rocket jersey running towards him. Instinct, most of the Celtics had thought at the time. In this league, you don't run at somebody to play peacemaker.

It had not been perceived that way by much of the public, and Washington knew it. This was a simple case of a scowling black man, a known enforcer, cold-cocking a soft-spoken white who'd never been known to initiate a fight. Did we even need the testimony?

You saw the film clips everywhere—Tomjanovich suddenly entering the picture, Washington wheeling, swinging, and Tomjanovich falling like a poleaxed sheep. But you rarely saw everything, Washington's defenders would say. You rarely saw the buildup, only the climax. On "Saturday Night Live," they did a skit about it, running the film in slow motion, while Garrett Morris, as TV commentator, cried prejudice. It was amusing in a raw way . . . just as the Claudine Longet Memorial Downhill had been amusing.

Unless you happened to be Kermit Washington, your case still pending, your salary withheld.

"Are you worried about people trying to provoke you when you come back?" I ask, finally.

"No," Kermit Washington says, quietly. "Because if there's another fight, I'm just going to pack my bags and go. Really."

Tuesday the 24th
NEW ORLEANS, LA.

Maybe Irv Levin should have some of his Hollywood set people build a mini-Milwaukee, complete with brewery façades, church steeples, and four inches of slush. Maybe he should hire some Polish-speaking extras and a few hundred teen-agers in Marquette T-shirts and send the whole thing on the road.

Because that may be the only way these guys are going to win a game away from Causeway Street these days. Gotta use a little environmental conditioning. It was 96–91 tonight in the Superdome as the now majestic (six in a row) Jazz made it nineteen losses in twenty-one road games . . . if you're still counting.

This time, the coup de grace was a 14-point fourth quarter, after the Celtics had rallied from deficits in every period, plus a large gap on the offensive boards . . . which Mr. Washington might have closed nicely.

It was over early in the fourth quarter, as the Jazz rolled up 15 points while Boston was struggling for two baskets. Their last two symbolized them all. John Havlicek, trying gamely to save a ball from going out of bounds, flipped it all the way to center court, where New Orleans forward Aaron James scooped it up and fed it to a bewildered Pete Maravich for an easy layup.

"When I saw that," said Rich Kelley, the Jazz's seven-foot center, "I knew we were in the driver's seat."

In the Boston dressing room, people are quietly stuffing equipment into bags. They aren't even sure what is missing now, or where these sad and useless evenings begin going down the drainpipe. All the Celtics know these days is what they can see in the standings, and simple arithmetic tells them that they are a worse basketball team than they were when Tom Heinsohn was fired three weeks ago.

They are still the second worst club in the NBA. They are still six games away from even the lowliest best-of-three, hello-good-bye playoff berth. And they have not won a regular season road game outside of the Milwaukee city limits since March 23 of last year.

"You wonder," says Dave Cowens, who played all 48 minutes—again. "What is the ingredient that is missing, that's taking the edge away from us, but giving it to somebody else? I think about it a lot, but even if I did figure it out, everybody on the team has to figure it out for themselves. It's a conglomerative effort. What can you say about this anymore? It wears on you after a while."

Part of it is the cold realization now that a coaching change does not necessarily bring miracles, that there is still the very stark possibility that this will be the worst season in Boston in eight years, that everything will come to an abrupt end on Easter Sunday in the Garden against Buffalo, that there will be no turnaround and no playoffs.

As it is, the Celtics need fourteen straight victories to even reach .500 by Washington's Birthday. Which would, by the way, bring their road record to 10–19.

"Two and 19?" Bing pondered, packing his bag for San Antonio and another night of tilting at windmills. "Never, not on all the worst teams I played for in Detroit, was it ever like that."

Wednesday the 25th
SAN ANTONIO, TEX.

He knew it was useless within five minutes . . . that it was going to be Frustration Alley all night, that he was going to have to signal Tom Sanders to get Dave Bing ready. It was The Foot again, just as Jo Jo White knew it would be.

"It's sore here," he's murmuring now, running his finger along the heel, moments after the 113–103 loss to the Spurs here. "And it's sore here. It's just not right, and the more I play on it, the worse it seems to get. It's all messed up."

He has had cortisone shots, and they have helped . . . for a while. He has tried exotic taping methods, extra socks, periodic days off. He has thought about everything. And all White does is buy time, a day or two here and there.

He plays magnificently in New Orleans for 42 minutes, scoring 20 points and running easily. Then he comes here walking on eggshells. If Cowens, sweating and fierce, was the image of the 1976 Celtics, White is their symbol now—troubled, hurting, and not quite sure what to do about it.

"What good is it doing for me to keep playing," he figures, "if it's going to be like this? I'm not helping anybody." So he is going to see Tom Silva, the team doctor, when the plane lands at Logan tomorrow, and they will talk about it.

He has always been Boston's Natural Man, playing a sport he loved with marvelous grace and ease, never questioning where the gift came from. He has played 486 consecutive games, the league's Iron Man, and most of them merely flowed into each other, painlessly.

But there is pain now, and only White himself knows how much. He will play on the foot one night, letting his instincts roam, and there will be no problem. He will come back the next, and find it swollen, the pain shooting through with every step.

He will have Frankie Challant tape it a different way, pattern #436, and pull on another pair of socks, and go out and shoot miserably, the ball bouncing off the front rim. And the cynics, seeing the impassive face and the erratic form, will mutter that Jo Jo White is bagging it. The season is shot, and White is going through the motions. White winces when he hears that. It's *my* foot, dammit. I've seen the X-rays. I've heard the midwife theories about bone spurs, about how a man can play on them if he wants to be a little Spartan about it. All I know is, it hurts. And I can't run on it.

So he motioned to Sanders last night less than seven minutes into the game, and watched the rest of it cloaked in his warmups. He watched his teammates, lashed on by Cowens, Bing, and a reborn Sidney Wicks, play respectably for three quarters . . . then fall apart with seven minutes left.

"Close again, huh?" Havlicek would say, after Larry Kenon had taken it away in one burst. "We go in thinking we're going to win. I don't think anyone here has a defeatist attitude. But we always have one quarter where we fizzle out, don't we?"

It was just another review of the whole season, in microcosm. Bizarre reversals of form, intermittent injuries, bunches of mistakes, all interspersed with brilliant moments that make you think a turnaround is only three days away. The only constant is the losses.

"Every night it's something different," Bing says, somberly. "The only consolation is that we're in every game, we're not getting blown out. But I just want to win . . . and I don't give a damn where."

Friday the 27th
BOSTON, MASS.

We had heard the rumors down in New Orleans—that Havlicek was going to announce his retirement, would have actually, if snow hadn't cancelled a Tapoff Club luncheon earlier in the week.

The Captain had laughed them off when I mentioned them then . . ."Misinformation," he'd said. "Rampant rumor. It'll probably get better every week, now."

Whether it's better or not, it's stronger today. The club has called a press conference for Sunday morning at the Garden. Of course, it could be anything from the retirement of Auerbach, whose contract ends this summer, to the sale of the franchise by Levin. Hell, anything sounds plausible at this point.

The most logical assumption is the departure of Havlicek, though. Hadn't he mentioned retirement to Auerbach before the season began? Wasn't he going to announce it at the B'nai B'rith dinner, until Auerbach talked him out of it? Hadn't his wife been lobbying for it?

"Yes," Havlicek had admitted, before the game at the Superdome, "Beth thinks it's time."

Time for a little serious sleuthing. It isn't going to be up there with Woodward and Bernstein poring through Library of Congress files, but it's a little more complicated than guessing tomorrow's starting lineup. First, call the Captain at home.

"Some guy from *Time* magazine asked me if I was going to a press conference Sunday," he says, doing the old soft-shoe sidestep, "and I said, 'Yeah, if they invite me to one.' "

Yeah, but is it going to concern your retirement?

Havlicek giggles. I can see him, lips tightened, beginning to smirk. "I don't think there's anything going on," he says. "I'm going to practice tomorrow, and I don't think you should have anything in the paper about my retiring."

Does that mean you *aren't* retiring, then?

Another giggle. "I don't really think that's an issue. Anyway, if I was going to retire, why should I give it to any one particular person? I haven't really talked to Red about it. But you can write whatever you want."

Ah, yes. Of course. First Amendment and all that. Didn't Ohio State have its own journalism school? Bollixed, I signal for Bob Ryan, the closest thing to divine intercession I can manage on short notice.

"Captain," he begins. "This is your biographer . . ."

Minutes later, he rolls his eyes. Havlicek is going to do the verbal minuet all the way through the weekend. Taking his nondenial denials as a departure point, I construct an orienteering course, marked by other conceivable, if unlikely, topics for a press conference. White's heels are a beginning.

No, the club says, no surgery is planned. Jo Jo is expected to play in consecutive game #487 against Golden State Sunday. "This announcement doesn't involve him," assures Auerbach.

The Washington reinstatement, then. Maybe the Celtics got secret word from league headquarters and are going to announce his arrival.

But Kermit's wife gave birth to a son yesterday. "I'm staying home with our daughter," he says. "Really, I'm not going anywhere this weekend."

And the league, when I call them, says they've received Washington's application for reinstatement, but hadn't told Boston anything—if or when—about it.

Auerbach hasn't made a decision about retiring. Levin isn't selling the club. In fact, he's pleased with the progress he's seen . . . the respectable losses, at least.

Gotta be Havlicek, I deduce, finally, returning to the obvious. I type three pages for the morning edition, saying, "almost certainly" that it will be Havlicek's retirement. There hasn't been this much speculation in the vicinity since the debate over the identity of "The Gong Show's" Unknown Comic.

As a final check, we decide to phone Will McDonough, the staff's resident Holmes. He covers the Patriots. but if anything is brewing, be it ever so gently on a distant back burner, he has a source— somewhere—that knows about it.

"Give me five minutes," he says. Then he calls back. "Havlicek," he says, definitively.

Sunday the 29th
BOSTON, MASS.

The Captain came in dressed for the television cameras before noon, with Beth and the children wearing their Sunday best, and he lined the whole family up behind a long table. "This has to be one of the worst-kept secrets ever," Red Auerbach would say, glancing over at John Havlicek, who was smiling, a little sheepishly.

"Contrary to what you think," Havlicek began, as the cameras whirred and flashbulbs popped, "Red's extending my contract for two more years. Seriously, though, this is my sixteenth and final year as a player. It's something I've thought about for a long time. I knew this would be my last year when I reported to camp . . . I'd talked it over with Red. This just seemed to be the appropriate time to announce it. It'll give people in the other league cities a chance to see me play once more."

The announcement was going to be made a week ago Friday, but a blizzard intervened, Havlicek would say. "Sunday, the storm was still with us. This was the next opportunity."

So unless the Celtics make the playoffs, the Captain will play his final game against Buffalo in the Garden on April 9, the day after his thirty-eighth birthday, when the club will hold a "day" for him, as they have for every retiring Celtic. His number will be retired, too, and hung from the rafters in the fall.

When he leaves, Havlicek will take away at least three league records with him—most games played (1,232), most playoff games played (172), and most consecutive 1,000-point seasons (16). He will have eight NBA championship rings. And he will leave as the embodiment of a tradition that may never be seen again.

"The career I've had has brought me great success and happiness," Havlicek is saying now. "Everything a player could possibly accomplish is something I've done. I've gone from one era to another with the Celtics. I'm more or less the last link between the Russell-and-Auerbach era and this one."

He had been passed over by the Olympic team in 1960—one of the great disappointments of his life, he would say—yet Havlicek was a marvelous all-around athlete. The Cleveland Browns had drafted him as a wide receiver out of Ohio State two years later, and had waived him reluctantly. They were coming off a championship year and already had an All-Pro, Gary Collins, to catch passes. So Havlicek had gone to Boston, where Bob Cousy would be playing his final season, and reported to Auerbach.

"Five minutes after he arrived," Auerbach would say, "I put him into a scrimmage. And then I turned to Ben Carnevale, the Navy coach—we were watching him together—and said, look what the hell we got here."

Havlicek could play forward or guard, shifting back and forth at a moment's notice, running . . . always running . . . yet never seeming to break a sweat. And he was durable—only forty-one games missed in sixteen years. If Auerbach had been the symbol of Celtic permanence, on the sidelines and in the front office, Havlicek was the symbol on the floor. He was Hondo, John Wayne in green sneakers, ready for whatever the hell came up.

Now he was going . . . sure, he'll be around, Auerbach said. John will have a definite and direct affiliation with the ballclub . . . but that was in the hazy future. There is the family now, Beth waiting patiently for a decade, and business concerns in Ohio.

He has talked to CBS about doing color commentary for their NBA basketball telecasts, and there are some fishing holes to be dealt with. "And," John Havlicek is saying. "I'd like to see what some of those islands look like in the wintertime."

After all that, the game with Golden State seems almost trivial.

Actually, the Celtics treat it that way, kicking everything away in the fourth quarter of a 99–88 loss. Nobody has much to say afterwards . . . except Jo Jo White, who begins softly, then lets the bitterness spill out. He had the heels looked at after the southern trip, he says.

"And did you come to an agreement on your playing status?" I ask him.

"I haven't come to an agreement with the club on one damn thing," he mutters. "And it's more than the heels I'm talking about, but I'd rather not discuss it. All I know is, there's some rotten bastards in this organization. That's all I'm saying."

He was not talking about the bad heels or the playing time (11 minutes this afternoon) or his role or the contract or the losing today, yet White was talking about all of them. He was not talking about something that just came up over the weekend—but he was.

"This goes back further than what's been happening with the team," White tells me. "It's dealing with my contract. It's dealing with a lot of things. I'm concerned with my foot, but it's not really that. It's a lot of things happening. Ask Red about the problems. Let him tell you."

So I do. Auerbach is downstairs in the team offices, smoking a cigar and watching Notre Dame play Maryland on television. He shrugs. "It's something I can't discuss," he says. "It's not a public-type thing. I hate to be so evasive, but that's the way it is. It's something we tried to do and thought we could get done. But other things arose that affected it. Nobody's really at fault."

Except the rotten bastards, to hear White tell it. Management had come to him last year, talking about a three-year extension on a contract that had two more to run. White wanted it guaranteed, and there hadn't seemed to be any major problem about it.

"Now, they throw in a new stipulation that the contract would not be insured," White says, angrily. "I go out there busting my tail for them, playing hurt, and they come back with some crap like this."

Neither side would go much beyond that, but it was no secret that Lloyd's of London was getting nervous about guaranteeing long-term contracts for aging athletes. They were said to be asking for annual physical examinations. White was thirty-one. He had persistent heel problems, and a contract that would carry both a substantial salary and a five-year term. All would be stumbling blocks from an underwriter's point of view.

White didn't want to hear about it. If it *was* a family, you took care of the members, and only Havlicek had been a member longer than White. When was the last time he'd missed a game—1972? Who always showed up at rookie camp? Who'd been voted the MVP when the Celtics won their last championship? Damn right. Irv Levin was wearing one of those rings, wasn't he? Why couldn't Irv Levin guarantee the contract? Lloyd me no Londons.

So White will go out to Lexington for practice tomorrow morning . . . and that is about as far ahead as he is willing to plan. He is not saying whether he'll play in game #489 against Indiana at Springfield Tuesday night, or whether he'll take the ten-day rest they've been talking about.

"At this point," Jo Jo White sighs, "I don't know nuthin'."

In six weeks, we will know it all, when White undergoes heel surgery and calls it a season. What they thought were merely bone spurs was also a deteriorating fascia, the supportive layer underneath the foot. Thinking of the pain it must have caused him, doctors would tell me that Jo Jo White had more guts than anybody gave him credit for.

FEBRUARY

Attrition Row

Wednesday the 1st
BOSTON, MASS.

He walked past the pinball machines and the lobby loiterers and came up the stairs by himself, dressed in jeans with a blue Lakers jacket under a fur coat and a green equipment bag over his shoulder.

"I'd like to see Mr. Auerbach, please," he told Celtics secretary Millie Duggan, who thought it was merely some well-mannered Italian kid from a Hanover Street playground hoping for a tryout. He was asked for his name.

"Ernie DiGregorio," the kid said, softly, adding the final dash of improbability to an already implausible day. In the course of six frantic hours, with phones ringing, Red Auerbach pacing, house counsel Jan Volk scurrying from cubicle to cubicle, and the league trading deadline looming, the Celtics

- found that Kermit Washington had been reinstated effective February 10
- traded Fred Saunders to New Orleans for a second-round draft choice
- mistakenly put Jo Jo White on the injured list . . . then yanked him off it
- plucked DiGregorio off the unemployment line for a ten-day look

Merely another business day down at 150 Causeway . . . if you're used to dealing in the atmosphere of a Marrakesh bazaar, that is. Just like old times for Auerbach, though. You should have seen him in the Far East fifteen years ago, his players would say, haggling over an ivory box or a teak chair. The more Byzantine the better, whether it was shopping or dealing.

Unless, of course, you have to set it all down in legalese or explain it to the press or inform the equipment men, coaches, and players.

By six o'clock, the Celtics are reasonably sure they have the necessary eleven men on their active roster, and that all of them know that they are playing Los Angeles here in ninety minutes . . . especially DiGregorio, who was a Laker himself until two days ago.

"The saga goes on, huh?" he jokes, as the L.A. writers do a double-take upon seeing him here. He was not going to play in Los Angeles. Jerry West had made that clear, almost from the day owner Jack Kent Cooke had brought him in, unannounced, from Buffalo in September.

"It was obvious to me from the first time I went to L.A. that I wasn't in their plans," DiGregorio figured. "But I'm not bitter about it. I'm not the kind of guy who gets bitter about things. If you walk around like that, you develop an attitude. I'm happy now. Yeah. I haven't played since December 29 . . . and I want to play."

With Charlie Scott gone, White hurt, and Don Chaney more of a forward than a guard, Boston was getting desperate for capable backcourtmen. The moment the Lakers released him, Auerbach found himself being lobbied.

DiGregorio had been a cult hero at Providence, the consummate street-corner ballhandler who'd gone to his neighborhood high school and then his neighborhood college. He'd loved the game with an ethnic passion, had embraced its simplicities, and at Providence, he'd found teammates that felt the same way. Kevin Stacom had played alongside him and Marvin Barnes, and they'd gone to the Final Four of the NCAA championships as sentimental favorites of anybody who'd ever scaled a fence to shoot baskets after dark on a cement court dotted with broken glass and Coke cans.

He had been Rookie of the Year with Buffalo, leading them to the playoffs and six tough games with Boston in 1974.

Two years later, after a knee had been opened, he was sitting on the bench, unused. The Lakers had never really wanted him; that had been the doing of a whimsical owner. Now, he had five games in Boston, with possibilities beyond that.

Ernie D., Red, the whisperers had importuned Auerbach. Why not? He's local, Red, that's 5,000 more people in the seats the first night he walks on the floor. He'll move the ball for you, he'll make things happen. Cost you nothing. Buffalo has to pay him until he's an old man, anyway. Why not?

Auerbach had shrugged and mumbled. Yeah, maybe, good kid, works hard. Dunno, though. Short (six feet, at best). Never been fast. The defense . . .

Ah, the defense. Ernie No D., they'd called him, watching him scramble back upcourt trying to regain contact with his man. You could lose DiGregorio in a forest of picks and screens without much trouble, the feeling went. You could outrun him. You could shoot over him.

To compensate, Auerbach theorized, you needed a Russell, a rejector, a monster defender underneath who could neutralize DiGregorio's deficiencies. Cowens was no Russell.

And yet, nobody since Cousy had possessed the talent—the gift, really—that DiGregorio had for finding the open man and getting him the basketball. He would come up the floor on stubby legs, a religious medal flopping around his neck, looking for his forwards on either wing, the head up, eyes riveted.

Then a hand would flick and the ball would go in the opposite direction. DiGregorio would have seen a slice of daylight, a man with a bit of open floor around him, and sent a pass whizzing away.

Wasn't he worth the risk? Nobody's playing defense on this club now anyway, Red. And remember, he's North Providence.

"We'll make a deal for this ten-day period," Auerbach had decided. "And if he makes good, then we make a new deal."

There is a last-tango feeling to all of it. If Ernie can't make it here, then . . .

DiGregorio knows that. "If it doesn't work out, it won't be like it's the first time it hasn't," he says, on his way to the dressing room to pick up his hastily personalized jersey. "I still have the confidence. I just haven't really been in a situation recently where people could say, 'Hey, Ernie DiGregorio can play.' "

Saunders, who will now watch the game from the stands in street clothes, feels the same way. There was a time when Heinsohn would start him, when he would come down the floor and take the first shot—his guaranteed, legs-atwitter ghetto jumper—just to get the juice flowing and the scoreboard working.

His defense, while enthusiastic, had never been efficient, though, and Saunders had all but vanished in the Sanders Era, piling up DNP on DNP, finding token minutes only when a Boswell was hurt or a Maxwell sick.

"Ever since the idea of trades started around here," he tells me, "I thought I'd be the most vulnerable man. My contract wasn't no-cut . . . it's just a rough business. Sometimes, they have to go with the percentages, the figures. I don't mind New Orleans. My alma mater's near there, the Jazz is a contender, the weather's cool. And I'll probably get some playing time."

And so, after two months, will Mr. Washington. He won't be allowed to practice, sit in on a chalk talk, or even attend a game on a complimentary ticket until the tenth of the month. He doesn't mind . . . and neither do the Celtics, who appreciate the advance notice from O'Brien.

"I know there was probably some pressure on the Commissioner to keep me suspended," Washington tells me, vastly relieved, from the Coast. "And there were probably people telling him that he should end it. I worried about the eye-for-an-eye thing. Maybe the Commissioner just looked into my past to see what kind of a person I am, and found that it wasn't the same as what people had been saying about me, I can't really be sure. But I am a quiet person. I hate publicity more than anything—good or bad. I just like everything quiet."

He will be in uniform for the New Orleans game here the night the suspension ends, and Auerbach will have seen two-thirds of the fruit from the Scott trade.

Speaking of whom . . . the Thin Man himself is donning Los Angeles blue and gold upstairs, number 11 forever, getting ready to come out as Laker game captain (and backcourt "maestro") and shake hands with John Havlicek.

Scott still shoots his classic rainbow jumpers and plays with hot-nerves enthusiasm, and the L.A. people seem pleased with him, particularly with the game he played at Cleveland last night.

"I don't have any animosity towards anyone here," he will say, shaking hands cheerfully. "I enjoyed playing in Boston. Made a lot of friends here. And I enjoy playing in Los Angeles now. It's just a situation that life takes you into. I knew that I wasn't the problem here. The solution? Well, that's what they told me. But you get too old in basketball to hold grudges against anybody."

Amid all these comings and goings, and all the dizzy tangents that turned the team offices into bedlam all day, the game seems almost frivolous. Yet it turns out to be the loveliest, wiggiest, most uninhibited 53 minutes of basketball of the year. Boston 103, Los Angeles 100, it was, in a Wild Mouse of an overtime that brought both teams screeching to the brink three times over.

And it had heroes that would have seemed impossible a month ago—Sidney Wicks and Kevin Stacom. They dropped in the pressure free throws in the final 13 seconds that crippled the Lakers, who were forced into mistake after mistake near the end, as West moaned and called them "dumb bastards."

"I don't have anything to say to anyone about anything," West would mutter. Down the hall, Stacom, who'd had his finest hour as a Celtic, playing 41 minutes and scoring 19 points, was in Utopia. With White missing and Havlicek shifted up front to replace an erratic Maxwell, he was getting his minutes ("the whole secret," he said, solemnly). And Ernie was back.

"Come to practice tomorrow," Stacom advised me, his eyes shining. "You'll see things you never dreamed possible."

Friday the 3rd
BOSTON, MASS.

For two hours, it was a simple case of mass amnesia—12,000 people forgetting there ever was a first half to this season. It was Friday Night Fever revisited, a throwback to the days when you could count on partying as soon as the third quarter ended, when you could make 9:30 reservations for veal marsala and red wine in the North End without worrying about missing anything.

You could do it all again tonight—the good times were back on Causeway Street, even with two men hurt and another sick. Sidney Wicks, Dave Cowens, and John Havlicek were the heroes—Boston 116, Washington 94, and a midwinter revival seemed in full flower.

The Celtics hadn't won three straight games since November. They hadn't seen third place in the division all season. Now with their most fundamentally sound game of basketball of the year— grudging defense, superior rebounding, crisp execution—they've held their last four opponents to less than 100 points . . . and pleased Prof. Thomas E. Sanders immensely.

"This was certainly our sweetest one," he nods afterwards. "No question about that. You start seeing good, solid give-and-gos . . . can't get more basic than that."

Something's happening here, Hoss. Something fine and natural and positive. And a season may just be salvaged if they can keep it going.

The kernel was there on Tuesday, when the Celtics finally blew somebody away down the stretch, drubbing Indiana. You could see the bud in the L.A. game. And now . . . now, they wouldn't mind seeing the All-Star break postponed until the sixth week of March and have Garden doubleheaders scheduled for the next twelve days.

"You almost wish you didn't have a break," says Cowens (who won't. He's starting center for the East in Atlanta Sunday afternoon). "Still, it's a pleasure that we can take a nice, deep breath and say, yeah, we're winning a few ball games."

Tuesday the 7th
INDIANAPOLIS, IND.

"Don't even bother writing," advises ace deskman Peter Accardi when I phone the office from Market Square for creative guidance before the game. "With all this snow, we'll be lucky to get one edition out of the building. Maybe for the P.M. Call again around midnight."

Not that the world is waiting anxiously for total coverage tonight. Lincoln wrote my lead a century and more ago: "The world will little note nor long remember . . ."

The Pacers, forced to hold a summer telethon to scrape together enough season ticket pledges to stay alive another year, have jettisoned as much of their pricy talent as they could, and much of what is left is either injured or snowbound tonight.

Only seven Indiana players—one under the league minimum— come out for warmups, and referee Don Murphy has to make an emergency call to New York for a ruling. Anybody who fouls out can stay in the game, he is told. Just assess an extra technical.

And the Celtics, who still can't win away from Causeway Street, have only nine able bodies—White is at home with the bad heels, and Curtis Rowe has a knee irritation. And if Jan Volk and Frankie Challant hadn't arranged for an early escape before Logan Airport shut down yesterday, nobody would be here at all.

By the time the fourth quarter rolls around, the body count is eight. Tom Boswell, going up for a jumper on Ron Behagen, comes down yelping, holding his shooting hand. No foul is called.

Boswell stares at the hand, seeing that the bone in the ring finger has broken through the flesh. Furious—and horrified—he runs over to Jess Kersey, the other referee. "Man," he screams, brandishing the hand. "You mean this ain't a foul?"

Kersey grimaces, and signals for Challant, who sprints down the sideline with a towel. "Aww, shit," Challant says, swathing the hand quickly and leading Boswell to the dressing room. Tom Sanders stares at the floor, and makes another mental subtraction.

Finally, after blowing a 16-point lead, the Celtics manage to hang on for a 92–89 victory, their fourth in a row. In the Boston room, I give Havlicek a small bottle of domestic champagne.

"To commemorate your first road victory outside the Milwaukee county limits," I tell him. "I've been carrying it around for only two weeks."

He smiles . . . and stuffs it into his traveling bag.

Wednesday the 8th
KANSAS CITY, MO.

Five little taxis all in a row, waiting to whisk us all off to Weir-Cook Airport and, ultimately, the Land of Oz. All of us, that is, except for Tom Boswell, who is standing in the lobby with his shooting arm in a sling, and six stitches in his finger.

"Dislocated," he nods, solemnly. "Yeah." Ten days to two weeks, Challant is figuring, which means no game tonight for Boswell, no return to the Garden, and no West Coast. And since the Great Blizzard has paralyzed Boston—Logan won't be open until the weekend—it means a number of days in a warm, comfortable place.

Atlanta? South Carolina, where he lives in the off season? "A vacation?" Boswell muses. "Yeah. Why not?" Can't play if you can't shoot. And you can't shoot with one finger swollen to Polish sausage proportions and held together with surgical thread. Boswell grins at the logic of it all. Alfred E. (What . . . Me Worry?) Neuman never had such a fine and practical attitude towards his work.

In a league where a third of the performers lived only from September to September, signing seasonal leases and keeping an open mind about places like Cleveland and Houston (you never knew, did you, when the phone might ring?), Boswell floated as an unfettered spirit, seemingly unconcerned with trading deadlines, playing time, or the waiver wire.

In Boswell's cosmos, the NBA was merely one pleasant way station among a variety of destinations, and public speculation about his potential, attitude, and unrefined talent didn't seem to worry him.

Bob Ryan, who'd covered him as a rookie, once summed up

Boswell nicely. "His attitude problem is that he hasn't got one," Ryan decided. "No attitude at all."

I'd mentioned that theory to Boswell once, and he'd nodded sagely. "Yeah . . . well, better no attitude at all than a bad one, huh?" The attitude, actually, was laid-back laissez-faire. You had no control over your destiny . . . at least your NBA destiny. You couldn't play basketball much past thirty-five. And they could let you go with a phone call—just set you adrift, like Cookie. Worry about it and it just messed up your head, not to mention your stomach.

So Boswell had settled in as a court jester, deflating royal attitudes from his perspective as a street-corner savant. The grin was devilish, the eyebrows raised. *So Shaheed think he can win the Bakeoff, huh?*

He would bestow nicknames in a moment's whimsy that would stick for an entire season. Dave Bing had been called Pee Wee for a while, until Boswell decided Disco would be more appropriate. *Man like to dance, didn't he, even at age thirty-four? Well then, Disco. Disco Dave.*

He would be the Wizard of Boz, showing you flashes of brilliance that justified everything they'd said about him. A rebounder. Strong, like Silas, but a better shooter. *This* year, he comes into his own. "You wanna know who could really do something," Havlicek would say, during an informal roster analysis. "Boz. I mean, that sumbitch can *play."*

All too often, though, the Wizard gave you mirrors, blue smoke, and amplifiers. Three years they had waited, finally thinking Boswell was on the verge, seeing it there for a week and then . . .

They'd tried him at center last year when Cowens was gone, alternating Boswell with Jimmy Ard, but the experiment had left Heinsohn dissatisfied and Boswell frustrated. *I'm not a center,* he'd say, shaking his head.

Once, after Ard had been thrown out of a game in Chicago for fighting with Artis Gilmore, Boswell had been sent in to deal with the 7-2 center himself. After watching Gilmore score 23 points and picking up a wreath of fouls trying to guard him, Boswell seemed near tears.

"John, John," he'd called from his dressing stall, "you've got to speak *out*. I get position on the man, and he destroy it, and they call *me* for pushing off. How am I gonna push the man? He's like a palm tree, just le-e-e-a-nin' in. I'm only 217 pounds now. How do they expect me to play him?"

Even under optimum circumstances (when he was paired with a power forward), Boswell's defense was haphazard and hopeful, which tended to reduce his value in Sanders's marketplace. They whistled fouls on him in threes—reaching in, holding, pushing—as Boswell whirled and grimaced. He would put up the hand, smiling, and you could hear them mumbling in the stands. What's he *smiling* for? What kind of an attitude . . .

It was an Oriental smile, once you'd seen it a few times, and there was no mirth in it. It was embarrassment, with a trace of confusion. Here I am, playing my defense, the smile said, and all I hear are whistles. The swollen finger was just another practical joke, intruding on the Boswellian cosmos. May as well grin . . . and head south for a while.

Thursday the 9th
KANSAS CITY, MO.

At the moment, Tom Sanders's greatest coaching decision has been the switch from the old Muehlebach Hotel to the massive Crown Center here, There are a few hundred restaurants, boutiques, food stalls, and bars at the Crown Center—enough diversions to keep a basketball player with a valid credit card occupied for a week or so.

Which suddenly became vitally important today, once the Celtics realized they could be stranded somewhere outside of Boston for the rest of their natural lives.

The itinerary said they were supposed to be here less than a full day—arrive from Indianapolis late in the morning, play the Kings at Kemper Arena at night (which they did, a 104-100 loss), and head for home today.

By now, though, we've all heard the horror stories from the Northeast—cabin fever mounting, martial law, soldiers brought up from Georgia to dig out the Yankees. Wherever you are, Governor Mike Dukakis is saying, you should only stay there.

So while Sanders runs a two-hour practice at Kemper this morning, preparing for tomorrow's Garden date with New Orleans that won't be, Frankie Challant has set up a hot line to the team offices and is scribbling down assorted cities, flight times, and train schedules. We can get as far as New York, he says, and bivouac there until Boston opens up. Or we can stay here and self-indulge.

Compared to the Muehlebach, a restored downtown hotel which once served as Harry Truman's campaign headquarters, the Crown Center is a pleasure dome.

Conspicuous consumption is the byword, as you wander from fruit stand to nineteenth-century apothecary to stereo shop, then board an escalator to do it all over again on another level. Sanders, after sampling the luncheon fare at one cafe, stops by a leather place and orders a dozen metal belt buckles with a Revolutionary message: UNITE OR DIE. He has them sent to the Garden, where one will be placed in each locker. Better than a fight talk any day. The Crown Center has its advantages.

Sanders had thought about such things as he created the new administration in his image. If systems, practices, and fine schedules could all be changed, why not hotels? Just because Auerbach had stayed there didn't mean you had to, Hoss. Especially if it didn't cost any more. If you chose a hotel near the arena, you wouldn't need a chartered bus, so you could apply the savings to the price of the room.

So we have left the Muehlebach to the ghost of H. S. T. We have moved from the Marriott to the Hyatt Regency in New Orleans, and may do the same in Atlanta. And there was serious consideration given to abandoning the idea of Oakland entirely, and staying at the Mark Hopkins across the bay. Gonna lose the game anyway . . . why not savor San Francisco? Ultimately, the thought of a bus ride in rush-hour traffic ended that fantasy, but Sanders's creative concern had not gone unappreciated.

If you spent seven months staggering off buses in variable weather (most of it forbidding) and playing a game and staggering back on, a hotel became a serious matter. Hell, in New York, they'd changed locales three times in a year (from the City Squire to the

St. Moritz to the City Squire to the Summit), and the team doesn't even stay overnight.

The St. Moritz might have had the fashionable address on Central Park South, nodding distance from the Plaza, but the beds were narrow and the shower nozzles poked you in the chest. Heavy liabilities for a group whose small people ran about 6-4.

The Summit, midtown East Side, could handle a rebounding forward comfortably. There was a good delicatessen two blocks away, and an all-night French restaurant around the corner. Ergo . . .

You became a connoisseur des hotels quickly if you traveled with the Celtics. Mention a league city and a dozen mental files would riffle in a dozen heads:

WASHINGTON PLAZA (Seattle). The best in the league by most estimates. A carpeted lobby big enough for a full-court game. Two blocks from the movies, the fresh-air market, the department stores. Twenty-four hour room service, radio speakers in the bathroom, and an incredible view of Puget Sound, the Lake, the Space Needle.

SWINGOS' CELEBRITY HOTEL (Cleveland). The room decor, with four posters, enormous pillows, and pastel colors was a cross between Louisa May Alcott and a New Orleans bawdy house, and it *was* on Euclid Avenue, one of America's grimmer thoroughfares. But Jim Swingos treated the Celtics like Oriental pashas, and the restaurant was a good one. They kept it open specially after games, broiling thick steaks while the bus returned from Richfield.

HILTON PALACIO DEL RIO (San Antonio). You could order breakfast by room service with grits and Mexican sausage, and eat it out on your balcony. And an elevator (just press the RIVER button) would deliver you to the Riverwalk and a stroll in the sun, with trees hanging overhead and the smell of barbecue everywhere. After the game, a row of taxis waited out front to take you to Mi Tierra.

GREENWAY PLAZA (Houston). Thick carpets, a walk-in closet and a telephone in the bathroom, with a Texas-size bed to sprawl on. If you grew bored, there was a theater in the basement, along with a couple of bars, a bookstore, and a gourmet food shop. The Summit, one of the league's nicest facilities, was right across the street.

EXECUTIVE TOWER INN (Denver). The courtesy van driver

knew you by name, and would pick up both team and luggage free of charge at the airport (a favorable point with Auerbach). And if a week of L.A.-to-Portland-to-Oakland had left you for dead, there was a health club on the premises. Whirlpool, sauna, all that.

There were little things from other cities that you remembered—the all-night coffee shops in Atlanta and Los Angeles, the sun-drenched swimming pools in Phoenix and Oakland, the Old World convenience in Milwaukee and Portland. You picked and chose your favorites according to a personalized creature-comforts shopping list, tailored to the often bizarre demands of oversized human beings stuck in a city for thirty-six hours without cars or local acquaintances.

You wanted a large bed (a large, *hard* bed if you had back trouble) with six pillows, a walk-in shower with overhead nozzle, a bedside alarm clock, and picture windows that overlooked mountains, an ocean, or both. You wanted round-the-clock room service, a same-day dry cleaners, a disco in the basement, and six movie houses across the street. You wanted someplace that was Manhattan in October and L.A. in February, where nothing happened much before noon or stopped happening much before four A.M.

For the moment, the Crown Center does nicely. But Sanders, after comparing dates, schedule obligations, and timetables, has called for an afternoon departure.

New York meets the criteria for an interim destination, he says, now that Friday's game (and probably Sunday's with Milwaukee) have been called off. We can be there by suppertime and stay at the Summit until Boston is fit for habitation. Plenty of places to practice, eat, drink, play. Three different ways to get home, gentlemen—air, rail, highway. New York, New York. A hell of a town, Hoss.

Saturday the 11th
BOSTON, MASS.

The airport is opened shortly after dawn, and *your* Boston Celtics are back on the first available flight, amid great civic apathy.

Cowens and Havlicek, who live in adjacent suburban towns, seek out a cab, since the driving ban is still in effect, with dire consequences for all transgressors.

"Forty-five dollars," says one nouveau capitalist. Cowens stares at him in disbelief. During a certified emergency, he feels, you should be at least public spirited, if not downright charitable. During the *last* blizzard a month ago, when a game had been called off and even buying a loaf of bread had been an effort, Cowens had tooled around Wellesley in his four-wheel-drive truck, scooping up pedestrians and delivering them to their choice of sites. One man had been hobbling along in a leg cast, plunging hip-deep into snow with every step.

"You're crazy, man," Cowens had said, and wound up taking him several towns away to a relative's house. Later, when it had come out in the papers, Cowens had been annoyed. It made it look as though he was making a play for publicity—all he'd wanted to do was help somebody out.

Now, a $45 taxi ride—more than double the normal rate—infuriates him. "Rip-off sumbitch," Cowens says. "I'll stick your head in the snow."

The cabbie, taken aback, goes defensive. "Well, it costs *me* $12 to watch you guys play."

Cowens considers this. "Well, then," he decides, *"you're* getting ripped off."

Monday the 13th
OAKLAND, CALIF.

No mistaking that voice as you come into the lobby of the Edgewater Hyatt Hotel. Johnny Most . . . in no uncertain terms.

"Ma'am," he is telling the desk clerk, "there is no man by that name with the ballclub. There has never been any man by that name . . ."

"John," he says, bringing me over as a witness. "Is there anybody named . . ."

"Zaid Abdul-Aziz?" I say. "Yeah. Due in tonight. A ten-day contract as a backup center." Most shrugs, and begins to laugh. A quarter-century with these people, and you couldn't make a simple declarative statement anymore.

Abdul-Aziz had been living on Vashon Island off the coast of Washington, working with his import-export business when the call came. He hadn't touched an NBA basketball in thirteen months, not since Buffalo had let him go and ostensibly ended a career that had spanned nine seasons and five cities.

He had come into the league as Don Smith, a first-round draft choice out of Iowa State, and had led the league in rebounds-per-minute one year. Along the way, he had changed his name and added poundage, but he was an experienced big man, and big men were valuable.

So Abdul-Aziz had been working out on his own at the University of Washington, and had gotten a tryout with Houston recently, but it had been too late in the season, they'd said. Maybe next year. Now, Boswell's injury and the Celtics' presence on the Coast have produced another opportunity, and before long, he is spotted in the coffee shop, a friendly, balding man who might be on a midweek business trip to the Bay area.

Havlicek, in his capacity as Official Greeter, goes over to shake hands.

"Hello there, Zaid . . . uh, Don . . . uh, Ziz," he says. "Welcome aboard."

Abdul-Aziz' eyes brighten. "Boards?" he responds, with great enthusiasm. "I'll get you some boards."

Havlicek is mystified for a moment. "Uh, yeah," he says. "Those too."

After twenty-four years, the Captain is beginning to wonder if the basketball gods aren't running him through the cycle again. The first time, sophomore year in high school back in Ohio, when there was no home gym, the record had been something like 4–19, and the frustration had been enough to make him burst into tears on court.

Now that the two home games have been postponed, the Celtics will have played eleven straight on the road by the time this trip finally ends in New Orleans, and will have been away from the Garden for a full month. Just Bridgeport H.S. all over again, losing record and all.

And the teammates won't even be the same as they were when Boston passed through this place in December. Charlie Scott and Fred Saunders have been traded. Jo Jo White and Tom Boswell are back in Boston on the injured list. And in their places are Abdul-Aziz and three former Lakers—Don Chaney, Ernie DiGregorio, and Kermit Washington, who'll play his first game since December 9 tomorrow night. Even Johnny Most, who's seen it all, hasn't seen this, when even a Hyatt employee knows more about the club than you do on any given day.

Tuesday the 14th
OAKLAND, CALIF.

For one very long moment after the buzzer sounded, he couldn't be sure why the people were running towards him. Kermit Washington had been hooted as soon as he'd stepped on the Coliseum floor here tonight, hadn't he, coming off the bench for Dave Cowens in the second quarter?

Now, six points, 14 rebounds, and three steals later, the fans were coming down smiling from the stands, heading in his direction, all of them unfamiliar faces.

"I'm very apprehensive about people running up to me now," Washington would say, after the Celtics had rallied around him for a marvelous 98–75 victory over the Warriors. "The letters I got, the people I saw on the street . . . most of them were more negative than positive. So now, when fans run up to congratulate me, I don't know exactly why. Do they want to congratulate me . . . or knife me? No, don't say knife me, it might . . ."

He does not want any more controversy. He never did. But Washington knows that the fallout from the one punch he threw at Rudy Tomjanovich is going to continue, that his debut tonight in a Boston jersey is only one more chapter in this harrowing saga. "It's not really out of the way," he says. "There's litigation coming, a number of things yet."

So he will approach it the only way he can—by playing basketball the way Kermit Washington has always played basketball and turning the other cheek to provocation.

Tonight, he gave the Celtics 25 minutes' worth of everything they'd dreamed about when they brought him in from Los Angeles.

He crashed the boards fearlessly. He scored his two baskets in classic Boston fashion, on a sneakaway and a back-door play. He rejected people in traffic. And he went to the floor with a thumping, screeching, banzai dive six—count 'em—times that rubbed knees and elbows raw and produced the three steals.

"Like a seal," grinned Cowens, who is a connoisseur of horizontal aeronautics and crash landings. "You know how they come down the chute at the zoo, sliding around on their chests, all wet? That's what Kermit looks like when he dives for the ball."

Godot never went to the floor like that . . . and the Celtics responded as though he'd been the vague savior they'd been waiting all season for.

It was the first time they'd won a game on the Coast since last February, when they'd come from 22 points down to beat Phoenix, and they'd done it stylishly. This was the same Golden State group that had scored 67 points in the first half against Boston in December, and sent Tom Heinsohn to his bench in desperation. Tonight they scored only 20 in the first quarter, and only 25 for the entire second half. That included a nine-point fourth quarter, during which the Coliseum partisans growled and hollered for somebody other than Rick Barry to take a shot. "Tonight is the best we've been able to play," Tom Sanders would decide. "No doubt about it."

And Washington, who played with confidence and courage, was

the generator. He'll be along for the rest of this Traveling Salvation Show, he says. Every stop on the tour.

"I'm going to Houston," he is saying now, flatly. "I don't care what they say. If they pay me to play, I want to play. Red says don't go, but I've got the plane ticket. If they want to pay money to come out and say anything let them. They're trying to make me out as controversial, but the truth is that I'm the boringest person in the world. Besides, if somebody wants to get you, they're going to get you. So I don't worry about it."

Thursday the 16th
PHOENIX, ARIZ.

What better place to rise from your own ashes? What better time to shoot 38 percent for two hours, foul out one of your starting forwards, go five minutes on one basket down the stretch, and still win a basketball game in a building that no visitor had left alive for more than two months?

And what better way than with the old, cobwebbed fundamentals—a helping, talking defense, brutal rebounding, and a lovely bit of thievery by the old Captain in the final six seconds. Just a little hands-on defense is all it was, the very thing John Havlicek had been using on his old Celtic buddy Paul Westphal.

"Hey, Havlicek's been holding me," Westphal had complained to referee Joe Gushue at one point, "and he's been getting away with it all night."

Gushue had shrugged. "What do you want me to do about it? He's been getting away with it for sixteen years." So why shouldn't he get away with it once more, and steal a 98–95 victory that sent more than 12,000 people into the parking lot mumbling to themselves.

"Here in Phoenix?" Cedric Maxwell had wondered, his eyes wide. "Well, John is John, a living legend."

It wasn't so much of a grab as it was a guiding hand that used Suns center Alvan Adams's momentum against him and brought all

81 inches of him down on Havlicek for an offensive foul.

And since the Celtics were leading, 96–95 at the time, and Phoenix *had* won sixteen in a row in the Coliseum, you might say it was a controversial call. Adams did.

He wondered sarcastically how he could have lost his balance so suddenly ... without a little help from a friend. "Now, how did I fall completely on his body the last five feet?" Adams asked, rhetorically.

Maybe with a little leverage from a man who's learned, over sixteen years, that the hand can be quicker than the eye ... even on the road. Across the hall, Havlicek assumed his best choirboy expression to explain.

"I just tried to get position," he would say, "and keep my feet on his and my hands on him, so that as Alvan gained momentum, he'd fall on me. So he started falling, and I started pulling. . . ." And they went down in a tangle on the baseline, with referee Tommy Nunez blowing the whistle and saying, no, no block. Offense.

It was a gutsy call to make in Phoenix, especially if you're a Chicano referee who happens to live here ... and it tied a bow on Boston's best stretch of the year. Two in a row and six of the last seven have been victories, and if you want to be optimistic about it and forget all those snow games that are going to be crammed into April, you can say that Boston is only one game out of playoff contention in the loss column.

And Tom Sanders, ever the optimist, is saying it. "You win one ... two ... three, and then you really begin to believe you *can* win," he says, as we pack for Los Angeles and another game tomorrow night. "I think we can win every game we play. But then, I've always thought that way ... even at Harvard."

Now he has his people thinking that way, too. Losses used to be blamed on brutal road schedules, lousy officiating, role confusion, and Tommy Heinsohn. Sanders didn't want to hear any of it. "The job just wasn't being done," he decided. "You're getting outrebounded. You're making twenty-some turnovers a night. Don't talk about percentages and atmosphere. Be serious."

Sunday the 19th
DENVER, COLO.

And now, it's time to play "How Well Do You Know America?" sponsored by Eddie Gottlieb and your good friends in Manhattan. After seven days and four cities, you tend to bolt out of bed, head aswim, when the wakeup call comes, groping for the curtains and a clue to your exact whereabouts.

No sun, so it can't be Phoenix. The air isn't brown, so we're not in Los Angeles. Ah, mountains, a little snow, religious programs on the tube. Must be Sunday . . . and Denver.

This is fast becoming Tennessee Williams material. "Attrition Row," you could call it, a compelling drama of life on the road, with another traveling companion missing every time the sun rises.

Today it was Dave Cowens who was sitting in a bed of ice at the Executive Tower Inn with three men—Jo Jo White, Tom Boswell, and Curtis Rowe—already back in Boston with various irritations, dislocations, and protrusions. That left nine workers on hand in a building where visitors had won exactly three games in twenty-eight tries this year.

So you could say that a 118–115 loss to the Nuggets could be tucked away as a moral victory, unless your name is Sanders and you care about things like blown fundamentals. Because in spite of the missing persons, the homesick blues, and heavy fouls on both John Havlicek and Sidney Wicks, this was Boston's game with five minutes to play. Even after the 114–106 loss at L.A. Friday night, a victory here would have meant a 3–2 record on the Western front, no matter what happens in Houston.

Instead, Denver went to their two big men, Dan Issel and Bobby Jones, and ran a clinic inside that ended it quickly. With Cowens back at the hotel, you could do that. In all, Issel and Jones scored 41 of their combined 51 points off low stuff—back-door plays, rebound action, affiliated free throws and the pick-and-roll. Understandably, Sanders, a man of precise execution, didn't want to hear the Attrition Row litany for very long.

"Attrition?" he would murmur. "You can use that, but our defense let us down. When they can run the pick-and-roll all night long—and I mean *all* night long—it's got to be the defense. It's hard to get more fundamental than that, and given the amount of time we've spent on it, we shouldn't have to pay that type of price."

So the free 'n' easy Coast feeling, when the Celtics thought they might play some of this trip on house money, has vanished. Not to mention a third of the club. Cowens, whose back is a mess of bruises from evenings spent alongside Clifford Ray, Kareem Abdul-Jabbar and Alvan Adams last week, is going to stay here for treatment. And Kermit Washington won't be going to Houston. Auerbach's orders. We're talking the eight-man minimum for Tuesday night. Even Travis had more men than that available at the Alamo.

Monday the 20th
HOUSTON, TEX.

He came out at noontime with the rest of them, dressed in a white warmup jersey that read HOUSTON in large red letters, and went directly out to his old spot—15 to 18 feet from the basket and straightaway.

And Rudy Tomjanovich began to shoot—long, soft arching jumpers that dropped cleanly, one after another. He ran a bit, joining Moses Malone, John Lucas, and the others in the half-court sprints.

But when the passing drills began, he walked to the sidelines, then left the gym through a side door to do a little jogging. After seventy-three days and two operations, Tomjanovich is worried about anything coming near his face.

"Right now, I don't even want to take a chance," he decided. "I want to play as soon as I can, but I'm not really ready for any competition or contact just yet. Eventually, I'm going to have to come to terms with this thing. I know that. Will I be gun-shy? I really don't know."

The battered face—fractured nose, broken jaw, fractured skull, damaged eyes, torn lip, loosened teeth, concussion—is almost healed now. The hole in the back of his left eyeball was repaired by laser surgery, and the torn tear duct in the right one will be fixed in April.

The wires have been removed from his jaw, and the only visible trace of the blow is a slight scar along his upper lip.

But Tomjanovich will not play basketball until the fall, when his professional recovery will begin. Until then, he will attend practice occasionally, watch home games from the bench in street clothes, and answer the flip side of the questions Kermit Washington has been hearing.

He prefers not to discuss the incident itself, presumably because of his pending litigation against the Lakers for damages. And he says he hasn't talked with Washington about it . . . and doesn't plan to. "I don't see what that would do that could make any difference now."

Rudy Tomjanovich would prefer to forget that the punch ever landed, and has said so. He would rather concentrate on pulling his career back together, and let the courts take care of the rest.

He has been working out on his own, he tells me, playing tennis and running. But today's workout, modest as it was, left him exhausted.

The shooting touch, so uncommonly easy and deft for a 6–8 forward, hasn't deserted him, but Tomjanovich knows that a light shootaround means nothing. Not until October, when he is playing in close with the elbows flying and hands in his face and bodies bumping, will he know how far he has come since December 9 . . . and how much lies ahead.

Tuesday the 21st
HOUSTON, TEX.

If you liked Ethiopia vs. Italy, you would have loved this one. This was tanks and eighteenth-century horsemen, eleven-on-eight. This was Houston 111, Boston 96, tonight—exactly what you'd guessed it would be the moment the Celtics walked onto the Summit floor. At practice yesterday, Tom Sanders had glanced across the gym at the remains of his Light Brigade, and thrown up his hands. "We have what you see," he said, softly. "We can't create any people for you."

Look along the bench and you saw three reserves—Kevin Stacom, Ernie DiGregorio, and Zaid Abdul-Aziz—two of whom had contracts that expire by Thursday. Commodity options were thin, to put it mildly.

So Sanders used everybody for a minimum of 20 minutes, mixing and matching as best he could. And the Rockets, who knew about injuries and life at the bottom, were kind enough to put Boston out of it early. The whole process took only an hour and 50 minutes.

"They took it to us in every way possible," Havlicek would sigh, after Houston had gone up 12–2 in less than five minutes, and went creative from there. He had played small forward on offense and guard on defense. Don Chaney had played guard on offense and forward on defense. Sidney Wicks had been the center.

"I'd like to say it was our best game of the year, that we played fabulous basketball," Rockets coach Tom Nissalke would say. "But in all honesty, they had so many guys out of position. . ."

So what began promisingly enough in Oakland and Phoenix last week has ended with three straight losses and enough personnel problems to suit a bored Soviet production manager.

And Sanders, who's thinking of changing his middle name to Job, just wants to get back to Boston and see a man about a hoss. Two or three hosses, preferably, to get his depleted roster up to strength before Friday's game at Buffalo. Time is beginning to run out, what with only twenty-eight games remaining and the Celtics still fourteen under .500 and four and a half games out of a playoff berth.

"I have learned the value of the conditioned athlete," Sanders says, sizing up the available bodies. He has eleven places to fill and thirteen people to fill them with, including three injured men and two whose contracts expire before the weekend.

So after tête-à-têtes with both Auerbach and Dr. Tom Silva, Sanders decides to activate Jo Jo White, sign Ernie DiGregorio to a contract for the rest of the season, and leave Curtis Rowe in active limbo. Later, he'll decide to put Rowe on the injured list, and will make a quick call to Bob Bigelow, a forward out of the University of Pennsylvania with a nice shooting hand and the deepest voice this side of "The CBS Evening News." Bigelow is a local—"from lily-white Winchester," he laughs—and Sanders has always liked him.

All of which leaves Zaid Abdul-Aziz as the odd man out. His ten-day arrangement would have expired Thursday, but Sanders decided to give him the news in Houston. So the former Don Smith ended his Celtic career without ever having seen Causeway Street, thereby assuring himself a place in the trivia archives. For a beer, who was the only man . . . ?

Tuesday the 28th
ATLANTA, GA.

Only one passenger train comes through town anymore—the Southern Crescent to New Orleans. There are no Hungarian restaurants within the city limits. And they're going to tear up Peachtree Street—again—for a new subway.

But they still have a basketball team here, and after what happened at the Omni tonight, Georgia folk believe there'll be a postseason for the first time in five years.

They made the announcement about playoff tickets with two minutes left, when the people were standing and cheering and the lead had climbed to an incredible 28 points. And after eleventh-man Claude Terry, celebrating a rare bit of playing time, had tossed up a wounded duck at the buzzer and owner Ted Turner leaped from his seat, the house organist pounded out the year's theme song along Techwood Drive. "Happy Days Are Here Again."

Atlanta 117, Boston 85, it was, and it was every bit as good—or as horrible—as it sounds. The Celtics merely played lousy basketball from the third minute onward, and absorbed their worst beating since the 132–99 job Seattle hung on them at Christmas time.

"Don't take anything away from them," Dave Bing would say, amid a healthy silence in the Celtics room. "They kicked our ass."

The Hawks, who hold the playoff berth Boston wants, simply did everything well that they have to do to beat people with more talent.

"The steals, the turnovers, the assists," Steve Hawes was saying, running his finger down the box score. "Those are the columns that are important to us, because we lack rebounding. And if we get the rebounding . . ."

Which they did tonight, decisively. Then the Hawks embarrass people. And the Celtics, who thought, finally, that they'd gotten it turned around, felt humiliated. After regrouping in Boston before the weekend, they'd taken the games at Buffalo and Piscataway, and were looking for a sweep (here and in New Orleans tomorrow) that would have brought them back into the race. Now, they're four-and-a-half games behind both the Hawks and Jazz, with only twenty-five left to play.

"We've got quite a bit to say about our own playoff hopes," Sanders says, somberly, as the gear is packed. "Hopefully, this won't be the response again."

MARCH

Bring Down the Numbers

Wednesday the 1st
NEW ORLEANS, LA.

I'd spoken with him by phone three times and lobbed questions from the back of a postgame media mob or two, but not until this morning, when we wound up side by side on the plane from Atlanta, did Kermit Washington and I really converse. After an hour, I regretted we hadn't done it sooner. He is hardly the boringest person in the world.

What he is, is what he'd said he was—a quiet, conservative man of twenty-six from Washington, D.C., who liked California weather, Eastern religions, and the Puritan ethic.

"You know, when I was growing up in D.C., they called me 'Good Livin',' " he told me. "I'd be walking towards some friends on a corner and they'd say, 'Oh-oh, hide the beer and cigarettes. Here comes Good Livin'.' "

He wasn't priggish, he said, but he had a conscience that worked serious hours, whether Washington liked it or not. "Like, I don't think I could ever fool around on the road, whether or not anybody found out. I'd know, and it'd really bother me. In college, a friend stole the answers to an exam once. 'I don't even want to see 'em,' I told him. He got an A. I wound up with a C. Good Livin'."

On a basketball court, Washington became a curious amalgam of emotions, a man at once unselfish, aggressive, reticent, and fiercely self-protective. For one moment, one night, they had gone out of balance and caused him three months of hell, loosing a flood of ugly mail and nasty phone calls.

Washington had picked up a stack of letters during the stopover in Los Angeles and thumbed through them en route to Denver.

"That's a bad one," he could tell, with one glance at the envelope. "That's another one." "KERMIT WASHINGTON, Animal," it read.

The contents expanded on the theme. One letter had been scribbled on a business memo pad.

TO: Kermit Washington
FROM: White America
SUBJECT: Niggers

Washington would shake his head, smiling sadly. What kind of a mind would write that kind of thing? he'd ask you. And the postmarks weren't all predictable redneck hamlets. They came from Denver, Houston, Los Angeles . . . even Boston. The only common denominator was the anonymity.

So he'd tossed away the mail and had hotel operators divert his calls to Frankie Challant for screening. And Washington had gone back to work.

The hooting had begun to decrease with each game, to the point where you'd hardly notice—at least from crowd reaction—when he came off the bench for a Wicks or a Cowens. But the life was lonely.

Washington had been a Laker for nearly five years, ever since he'd turned pro out of American University. He'd bought a home on the Coast and liked it there. Anyway, you didn't want to move a wife and two small children to Boston in the middle of the worst winter in recorded history.

So Washington had moved into the Sheraton-Boston, where the Lakers stayed whenever they were in town, and was planning on living out the season there.

"I change rooms," he assured me. "I go from the Charles River side to one overlooking Copley Square. The only difference is, when you lose, you're at least able to come home and your wife says something nice. Here, my hotel walls are there. Win or lose, they say nothing."

Still, Washington likes Boston, and is grateful to Auerbach for the chance to play regularly. When his contract expires this spring, he says, he'll simply renegotiate. No bidding wars on the free-agent front.

"Why chase money?" he says. "I see some people who are lucky to be in the league asking for crazy contracts. Doesn't make sense."

Washington's own salary is reputed to be around $150,000, decidedly less than his worth. An unselfish power rebounder, on the NBA market, was worth more than anything but a starting center, an accomplished playmaker, or the very best shooting forward. You could count the quality performers on your fingers. With a good option year, Washington could demand $250,000 easily, maybe more, if he caught somebody like New York in a desperate moment.

And he could use the money. O'Brien's fine and the suspension had lifted a third of his salary, and there were legal fees upon legal fees, with daylight still a long way off.

"Think I don't want to make the playoffs?" he asked, entirely rhetorically.

Yet by midnight tonight, the playoffs have never seemed so distant. The Celtics came here with the best chance to make up ground in one evening that they've seen in a month. Atlanta was losing at New Jersey, and with only four minutes to play, Boston had left the Jazz for dead, 95–88.

And in a horrifying final two minutes, Sidney Wicks and John Havlicek each missed two free throws (with New Orleans leading by a basket each time), Dave Cowens was ejected for the first time in his career, and Dave Bing missed on a penetration drive that would have won it in the last three seconds. Jazz 101, Celtics 100—and Sanders was furious about it.

"That," he muttered, "was a gift. New Orleans worked pretty hard in the last part of the game, but we made it easy for them, between guys not knowing the plays and Dave blowing his top. No excuse for that. We're supposed to be professionals. Shit, I haven't seen a player change a call yet."

Rich Kelley, the Jazz's seven-foot center, had gone up over Cowens's back underneath, but referee Paul Mihalak had whistled

Cowens for pushing, and sent Kelley to the line in a bonus situation. Three to make two with 2:13 to play.

Cowens, incredulous, had stalked Mihalak, yelling at him, and upon seeing the "T" sign, came up with one of his own for Mihalak, his face twisted into sarcasm and disgust.

Mihalak thumbed him out, Kelley made both free throws, Gail Goodrich converted one of the technicals, and it was 99–97 and slipping away.

Afterwards, Cowens sat scrunched in his dressing stall, his head hung. He had violated Sanders's first commandment: *THOU SHALT NOT BE UNPROFESSIONAL.*

If you played for Auerbach, you'd had it drilled into you. You came to camp in shape. You knew the plays. You accepted your role. You made the intelligent play. And you kept your poise, especially down the stretch, which is where an evening was decided.

"Technicals don't do anything but cost you ball games," Cowens would say, upset with himself. "You're just helping 'em out. It was a real amateur mistake."

And it cost Boston a full game in the playoff race, with tomorrow's Garden rematch with the Jazz now taking on Custeresque proportions.

Saturday the 4th
NEW YORK, N.Y.

It was in the charts, even before they came down here this morning. The Captain could have told you that on the flight from New Orleans this week.

"The rhythms were down, right?" he nodded tonight, after the Celtics had been beaten, 99–91, in the final seven minutes at Madison Square Garden. The Gotham press corps, accustomed to more conventional losing analyses, buzzed in confusion.

"Bad biorhythms," Havlicek continued. "Physically, we were in a down cycle . . . and we didn't put the ball in the hole. What can I say?"

You could blame officials Jack Madden and Mel Whitworth for their myopia, which was the popular pastime in the Boston dressing room afterwards. Or you could look to the rhythms, which Havlicek has been studying ever since somebody gave him a calculator.

He'd taken it out on the team bus before Friday's flight to Logan, and quickly computed everybody's rhythms—physical, intellectual, emotional—for the weekend. If you gave him your birth date and your wife's or lover's, he could do a full relationship analysis.

Somewhere over North Carolina, the Delta stewardesses hear about it, and come over for a reading. Havlicek gets the birth date, punches the buttons, and raises his eyebrows.

"Have you and your boyfriend been getting along together physically?" he asks one woman, clinically. She blushes, as her colleagues giggle. "Not really, I guess."

"Didn't think so," Havlicek says, gravely. "Four percent compatibility." Tom Boswell, sitting across the aisle, can't believe the true-confessions potential here.

" 'Cek," he says. "Where do you get those machines? Yeah."

Sunday the 5th
BOSTON, MASS.

It was enough to make you believe in magic again, to believe that there will be evenings of wonder and drama on Causeway Street this month and a second season in April. It was a lovely old-time blowout of Noo Yawk on a chilly Sunday afternoon—Celtics 112, Knicks 94, for your records, and if you were sitting next to the B.U. sophomore from Queens, it was enormous fun.

From the moment Don Chaney popped a 14-footer 27 seconds after they went up for the tap, Boston never trailed, rolling up leads of 12–3, 27–14, 50–30, and 80–50 on the way to their earliest garbage time of the year. And along the way, the Celtics laid on their best *DEE*-fense in memory, limiting New York to 18 points at the break, 30 at halftime, and an incredible 50 after three quarters.

By then, all five Boston starters were resting comfortably, and

Tom Sanders was letting Ernie DiGregorio run the cleanup detail. After a forgettable week—a horsewhipping at Atlanta, a collapse at New Orleans, a close shave with the Jazz here Friday, and last night's hair-puller on 33rd Street—it was fun to watch the Celtics enjoying the fruit of a laugher they'd worked hard for.

"I remember a long time ago we used to sit on the bench and relax like that," Don Chaney would tell me afterwards. "And watch the game in the fourth quarter." He smiled, a little sadly, and I felt badly for him.

Chaney had been Boston's first-round draft choice in 1968, coming out of Houston where he'd played with Elvin Hayes on the team that had beaten UCLA and Lew Alcindor. As a rookie, he'd lived through the most bizarre—and rewarding—season in Celtic history. They'd finished fourth in the division, yet wound up shocking the Lakers at Los Angeles for the championship.

Chaney had been here for everything that followed, the two struggling years after Russell had retired, the Renaissance, with Cowens and White and Havlicek and Silas and Nelson, and the return to glory in 1974. He was the defense guard in the role-scheme, swatting balls away with oversized arms, rebounding faithfully.

He was The Duck (what else did you call a kid named Donald? It had followed him) and everybody liked him. But he'd played out his option in 1975 and gone over to the ABA, to the Spirits of St. Louis, hearing Auerbach's growls in the background. The goddamn ABA. When the Spirits folded in 1976, Chaney had signed with Los Angeles as a free agent. Now he was back in Boston, and the cycle had come round and was heading down again. Heinsohn had been fired. Nellie and Silas were gone. Havlicek was going. White was openly unhappy.

And Chaney was a forward now, starting alongside Cowens and Sidney Wicks, who was wearing Chaney's old number. "Got to get used to the punishment," Chaney would say, smiling. "The elbows, the shoving. It's *different* up there." Different all around. Sometimes I'd come in after games and see Chaney sitting at his stall, gazing quietly across the room, another loss just minutes old, the playoffs slipping away, the end growing nearer. Today . . . today belonged to the Renaissance.

Tuesday the 14th
BOSTON, MASS.

An hour before the tap, he was sitting in the loge seats, staring up at the retired jersey numbers hanging from the rafters. "I saw what Satch was saying in the papers," Detroit coach Bob Kauffman says, as I come looking for pregame notes.

"They still think they have a chance, don't they? They still think they're going to turn it around? Well, you bring back Russell and Cousy and Heinsohn and the Jones boys. Put a 14 on somebody, and a 6 . . . and maybe the numbers will bring 'em back."

For one evening "the numbers"—the future numbers, that is, specifically 17 and 18—worked their magic. John Havlicek and Dave Cowens tore the game away from the Pistons tonight, and they did it with one of the sacred Celtic relics—the back-door play.

Twice in the last three minutes Cowens found Havlicek alone under the basket for three-point plays to give Boston a 99–95 lead after they'd trailed for the entire second half. The final was 105–98, and it kept this frail fragment of a season alive, even as Cleveland was beating Houston easily at the Coliseum, which is the next port of call.

"You wouldn't believe what they were saying to each other out there," Kevin Stacom would tell me, after the Pistons came apart like a cheap sub-economy compact in the fourth quarter. "Pass *me* the ball, mother*fuck*er."

While the faithful might have viewed it as a Boston comeback in the grand tradition, it was considered a master job of bungling by the Detroit players, who are three and a half games behind Milwaukee in the race for the final Western playoff berth and needed this game badly.

Some of them, including Bob Lanier, their brooding captain, felt it had been Kauffman's fault. He'd had both Lanier and guard Eric Money, his two best scorers, gathering dust on the bench together when Boston made its run.

Others, remembering how the Pistons had been outscored 14–3 in the final three minutes, looked elsewhere. "Look in the damn mirror, motherfuckers," one of them yelled in the dressing room afterwards. "Why don't you try *that* some morning, huh?"

Dave Bing, who spent his nine years in a Detroit jersey and had had his fill of that kind of talk, shook his head. "Hey," he says, "let 'em have all the problems they want. We got our own."

Like a 25–39 record with eighteen games to go and a plane leaving for Cleveland tomorrow night.

Thursday the 16th
CLEVELAND, OHIO

They belong to "the numbers" now, to the loss column and the games behind and the twenty-four days that are left to them. You can talk about improved play and how much the guys all want it, but every loss adjusts the numbers upward and downward, and none of them are doing the Celtics any good.

Cleveland 112, Boston 102, it was, and it was over as soon as the Coliseum clock began running in the fourth quarter. Austin Carr made a layup, Campanella Russell popped one from the key, and Terry Furlow hit a 15-footer—all within 81 seconds—and the margin was 13 points and it was gone.

So the Celtics lost their fifth straight game on the road. They lost their third to the Cavaliers, and with it, the season's series that will serve as the primary tiebreaker, should the two clubs finish in a tie on April 9. And they fell a full seven games behind Cleveland in the race for the final Eastern playoff berth with seventeen to play.

Which means that anybody who still has a shred of optimism should write a nice note to his favorite Pacific Division coach and ask for a bit of charity this weekend—like a 20-point victory over these Atlanta and New Orleans people. That's the way it is, crazy as it might have seemed last September.

"I think we really have to have help," John Havlicek is admitting finally, having inspected every available cloud for traces of a rainbow. "At one point, I thought we really weren't going to need any, but now . . ."

The margin has shrunk to almost nothing. The Celtics have to overtake two clubs to get even the meanest best-of-three, on-the-road playoff spot. And Dave Cowens stares at the floor when you mention it.

"I got a feeling," he says tonight, "it's gonna be a short season."

Cleveland—Richfield Township, actually—is no place to look for helping hands. Boston hasn't won in this building since it clinched the Eastern Conference title two years ago, and two bad spurts, one at the beginning of each half, were enough to take them down tonight.

I'm thinking about that back at the hotel, when the elevator door opens and several members of The Tubes, an androgynous punk-rock group, crowd on. This *is* Swingos' Celebrity Hotel, after all.

The men are wearing jeans, platform heels, and satin athletic jackets—their road uniform. The women are something out of Charles Addams—the skin chalky white, the hair straight, the gown sleek, Morticia-style.

"You with the Celtics?" one of them asks.

"Yeah," I nod. "I travel with them. A writer."

"They lost, right?"

"Yeah. Usually do out here. Bad city."

One of the women is sympathetic. "Like Chicago," she offers. "We always have a bad gig in Chicago. The truck never arrives, the equipment breaks down. You know?"

Sure.

Saturday the 18th
BOSTON, MASS.

Z-z-z-z-z-z.

If you liked *Coma,* you belonged here this afternoon, watching two basketball teams on life-support systems, kept alive by inertia and "the numbers." The Kansas City Kings hadn't won a road game in a month (they were 6–27 on the year, actually), had taken an 11-point licking at Philadelphia last night, and grabbed "the Midnight Special" for Logan Airport.

And the Celtics, living day to day and looking for outside help, were playing their third game in forty-two hours, with another coming up here tomorrow afternoon against Denver.

Together they produced one of the great spectator snores of the age, a 117–110 Boston triumph that kept the home forces breathing in full view of 8,894 of the dedicated . . . but not much more.

"Every time I looked up at the clock," John Havlicek would tell me, yawning, "I thought it would be farther along than it was." He'd seen *Coma* and read the book, so he was familiar with enforced somnolence.

The game, actually, had been flash-frozen on January 20, when heavy snow kept the Kings from getting any further east than O'Hare Airport. They weren't going to be in the remote area again until this weekend so both teams merely dropped the date in between last night and tomorrow afternoon. And the Celtics, who ravaged Phoenix yesterday to stall their magic elimination number at nine, just pretended it was a Coast trip, where this sort of thing is commonplace.

So the pace was leisurely, and I spent most of the afternoon cracking peanuts next to Bob Bigelow, who'd played for both teams this year. The Celtics had let him go with a hearty handshake after his ten-day contract had expired, and he'd just been keeping in shape, playing pickup games and doing clinics. This was a social call.

"Scored 58 points in a game at New Haven last week," he tells me. "But don't make a big thing of it. We were playing against a bunch of old guys. Actually, I've been doing more volunteer work than Clara Barton."

Presently, I mentioned Ernie DiGregorio, and what a shame it was that he was spending night after night on the bench. We could use some offensive pyrotechnics about now, I guessed. Bigelow laughed.

"Hey," he said, "you're looking at the undisputed *king* of the DNP's. A hundred and four in two years. Glenn Hansen and I . . . every night, we'd sit on the bench together and look at girls in the stands. Hey, up there, Section 107."

The Kings had drafted him in the first round three years ago, then never used him. Bigelow had explained their rationale for me, but I'd forgotten it. Either it was too complicated or it didn't make sense. Maybe both.

We pass a pleasant afternoon together, glancing up every so often to make sure the game is still in progress. Later, Bigelow visits both locker rooms, with postgame greetings for all. He was good company, and I'd begun to regret he hadn't been around all year. After five months, camaraderie had begun to be the only reason to keep interested.

Sunday the 19th
BOSTON, MASS.

No, Red Auerbach hasn't thought about bringing in The Bee Gees to sing "Stayin' Alive" instead of the national anthem this week—but he should. Because "The Star-Spangled Banner" just doesn't make it now that the Celtics have grabbed the calendar and the loss column in a full-nelson, trying to squeeze a dozen more victories out of the last twenty-one days.

What they achieved in just forty-two hours at the Garden this weekend was merely remarkable after stepping off a plane from Cleveland—and their fortieth loss—Friday noon. There was the 115–108 victory over Phoenix that night. The bleeder at Kansas City's expense yesterday. And today, a 122–95 mauling of Denver that stands as the Celtics' finest hour of the year.

"Has to be the best," decided Tom Sanders, after the Celtics had throttled their guests with an awesome second quarter and ended it by halftime. "That's what I might term, mildly, a very powerful performance."

And it was the Golden Era backcourt, a thirty-seven-year-old John Havlicek and thirty-four-year-old Dave Bing, that did it. Of a possible 288 minutes at guard, they'd played 230 in the three games, pausing only to swig water during timeouts, take a short blow now and then, and go back out to work against younger legs.

"You're going to be eligible for a lifetime MTA pass before long," I told Bing, after he'd finished up with 32 minutes, 15 points, and eight assists today. He'd laughed, and looked over at Havlicek, who'd scored 27 in his 38 minutes. " 'Cek and I ... we're gonna need one if this keeps up," he said, before heading off to the whirlpool. Someone had stuck a swatch of tape on it, christening it the USS *Pee Wee-Chief,* because Bing and Jo Jo White spent so much time soaking there.

Bing liked the minutes, actually. After a year as a bench ornament in Washington, it was nice to feel needed, even if it was only for hosing down the smoking rubble. And Havlicek would play all 48 if you'd let him. His body functioned more effectively under heavy use, he thought.

"Aren't you worried about running those guys into the ground?" I'd asked Sanders at one point. He'd given me the "Be serious" look.

"If things don't work out," he said, "they can have all the rest they can handle. And if they *do* work out, then, after the playoffs, they can have all the rest they can handle."

Tuesday the 21st
LANDOVER, MD.

We've seen this story before on Sunday afternoons, with tympani and slow violins and actual footage of Axis soldiers slogging through rubble on the way to 1945.

"The curtain descends," the titles said, and somebody with a bowel-deep voice talked about time running out and the world closing in on all sides.

The symbolism may be a little heavy—I mean, there *have* been forty losses already—but the parallels are real enough for the Celtics, who find themselves running short of days and bodies all at once.

Tonight they could put only nine men on the floor, and that included Dave Cowens, who'd turned his stomach inside out with bad swordfish last night.

Curtis Rowe was back home with his bum knee. Don Chaney made the trip, but his sore heel put him into street clothes after an abortive warmup. And if Cowens, who wasn't going to come down at all, hadn't caught a late flight, it would have been Minimum

Time again, in a building where Boston hadn't won in two years.

Not that it made much difference, anyway. The Bullets—or more precisely, Elvin Hayes—did exactly as they pleased from the tapoff, shooting long and rebounding close, and the deficits looked familiar—16–6, 26–14, 52–36, 72–56. The final was 119–107.

Nothing much you needed to say after that, except when can we get *out* of here?

"There's a 2:30 A.M. red-eye out of Baltimore," I inform Cowens. "Interested?"

He is, and he says a few others might be, too. A full evacuation by moonlight. After Cowens refills his stomach and I finish up Sob Story #41 on the season, we walk outside to find the rental car.

The Capital Centre, a modern and massive cavern of the winds, was plunked down in an old soybean field, an air ball away from the Beltway. A chill mist envelops everything as we walk across the parking lot . . . could just as well be midnight in Kentucky.

"Frog-giggin' weather," Cowens decides, cocking his head. "I can hear 'em now." Damn right. Go out in a boat with a flashlight and a modified trident and look for the whites of their eyes. Get a bagful. Cowens did it all the time back home with his buddies. Most natural thing in the world.

He was a good ole boy at heart, and simple pleasures delighted him. I'd never seen him happier than he was at his Derby Day barbecue last year, standing behind his grill with an apron around him, sleeves rolled up, the smoke rising. Steaks, ribs, bratwurst, beans, beers. And later, as they were calling them to post on his TV inside, Cowens had come around with juleps. Fresh mint and natural sugar. Yes, suh.

He'd called the house a few days before, when I was in Philadelphia doing a playoff game, and talked to my wife. "How ya doin'?" he'd said. "This is Dave Cowens, and I was wondering what y'all had planned for Saturday. Back home, Derby Day's pretty big and . . ."

If he'd been in Kentucky, he'd tell me, he would have been there. Get a few cases of beer and some buddies and drive down to Churchill Downs. Take your shirt off and roam the infield.

Essential pleasures were the best ones, weren't they? David Cowens didn't need much in the way of material goods—a wool jacket, a parka, wing tips, trousers from a suit, a necktie, and a tweed cap would do for a road trip. Jeans and a work shirt were enough at home. Tool around in a truck, live out of a second-floor flat in the suburbs.

Like Hemingway, it was more important to him to know *how*—how to tune an engine, run a store, drive a taxi. Yet Cowens had an attention to detail and a perfectionist's drive. At his summer basketball camps, he'd oversee everything from sweat socks to Wednesday's lunch. And during the season, he'd carry a briefcase on the plane with him, stuffed with brochure layouts and guides from the Small Business Administration.

And when he went to the Far East to do his clinics, he'd scowl at botched plays. "Next guy who makes the same mistake twice takes a lap around Japan," he'd say, as the interpreter squinted and shrugged.

Living through this season galls him. Cowens has never played on a losing team, not even at Newport Catholic. And despite his own Olympian contributions, he feels confused and humiliated. Tonight was just another two hours spent chasing shadows. Didn't need to stay overnight.

At the hotel, we pick up Chaney and Sidney Wicks and head for the Baltimore–Washington Parkway, doing an easy 70 on empty road with light disco playing on the radio.

"Hey, Duck, what kind of music do you like?" Wicks wants to know.

"Well, to tell you the truth, my tastes are kind of stagnant at the moment," Chaney says.

"Musical stagnation, huh?" Wicks says, pondering it. "Well, I dig it *all*. Disco, rock, jazz, blues. Everything."

Donna Summer, the disco queen, is his high priestess, though. On a transcontinental flight, Wicks always had the headphones on before anybody else, and you could tell when a Summer cut came on. Wicks's eyes would close, his mouth would open, and his hands would move. "Love to Love You, Baby" could send him off into another rhythmic galaxy.

They might have called Bing Disco, but Wicks was the man for that. He went to discotheques religiously, where he cut a striking figure at 6–9, the clothes fitting tightly. With the beard and the penetrating eyes, he looked like a sheik. Omar, somebody called him once, seeing him emerge from the showers draped in towels. Looks like Sharif, heading for his war camel.

He *was* intrigued with movies—Sidney Abdul-Hollywood, an L.A. writer had dubbed him once—and Havlicek once told me that Wicks had appeared in films himself. Basketball was simply another form of self-expression, like dancing, or popping your fingers to disco tapes 20,000 feet above the earth.

There are no headphones on the Delta flight to Boston, but there is Ernie DiGregorio. He is sprawled in a first-class seat as we board, arms and legs flung out in an *X,* a blanket pulled up to his chin.

He is the undisputed Red-Eye King, hunting out obscure 2:00 A.M. flights from Denver and Houston that will get him back to Boston, and ultimately, Rhode Island, a dozen hours early. A friend will pick him up at the airport, he says, and he'll be having breakfast with his wife and two daughters when most of his teammates are still struggling out of bed in a Sheraton somewhere.

Gradually, DiGregorio comes awake, and we chat. Cowens, leaning forward, wants to know what it's been like for him, gathering dust now, his playing time shrunk to three or four minutes a night.

"It bothers me," DiGregorio admits, "but it doesn't bother me like it should bother me. You know what I mean? Because if it did bother me like it should bother me . . ."

He'd turn bitter . . . or go crazy. Or both. He learned a long time ago, he says that it didn't pay to worry about things like that. It was not a predictable life or an orderly world, and you did best by expecting nothing.

Hadn't DiGregorio grown up in a working-class Italian neighborhood, played for North Providence High, shot free throws by himself, hour after hour, when everybody else was on their way to the beach?

And one day, hadn't he risen to find himself a millionaire, guaranteed $50,000 a year for the next thirty years by the Buffalo Braves? Hadn't he been able to build himself a mansion in Lincoln with a library?

A library? friends had puzzled. Didn't know your scholarly interests ran that deep. No, DiGregorio was supposed to have said.

But I always thought it'd be nice, so when I had friends over, I could say, Why don't you step into the library?

But if you knew Ernie—and nobody knew him better than Kevin Stacom; they were flip sides of the same Irish-Italo coin—you knew that the money, the library didn't mean a damn to him, really. He wanted to play, and he would play in a YMCA in Des Moines if that was where he could get his minutes. Pay me $100 a week. Pay me nothing. It don't matter.

But there were precious few minutes for him in Boston—the players aren't used to his passing yet, the reasoning went. Maybe in the fall, after a training camp . . .

Now, he was just another casualty of a forgettable campaign, slogging through the rubble, waiting for the curtain to descend.

Friday the 24th
BOSTON, MASS.

Sheriff Ray Bledsoe had the words for Butch Cassidy and the Sundance Kid eighty years ago this spring once the fences had begun closing in. "It's over," he told them. "And you're gonna die—bloody—and all you can do is choose where." Which is what the Celtics are hearing around them now, as the days slip away and the losses mount. Tonight's hurt . . . badly. It was Boston's game with six minutes left. The lead was five points and holding steady. With 10 seconds left, the Celtics still led by a point, and had the ball. But Dave Bing's hurried jumper bounced off the rim, and Chicago had possession with time for one shot.

The inbounds pass, intended for Mickey Johnson, had been picked off by Kermit Washington, though, as Johnson fell down. But referee Jake O'Donnell whistled a foul on Washington—from his vantage point on the baseline, he thought Johnson had been pushed. You didn't just fall that dramatically, he thought. So Chicago got the ball back, and with one second left, Johnson threw in a twisting fallaway jumper to win it.

Later, they ran the videotape machine back and forth, back and forth a dozen times, the Celtics standing around cursing with each replay. Washington had never touched Johnson from a side view. He'd just lost his balance jumping for the ball. It was a clean steal. Still . . .

"We should have put the game out of reach long before the end," John Havlicek would tell me, softly. Chicago had lost twelve of their last thirteen games on the road, after all. And there had been bickering in the Bulls' locker room at halftime, when Boston had had a comfortable lead. You put teams like that away early. Auerbach had insisted on it.

Sunday the 26th
SEATTLE, WASH.

Not to become overly morbid about it or to bury these people before their time, but if you know a nice old lady named Dowd or Callahan who owns a black dress and a good set of tear ducts, sign her up soon. Because there's going to be a Celtic wake coming up. The only question is when . . . and where.

That seems almost certain now that another day has gone awasting. Another loss—number forty-three—has been added to the down side, and only ten games remain. Today's defeat was neither very remarkable nor very numbing. The Celtics simply let an eight-point, third-quarter lead slip away in a cloud of Sonic exhaust and lost going away, 112–101.

"Just one more loss," conceded Tom Sanders, "and I think we've seen it. I'm not holding out straws. That's just the way I see it." He'd been following the numbers as closely as anybody. Last week, as a mathematical/adjectival reminder to the gentlemen, Sanders had posted a playoff chart in the dressing room—BOSTON'S CHANCES: GREAT 42–40, FABULOUS 41–41, OUTSTANDING 40–42, REALLY GOOD 39–43, TIGHT BUT O.K. 38–44, A PROBLEM 37–45, AFTER THAT . . . A MIRACLE, WITH HELP FROM ALL OTHERS. As each figure had become impossible, Sanders had crossed it out.

It is going to take pontifical intervention to do much for Boston at this point—unless you think the Celtics can win their final ten games, including the rest of the God's Country Trilogy at Portland tomorrow and Denver Wednesday. Even so, two of their three rivals (Cleveland, Atlanta, and New Orleans) will have to come unglued at the same time.

That might not have been entirely necessary last week, but after Friday's sorry loss to Chicago and today's defeat here, there is simply not that much luck in the universe—Irish or otherwise.

And it has become more than a matter of luck. The Celtics are simply being beaten now, beaten with their own hallowed techniques. When the Sonics wanted the game today, they simply cranked up their fast break and sprinted away with it. "If we could get running," coach Lenny Wilkens would say, "I knew their transition wasn't very good." You never thought anybody would be able to say that about a Boston team. And Paul Silas, playing in Seattle green now, was a little sad about it afterwards.

"To see them play like that . . . the guys not really caring . . . it was really sort of frustrating for me," he'd tell me. "I didn't really enjoy playing against them. The fight, the spirit, it wasn't there. When you played the Celtics, you'd be in a battle and you enjoyed it. You hoped it would always be that way. This year, it was almost like they were a laughingstock."

Monday the 27th
TILLAMOOK, OREG.

Hangin' out at the Wilson Hilton, where the river roars all night outside your window and lumber trucks rumble along the two-lane blacktop up above.

"Wanna fish for some steelhead?" the Captain had asked, before we'd ever left Boston. "I met a guy out in Oregon last time who said he'd take us. I'm supposed to give him a call."

Always wanted to do a full Hemingway. Big Two-Hearted River and all that, even though I haven't been fishing since 1957, when I lost my beginner's rod in the Cape Cod Canal. No problem,

Havlicek says. The guy—Bob Zwand is his name—will pick us up at the airport as soon as we get off the plane from Seattle. He has all the gear. We'll take the Bird along with us, and go right out to the cottage."

Zwand appears on schedule, a good-natured man, totally accommodating. We drive downtown, to Portland, so I can hand in a game story at the Western Union office, and then head out to a rendezvous spot, a Denny's Restaurant somewhere in suburban Oregon. Portland is a delightful town, with bridges crisscrossing everywhere, two rivers (the Columbia and Willamette), green hills and fresh air, with buildings out of 1934 alongside new high rises, a town where they sell hot dogs on street corners in the afternoon rain and cab drivers still say, "Jumpin' Jehosophat."

Within 20 minutes, you can be alone with the trees and the stars, heading for a river where you can fish all day without seeing more than half a dozen human beings.

Before midnight, we're at the Wilson Hilton, a pleasant wooden house at the foot of an embankment, with hills looming up around. Everything you would need is here—bunk beds, a wood-burning stove, bathroom, and affable fishing companions. Jim and Dave Farley, brothers, will be the boatmen. Dale Ott will be the comic philosopher.

By six o'clock, we're putting gear into the trucks, as the fog rises up everywhere. The air is chilly, and the only sound is the river rushing by a hundred feet away. Surrealistic, is what it is.

"I've been out here some days when everything the good Lord could throw at you he's done," says Ott. "Snow, hail, 50-mile-an-hour winds, fog. Break the ice and row across to the hole. Spook all the fish, row back to the bank and wait. Go back again, cast for 'em and catch 'em."

Jim Farley, who runs a flower business in Gresham, laughs. "There is no truth to that whatsoever," he says.

"The hell there ain't," Ott replies, convinced.

Ott, in no particular order, is a graphic designer, fisherman, and Trail Blazer season-ticket holder. He has definite theories on a) the state of professional basketball and b) Sidney Wicks. His traveling companions are interested parties, but somewhat less avid.

"I was awful," says Zwand. "After I got cut from my high-school freshman squad, I caught on with an industrial team. And the first night I got my suit, the star forgot his tennies. I had to give him mine, and sit on the bench in my stocking feet. Life is cruel, gentlemen."

Zwand, who is white-haired and nicely rounded, *can* fish, though. Nestucca Fats, they call him, because nobody finds as many steelhead trout in the Nestucca River as he does.

Whether we'll find any in the Wilson River today is questionable. The winter run had been over for nearly a month, but the Celtics couldn't get here any earlier. "Most people think the fishing's done by now," Jim Farley says, as we head into town for breakfast. "Most of the intelligent people, anyway."

Breakfast is country-substantial—eggs, toast, sausage, home fries, coffee, juice—and we eat it at the Big Cheese Grill. This is famous dairy country, and they send their cheese all over the world. The coin-op laundry across the street is the Little Cheese.

"Is there a high school here?" I ask Ott.

"Limburger High," he nods.

By eight, we're on the river, having unloaded two boats and slid them down a mucky bank onto the sand. The trees—there are trees everywhere—are still shrouded in mist. The air is crisp and clean, the water sparkling. Switzerland, I think. No wonder they tell everybody it rains all the time. They don't want everybody coming up here to spoil it. DON'T CALIFORNICATE OREGON, the bumper stickers say.

The Wilson is narrow, deep in some spots, but in others, boulders lie just below the surface that can poke a hole in the bottom of a boat. Dave Farley, who's just had this one built to order, does not seem alarmed by this, nor by my tendency to hang lures up in trees. He is the old pro among us, with the "Oregon Guides and Packers" patch on his shirt.

He knows every hiding place in the river and handles the boat skillfully, pulling hard against the current, now turning left to inspect the unseen holes where steelhead like to hide.

"Steelhead spook easily," he is saying. "Not like a salmon."

"Yeah," Zwand says. "Salmon are so damn dumb they'll hit anything."

As we drift downstream, time seems to be suspended. You can pass two hours without seeing another fisherman or hearing anything but the whirr of the casting reel, the burbling of the river, and the distant whine of truck tires on blacktop.

The winter was rough here—storms tore away huge chunks of the bank on either side, felled trees, and turned the river swollen and angry. Still, some people take the risk of building houses—if frequently on stilts—because they love the area, and we pass A-frames, cottages, and ranches perched on the bank.

By now it's noon, and nobody's even come within spooking distance of a steelhead. Looking upstream, we see Havlicek and Ott standing, casting, reeling in, casting again. Nothing.

Then Zwand hits something—"Damn!" he yells, and there is a distant splash . . . and then, nothing. As the afternoon wears on, resignation sets in. We are late, after all. The others talk about coming here in midseason with the Wilson choked with fish and even rank novices finding steelhead. Later, as the buzzard circles lazily overhead, we pass tin shacks on either side.

"Old farts use 'em," Zwand says. "They cast out into the middle of the river, then put the rod into a holder with a bell, to signal 'em, and then go back inside to lie to each other and hear the rain fall."

As suppertime approaches, there is only a mile or so of river left to fish, and Farley is desperately pulling from side to side, searching every possible hole that's ever produced a trout. He seems a little embarrassed, bring these people all the way out for nothing, after all the steelhead we found here.

Havlicek doesn't seem to mind. I've rarely seen him more at ease, in fact. He loves the outdoors and the intricacies of fishing, and he escapes to them during the offseason. Last summer, he and Stacom did some fishing in Maine. "You'd love it," Havlicek had told me. "Eat all you want."

And he had gone off to Montana with Indiana coach Bobby Knight, a former college teammate, and some friends, getting as remote as possible, with horses and pans for frying trout and hip-waders. You had to break the ice in the water basin to wash your face in the morning. "Just packin' up," Havlicek had said, a satisfied smile spreading, "and hangin' out."

He had asked Tom Sanders for this day off two months ago, as much for the pleasant isolation as anything else. Any trout would be a bonus.

"Damn," Dave Farley says, as we finally head for shore. "I *hate* getting skunked. And we fished this river hard." Ott promises they'll send along some steelhead—canned—to Boston, and we head back to Portland and another Hilton. The next night, at Memorial Coliseum, the Blazers will bid farewell to the Captain, giving him— among other things—a graphite rod.

"We went looking for steelhead," Havlicek will tell the crowd, "and we got skunked. So you owe me one."

Tuesday the 28th
PORTLAND, OREG.

The jerseys—white, clean, and crisp—are draped neatly on red hangers on every locker in the home dressing room here. WALTON, they read, GROSS, STEELE, NEAL. Nobody used them tonight, and if you would ask coach Jack Ramsay if they will be used next week or next month, he would shrug and use the word "hope" in every sentence.

Jacky Dorsey, Dale Schlueter, Corky Calhoun, and Willie Norwood are the Trail Blazers these days, fitted in and around what remains of Ramsay's NBA champions. So beating Portland at Memorial Coliseum before the usual frenzied 12,666 (and a closed-circuit audience downtown) doesn't have nearly the cosmic significance it did at Christmas time.

Unless, of course, you are the Celtics, and a road victory over a .500 club of any denomination is cause for wild cheering and chilled wines. So Ramsay and the entire state of Oregon received about a third of an ounce of sympathy last night after the Celtics rolled up a 19-point lead on "the remains" last night and ended with a nicely preserved 104–92 victory.

It was the Mathematically Dying vs. the Physically Depleted—a lovely sort of brawl—and you could hear the catcalls all night from season ticket holders who'd watched Portland riddle the Celtics by 44 points here last year. If Walton's foot hadn't gone bad, they muttered. If Gross hadn't busted the ankle. If we hadn't had to sign up every unemployed former NBA player to fill out the roster.

"Hey Boston," one man had howled during a timeout, "how's it feel to beat a City League team, huh?"

Right now, absolutely effervescent, considering the alternative.

Wednesday the 29th
DENVER, COLO.

Numbness. You stared at the scoreboard, as the people spilled out of the stands and danced on the floor, and caught a glimpse of a raging Dave Cowens chasing referee Joe Gushue, demanding that he explain the unexplainable.

How could he have called a foul with 15 seconds to play on something like that, on an accidental brush of one player's hand by another's? How did you take a 106–101 Boston lead with 59 seconds to play and make it a 109–106 loss, just like that?

"He said he'd call it the same way anytime," Cowens told me, his voice heavy with disgust, after Gushue had nailed him with a cheap backcourt foul and turned the entire game around. "And I said, 'Man, you *know* it's a different situation. Give him three shots and put 'em ahead on that?' The whole goddamn game comes down to that?"

Yup. And a season, just when it looked as if the Celtics might force the issue at least until the weekend, and the Garden showdown with New Orleans. They had controlled this one from the start, passing and breaking and shooting with lovely fury, leading the Nuggets at every juncture.

And as the final two dozen seconds were ticking away, and Cowens reached in to slap the ball away from Denver's Tony Roberts, Gushue's whistle blew and it was gone.

Even Roberts, a rookie, was surprised. Most referees would have let it go. "He fouled me, yeah, but we were going down the floor and

Ralph Simpson had the ball," Roberts would remember. "And all of a sudden, our bench started cheering. And I said, not me. Not me going to the foul line. I was shocked."

He made his two shots, and "the numbers" dropped another notch, even with the Jazz losing at home to Los Angeles. It is one with Cleveland now, and three with New Orleans and Atlanta. Kindergarten integers.

Friday the 31st
BOSTON, MASS.

You'll see them tomorrow—"Saturday Night Live" as the Not-Ready-for-Prime-Time Players—performing their own version of "Franco Takes Turn for Worse."

Is the Celtics dead, as Charlie Dressen used to say? Nope, just seems that way, although they grabbed themselves by the throats and twisted their necks another full turn tonight before 13,000 of their dearest friends at the Garden.

This time it was San Antonio 120, Boston 117, as the home folks blew a 17-point second-quarter lead, then got themselves outscored, 13–1, down the stretch to kick it away entirely.

So Cleveland is out of reach now, and a loss to New Orleans here tomorrow or an Atlanta victory at New Jersey Sunday would end it. And all the nine days in April would be good for is screwing up a good draft choice.

What happened tonight was travesty enough for a full month, since the Spurs had absolutely no reason to win here. They'd clinched the Central Division title and a first-round playoff bye last night by beating the Cavaliers. And they'd begun the day with the worst possible combination—waking up in an airport motel in Cleveland with champagne hangovers.

"I don't think nobody went to sleep last night," Larry Kenon would say, whooping. "I know I didn't." So Doug Moe, the coach, had pulled all five starters before halftime, conceding it. And the Spurs still won it going away.

They are not what they were a year ago, when they'd swoon at the sight of green. They play loose and hard and hungry, even hung over, making their fourth stop in as many cities in as many nights.

"We *like* to play a lot of games in a row," Moe said, gleefully. "Hell, we're from the ABA." A long time ago. Now, the San Antonio *Light* spreads the Spurs—CHAMPIONS!!!—across its first four pages. The mayor urges everybody to go to the airport to welcome 'em home. And nobody worries about best-of-threes anymore.

Used to be like that here.

APRIL

Locking the Door

As March has become April and the playoffs are merely a fragment of a figment, the theme song along Causeway Street has become "Stayin' Alive." And the man they call Travolta has memorized it, note for note, line for line.

The Celtics may tease Kevin Stacom about his *Saturday Night Fever* fetish, but tonight his wild-eyed, open-mouthed enthusiasm (and his career-high 22 points) swept through them infectiously.

And what had been a 20-point deficit 14 minutes into the evening turned into a giddy 119–108 Boston disco dance that dealt New Orleans a staggering blow, and kept the Celtics alive. At least overnight.

Stacom accounted for most of that with one brilliant burst in the second quarter, when he wiped out the Jazz's 39–19 lead by setting up four baskets and scoring four points himself. Then, in the fourth quarter, he unloaded a 12-point barrage, with DiGregorio looking for him and Stacom swishing jumper after jumper.

"All you have to do is move," Stacom would tell me. "Ernie gets things in motion, and we get running. That's the way this team has always played. That's the only way to play."

It was a simple game, Stacom would tell you. You played defense, you looked for the open man, you took your shot. Fundamental. You didn't need a complicated system, boxes of chalk, or intricate zone presses. You knew how to play the game if you'd come this far. *Play* the game.

He'd been with the club four years and got his ring in 1976, when they'd all embraced in a last hurrah at Phoenix.

This year, when the losses had piled up and Stacom was watching teammates stand around, walk through plays, and throw up junk from outside, he'd romanticize about the old days—intensely—over beer.

"I wish you could have been there for it," he would sigh. "Nellie, Silas . . . they were *men.*" Stacom was the last of them, the only Celtic who knew the words to "The Rising of the Moon" or could find his way to Kerry.

He was a Catholic from Queens, Holy Cross H.S., and he had a teen-aged sister named Noreen and a couple of aunts who liked a sip of whisky now and then.

You would see Stacom slipping lightly up the street on the road, going after a cold Heineken and a game of pinball, and he'd be wearing a long tweed overcoat and a scalley cap, the thick, curly hair bushing out underneath. He looked like a courier for the IRA Provos, and he had a fine Hibernian cynicism.

"What are they telling you?" he'd want to know, and I'd say, "Well, the front office says . . ."

He'd grin, the head moving up and down. "And you believe that, right?"

He kept his own counsel, answering postgame questions laconically if he didn't know you, but Stacom had more philosophical depth than most people suspected . . . and more nicknames than anybody in the dressing room. He was the Stakeman, the Snake, Pit (because he sweated freely during a game), but mostly, he was the Bird.

"Can you believe that guy," someone had remarked, after Buffalo's Bird Averitt had gone one-for-twelve with long-range jumpers in a game against Boston last year. "Hey," Havlicek had responded, pointing to Stacom, who'd gone one-for-ten. "We've got our own Bird."

On the road, he'd read Kafka and Dostoevsky when most of us

were flipping through *Inflight* magazine (or worse). "Listen to this," he'd say, quoting a passage from *The Idiot* about dullness in great men. "That's great shit."

Once, he'd likened himself to the Kafka character in *The Metamorphosis* who wakes to find himself a beetle. Inwardly, I haven't changed, he'd say, when Heinsohn inexplicably had him on the bench. But . . .

Now, he was Travolta. I'd come into the room before a game and spotted him in the bathroom, shaving.

"Seen *Saturday Night Fever* yet?"

He'd nodded and began singing in a Bee Gee falsetto . . . "Oh you can tell by the way I use my walk I'm a woman's man . . ."

He was still the kid from Queens, a little bit awed by the City, but defiant of it. He loved the scene from *Fever,* where the Brooklyn kids are going back across the bridge to Bay Ridge. Stopping the car, they look back at the skyscrapers, and bring the arms up, middle fingers pointed.

That's what's going to happen this month, I'd told him. You guys are going to make a fantastic comeback, reach the playoffs, and draw the Knicks in a best-of-three. Games are 1–1, the finale at Madison Square Garden. New York leads by one, six seconds left, you bring the ball up, looking for Havlicek and the Ohio play. No chance, so you drive to the top of the key, and let it go, the shot falling as the buzzer sounds, and the whole building going quiet. And then you run to center court, staring at the balcony, and do it.

He'd smiled. And you *believe* that, right?

Sunday the 2nd
BOSTON, MASS.

The End—officially—came at 3:59 EST by the Garden clock this afternoon, just after Indiana guard Mike Flynn had dropped in two free throws with two seconds to play.

Maybe we could have run a comparative time check with the Omni people, since Atlanta was beating New Jersey there simultaneously, making the Celtics' disappearance doubly certain.

But it was more symbolic to think of the burial coming here, where the worst foul shooter on the worst team in the Western Conference seals the lid on the most forgettable basketball season in Boston since 1970.

As it was, the Pacers had come here without two men. Coach Bobby Leonard, who'd given the season up for lost, was off scouting something called the Pizza Hut Classic, leaving assistant Jerry Oliver to run the show. Four of their nine men were playing on sprained ankles, and forward Ron Behagen worked most of the afternoon with one black Adidas sneaker and one white Converse.

Yet they hung on Boston's shoulder all day long, and when the deal went down, Indiana simply grabbed the game away, just as the Spurs, their old ABA cousins, had done here Friday night.

"I don't think it's the same Celtics I played against with Phoenix in the playoffs two years ago," Ricky Sobers would tell me. "They still had a mathematical chance today. Maybe we just wanted it more."

It was a moot point, actually. By the time the Celtics hit the showers, word had arrived about Atlanta's triumph, which would have rendered a 100-point Boston victory meaningless.

"It's all over but the draft choices now, right?" John Havlicek murmured. "We'll try to win the games we have left, of course, but . . ." It will all have the taste of flat beer. For the first time since 1971, there will be no playoffs for a team that practically invented them.

You can point at the games that got away—the Andrew Carnegie Memorial at New Orleans on March 1, the last-second loss to Chicago here a week ago Friday, the huge second-quarter lead blown at Piscataway in October, the 59-second debacle at Denver last Wednesday . . .

"When they're that easy to point out," Dave Cowens would muse, his face solemn, "you know you really screwed up."

And it isn't over yet. Unless the Celtics can win three of their final five games this week, they will have lost more games than any Boston club in the thirty-one-year history of the franchise.

Don Chaney had played on the worst one, the 34–48 club of 1969–1970, the transition year between Bill Russell and Cowens, when Henry Finkel had been the center and Boston had finished twenty-six games behind New York.

"We didn't really have the veterans," Chaney tells me, softly. "But we hustled. We tried that year, we really tried hard. This year . . ."

The fantasy was that he would make it Friar Heaven for one night, that he would let 11,000 people bring back 1974 and revel in it . . . when it was Ernie and Kevin and Marvin and PC in the Final Four, and every night was a party.

Hell, the season was over. Why couldn't Tom Sanders turn showman, starting Stacom and DiGregorio in the backcourt and letting them improvise? Might as well entertain the customers if you weren't going to beat anybody.

Sanders hadn't even bothered saying no. He'd merely come back with The Look. *Be* serious, it said. So Havlicek and Bing go out for the tap tonight against Washington with Stacom as third guard— the usual arrangement—and except for six minutes at the beginning of the second quarter, DiGregorio rides the bench.

He stands at the edge of the huddle whenever Boston calls time, nodding to acquaintances in the stands, looking for the family. And finally, with the third quarter winding down and the Celtics trailing by 16 points, Sanders motions for him. Go in there with Stacom.

It takes him precisely 30 seconds to score, driving down to the left side of the lane and tossing up a runner. Two minutes later, he throws in another from the right side and the Civic Center . . . *Er-NIE, Er-NIE* . . . is beginning to shimmy. They come out for the last 12 minutes and DiGregorio nods to Stacom. Go for it.

Ernie comes down now, legs pumping hard, the head up, ball high, eyes darting. He sees Stacom coming across the lane, open for a fraction of a second, and fires him the ball for a reverse lay-in. A minute later, he sees Stacom again on the baseline, 17 feet from the basket, and ships another pass across.

Thirty-five seconds later, Stacom returns the favor, same pass, same place, and the noise is fantastic. "That's the way it's supposed to be," DiGregorio tells himself. "And it's been a long time, too."

With eight minutes left, the Washington lead is down to ten, and DiGregorio is launching another one from the baseline, the right hand cocked over the shoulder. The shot drops cleanly, Larry Wright fouls him, and Ernie goes to the line to make it seven. As he waits for the ball, he makes the sign of the cross.

It *does* seem to come from another realm. Looking at the running score sheet later, it appears that nobody else was on the court.

7:26 DiGregorio 19 lt. base
6:32 DiGregorio rt. top key
5:47 DiGregorio leaner in key

Eleven points for him now, the deficit still seven, but the tide turned, the crowd impassioned, sweeping him along. Then, just as the clock passes five minutes, Stacom snags his foot on Elvin Hayes's ankle and falls heavily, grimacing, the ankle sprained.

For a moment, as they help Stacom off ("Guess *your* season's over, anyway," Washington tells him), there is no sound in the building. The spell is broken, the connection suspended. But when the teams are whistled back on, DiGregorio kisses the crucifix around his neck, and goes out alongside Bing. And simply takes the game into his own hands.

A bomb from the right side drops. Then Hayes travels, and DiGregorio comes back, all alone, driving the baseline for a lay-in. The Bullets miss at the other end, and here is Ernie, all 72 inches of him, going up with Cowens and grabbing the rebound away. Cowens, who's rarely had to worry about any of his teammates challenging him for a loose ball, is astonished.

"I look over," he tells me later, "and I say, what the hell are *you* doing here, skying for rebounds. Super fly."

As the crowd howls, DiGregorio comes back up the floor, running alongside the press table, his eyes on the hoop. The expression on his face is surreal, a cross between mania and desperation. He looks as though he is going to burst into tears.

He drives in alone, with Wright scrambling to cover him, and lays the ball in, drawing a foul. When it drops, the score is Washington 105, Boston 101, and more than three minutes remain.

"That is how it used to be," says Bill Parillo, who'd covered

DiGregorio in college for the Providence *Journal*. *"That* is the way it was. Every night."

But DiGregorio is exhausted now, his legs wobbly, the breath coming in gasps. He has been on the floor for 14 minutes without a rest, and Sanders is worried that he will start coming apart, forcing passes, making mistakes, and that the game will get away.

So DiGregorio comes to the sidelines, as the ovation washes over him, the last one, in all likelihood, he will ever hear in his hometown. He looks down at the floor, walking slowly, and a smile spreads across his face.

The game *does* get away, Washington winning by nine, but nobody really notices. There was a reaffirmation here tonight. The kid can *still* play. Twenty-four points, seven rebounds, four assists.

"It felt good to play in front of my family," he says later, as the well-wishers crowd around. "At least they went home with a smile. That's all that matters to me."

Going out, he spots Dave Gavitt, his old coach, who'd recognized his gift and built around it, and sworn he could play in the NBA.

"Coach," DiGregorio says, shaking hands, "I told you, you wasn't wrong."

Friday the 7th
BOSTON, MASS.

Just for the sake of formality—and for archivists who like to squirrel such things away—it was Detroit 111, Boston 109, tonight, a meaningless result for two teams headed nowhere. Except that it was loss No. 49, which officially brands this as the worst season in the history of the franchise. Even if the Captain scored 80 points and ascends into heaven Sunday afternoon, that won't change.

The Pistons, whose own playoff hopes went a-glimmering a while back, too, found themselves in command for most of the evening, and had a four-point lead with four seconds left, when the Celtics called time to blueprint a miracle.

"They're going to Havlicek," coach Bob Kauffman said, excitedly, in the Detroit huddle. "Same play as last time." Several Pistons yawned.

"Hey," Kauffman said, "I've seen a lot of crazy things happen in this building."

"Man," one player said, finally, before turning his back. "Not even John Havlicek can score four points in four seconds."

Sunday the 9th
BOSTON, MASS.

He'd rented the tuxedo—jacket, shirt, studs, cummerbund, black tie, all of it—because he thought that was how a man should go out after sixteen years.

"A special day," John Havlicek is saying, just before noon, "and you should wear special clothes on special occasions."

You should arrive at the office early on your final day, he figured, garbed in formal wear, and drape each article on a separate hanger. You should put on the uniform slowly, making sure the shoelaces are straight. You should have your speech written and rehearsed and shake hands with everybody from the owner to the cop at the door.

And then you should take a deep breath and try to keep it all from crashing in on you. There was only so much of it you could control. He knew about the gifts. They'd been holding halftime fetes in every road city ever since Havlicek had made the announcement in January. There had been a solid gold money clip in Oakland, an outboard motor in Seattle, a resort vacation from Denver. And in Philadelphia, they'd unloaded a mountain of local goodies on him, everything from scrapple to a Liberty Bell, seventeen items in all. We'd carried them back to Boston on the midnight plane, shoving cakes and hockey sticks under seats. Tom Sanders had wound up with the ten-pound kosher salami, trailing it behind him as we walked down the corridor.

Today, they've piled the gifts at center court, something from every conceivable merchant from the North End to Freeport,

Maine, and rented a truck for Havlicek to take them home in.

And out in the lobby, a security guard stood watch over a $50,000 mobile home, custom-ordered by the club. Havlicek had been dreaming about it ever since I'd known him. "Remember when we went to that recreational vehicle show in Seattle?" he'd say. "Well . . ."

If you'd been to any of the other "days" they'd had for retiring Celtics, you had to smile at that. Usually, a man was given a Cadillac, but he'd have had to turn in his own car in the bargain. For a camper, fully accessorized, they'd joked, Havlicek would have to sign over his soul.

There *was* a bit of a "King for a Day" aura to it, but Havlicek had come bearing gifts, too. Last night, he'd had specially designed belt buckles, with a Celtics logo and his number, for everybody connected with the club, from secretaries to stat crew members.

And for people he'd traveled with and shared airport breakfasts and bus rides with, there was an engraved gold pocket watch. TIME FOR A FRIEND, it said inside. JOHN.

He'd thought of everything—everything but the enormity of the building and the crowd. When he'd gone out for his two-layup fetish (he'd always taken two, just after the teams had been whistled off, it was a Celtic tradition he'd inherited), they'd given Havlicek an ovation, and it surprised him. "Didn't know they were waiting for it," he thought.

And when he'd been introduced with the club, he'd gone out to midcourt for two deep bows, the noise tumbling down on him. The Garden had been sold out for weeks, and there were green-and-white banners hanging everywhere. "The Buckeye Stops Here," one said.

Then, lips trembling, tears brimming, Havlicek had run to the sidelines, waving his hand in a circle above his head.

"Let's *go* already," he yelled to his teammates, as the roar rose, crested, and rose again. But the noise continued—for eight full minutes—laced with a rhythmic *HON-do, HON-do, HON-do.* Nothing to do but wait it out, as the Celtics applauded, too. Dave Cowens, who'd given Havlicek a Cuisinart set from the players, sat alone on the bench, staring straight ahead, whistling, the fingers in his mouth.

And then Havlicek took his team onto the floor for the last time. We'd talked about how he wanted to play the final game against Buffalo. All 48 minutes, I'd said. And the last basket has to be a dunk, just like the first one in 1962. Havlicek had grinned. There was a certain symmetry to it.

"I'll do everything just a little bit slower," he'd thought, "so I'll remember it." Tom Sanders started Havlicek in the backcourt with Dave Bing, where he quickly set up four baskets, but nothing of his own was falling. A jumper from the top of the key missed. A fallaway bounced off the rim. Another was partially blocked.

"I'm shooting a bunch of bricks today," he said, during one timeout.

"Nervous?" I wondered.

"No," he shook his head. "I've got the strength. That's not the problem."

Finally, with 44 seconds left in the quarter, Kermit Washington got a pass to him, and Havlicek slithered through the lane for a basket that brought a roar.

There were two more in the second quarter, but Havlicek was taking a beating now. His hand had gone numb for a moment after one defensive whack underneath. Larry McNeill's elbow had cut his lip. And they'd called three fouls on him before halftime. Sanders had had to sit him out for three minutes.

Havlicek gave his halftime speech through swollen lips, trying to keep from breaking down. "A lot of deep breaths," he said. "It was the only way." He thanked Red Auerbach for drafting him, his family—Beth, Chris, Jill, and his mother—for supporting him, and the fans for backing him.

"You provided me with many thrills," he told them. "I'm going to remember most you people in the stands, and the flags hanging above me. What more can I say? Thank you, Boston, I love you."

He'd gone to the sidelines then, as the teams came out for the second half. "O.K.," John Havlicek told the Celtics. "Let's blow it out."

By now, the game was hardly an issue. Boston had taken a 12-point lead into the dressing room, and they expanded on it at will. The only question now was the dunk. Could they sneak him away for one?

"I'll look for him," Ernie DiGregorio had vowed, back in the first quarter. "Are you shittin' me? Every time up I'll look for him. You watch."

Sanders had sent him in with two minutes to play, and moved Havlicek to the frontcourt. "I'd like to be able to free-lance," Havlicek had told him.

So DiGregorio looked for him . . . and the last two minutes were magic, with 15,000 people screaming and stomping, and Havlicek running like a madman.

"Let me play the last two," he'd told Sanders. " 'Cause I want to be on the floor at the end."

Only 1:09 remained when DiGregorio finally found a swatch of daylight and got the ball to Havlicek for a driving lay-in. There hadn't been room for a dunk—Poodles Willoughby, a journeyman of no particular distinction, didn't want anybody making history on *him*.

Eleven seconds later, DiGregorio found him again . . . and again, Havlicek had to settle for a reverse lay-in. With 41 seconds to go, there was another chance, but Havlicek's shot bounced off the rim and he'd had to pop in the rebound from the lane. They fouled him on his last real chance 12 seconds later, and Havlicek made one free throw, his 26,395th career point in his 1,270th game.

"I kept easin' away for the dunk," he would say, "but I just couldn't get it done. I would have tried it, though. You better believe it, after all the other stuff I was missing (he was eleven for thirty-three on the afternoon). I figured, throw it all up. Bring out everything I've ever known. Back home, I've got a basket in my backyard. It's about seven feet high, for my son. Maybe I can go home and dunk one on that."

Finally, with 15 seconds left, and Buffalo's Scott Lloyd at the free-throw line, Sanders motioned for Bing.

"John, I want to take you out," Sanders had said, earlier, but Havlicek had shaken his head. "I started my career running and I want to end it running."

But now, Sanders figured, the time was too opportune. Bing, who'd dressed next to Havlicek all year, ran in and embraced him. So did Don Chaney, who'd spent nearly eight years on Boston teams with Havlicek and shared two championships with him.

Then Havlicek walked to the bench, raised his hands to the crowd, sat down ... and sobbed, staring up at the clock, a towel around his neck. His face was twisted, the lower lip quivering. It ended 131–114, and they hurried him out, with police all around, to an all-comers mass press conference, where he gave his final interview, bloody gauze stuffed in his mouth.

A telegram was waiting for him. HAVLICEK, it read. HONDO IS WATCHING. CONGRATULATIONS, JOHN WAYNE.

"Maybe I'll give him a call," Havlicek said. "He's been a big part of my life. I've never met the man, but I've carried his name around for a good part of my life."

Long after the movie had been forgotten, they were going to remember the nickname. Havlicek said he'd been watching a television collage of his best moments earlier in the year, his family gathered around. "Chris and my wife got teary-eyed," he would say, "and then Chris went upstairs. Later, Jill went up to see him, and came down. He's still up there crying, she said. So I went up, and he had all the pictures that had been taken of us together, and some of me as a child, and he'd spread them on the floor. And he was just staring at them, sobbing."

They were going to have a party for him at a Boston disco afterwards—just eight hundred of his closest friends. But Havlicek wanted to stall a bit, savoring it. Long after the crowd had cleared out of the dressing room, he was still in his uniform, talking to stragglers, reminiscing. He remembered the first game he'd seen in Boston, the playoff with Philadelphia, when Wilt Chamberlain had gone after Sam Jones, and Jones, terrified, had picked up a photographer's stool in defense. He'd eaten his first Boston meal in the Hayes-Bickford cafeteria across the street. And on his first day as a Celtic, Frank Ramsey had come over to welcome him. He'd remembered that, Havlicek said, and he'd always tried to go up to rookies himself in later years.

Finally, Walter Randall, the clubhouse man, had come over. It was 5:30, nearly two hours after the buzzer. "Hey, John, turn out the lights when you go, will you," he'd muttered. Havlicek had nodded. And after he'd showered, folded the uniform, and cleaned up around his stall, stuffing everything into a cardboard box, along with the final stats—41 minutes played, 29 points, 9 assists, the basic Havlicek line—he'd slowly dressed himself in the tuxedo, putting the studs in one by one.

Then he made sure the windows were closed and the lights turned off and headed for the door. Suddenly, he stopped, and fished through his jackets for his championship ring. "Knew I had one in here somewhere," he murmured.

And then, with the box bulky under an arm, John Havlicek locked the door on an era on Causeway Street.

EPILOGUE

Chicken Man

The Reconstruction, Irv Levin vowed, would begin immediately; he had already told Red Auerbach "to spare no effort or expense." The phrase conjured up images of Carnegie or Rockefeller waving a vague hand in the direction of midtown Manhattan, and I couldn't help smirking when I scribbled it into a notebook.

Thumb through the club's press guide and you saw Levin described as "a total businessman . . . a man of creative talents and staggering achievements . . . a major figure in the worlds of sports and motion pictures."

The composite was a latter-day Irving Thalberg and Jacob Ruppert, a dynamic figure equally at home on Rodeo Drive or the Garden, concocting a blockbuster movie package on one phone and sealing a deal with the Lakers on the other.

You rarely saw Levin on Causeway Street, and that helped perpetuate the aura. He thrived on distance, on the illusion that there were weighty matters that required his attention in Israel and New York and Los Angeles. Later, when there were messy issues to be dealt with and accounted for—the firing of Tommy Heinsohn, the presence of Sidney Wicks and Curtis Rowe, the contract problems with Jo Jo White—it made it easier for Levin to deflect accusing fingers elsewhere.

Auerbach fired Heinsohn, Levin told me. It was Auerbach and Heinsohn who really wanted Wicks and Rowe. It wasn't my idea to get involved in the White negotiations. Red asked me.

Nobody believed him in Boston, and Levin was stunned when he finally realized that. He had stepped to the microphone at midcourt to present the camper to John Havlicek at the Garden and the booing had been shocking and ugly.

I never knew, Levin would tell me, weeks later. Maybe because he didn't want to, I guessed. There were times when he reminded me of a Back Bay slumlord, tanning himself in Palm Beach while his tenements sagged with rats and neglect. He would drop by once a year and profess dismay . . . migawd, why didn't you tell me about the roof and the windows and the boiler? . . . and quickly check on that midnight flight out of Logan.

You heard talk about what a benevolent owner Levin was, how he'd spend the money and let Auerbach run the show, another Walter Brown, folks, just when we thought the good old days were gone forever.

But you also heard the whispers about the debt service, about how deep those pockets really were, about how the Celtics better never miss the playoffs because they needed the cash flow as much as ever. The season had cost Levin a quarter of a million, the speculation went. It was easy to play Carnegie when you were drinking champagne and wearing a ring and counting 15,000 heads in the Garden for two months of playoff games.

I want to see how you'll react if we ever start losing money, fans, and games, Auerbach had told him once. *That's* the test of great ownership.

All Levin's talk about damning the expense was fiscal bravado, you thought. This is merely 1970 all over again—an aging club, a retiring legend, a tight budget—and the only solution is the classic one. A good drafting position and Auerbach's horsetrading instincts.

And even in Boston, you heard the skepticism about Auerbach. The game is beyond him now, the talk-show callers would say. Look at the draft choices, the Steve Downings, Glenn McDonalds, Tom Boswells, Norm Cooks, all of them pissed away. Look at Westphal, the cornerstone at Phoenix now. Look at Silas, playing for the NBA title in Seattle.

Talking to Auerbach as the season progressed, I had frequently come away troubled. "Boy, when things go wrong, they really go wrong," Auerbach would moan, running down the litany—the injuries, the collapse of the Civic Center roof at Hartford in midwinter that had screwed up the schedule, all that. Does he really believe that's the reason, I wondered?

He didn't. Weeks after Havlicek had locked the door, when Washington and Seattle were playing for the championship, I'd met him for dinner at Duke Zeibert's, and we'd gone up to his condominium out on Massachusetts Avenue for a nightcap. And he'd laid it all out for me—every disturbing little incident, every personality conflict, every flaw that had turned the season sour from the start.

He had known about everything—what the players were saying about Heinsohn, who was saying what before the game in Washington, who was eating popcorn before the debacle at Seattle, who cared and who didn't.

And Auerbach had kept it to himself, because he had always operated that way. You never solved anything in the newspapers. When the season was over, you did what you had to, waiving or trading or chewing ass.

The refurbishing began on June 9 with the college draft. The 32–50 nightmare had been good for one thing—the sixth choice overall—and Auerbach used it to get the shooting guard they needed, taking Freeman Williams, the national scoring champion from Portland State.

He had the reputation as a mad bomber in the Lloyd Free mold, and some true believers winced, but Auerbach said, no, no, we checked him out. He'll pass the ball and he can play defense. We aren't crazy.

The Scott trade had also produced the Lakers' second best pick in the first round, which turned out to be eighth. And Auerbach, ever the Byzantine gambler, spent it on the rights to Larry Bird, a magnificent white power forward out of Indiana State, by all accounts the best player in the draft.

Bird was a junior-eligible (he had transferred from Indiana, and his class had already graduated), and had the option of either signing or finishing out his senior year. Everybody wanted him, but nobody wanted to risk a high choice on an uncertainty. Bird was going to stay in school, he said, and most clubs wanted immediate help.

If you drafted Bird, you owned his rights for a year. He might change his mind in the interim. And even if he decided he'd rather play in Phoenix or Portland, you could always recoup your investment by dealing his rights to the club he'd chosen. So how much of a gamble was it?

The backup center for Cowens could be acquired somewhere else (that had been the other obvious need) and even as the draft was going on, the Celtics were announcing that they'd come to terms with Kevin Kunnert, the seven-foot reserve from Houston who'd played out his option.

Levin seemed pleased when I saw him a week later at the league meetings in San Diego. He thought the draft had gone well, was looking forward to a stable autumn. Everybody would be at training camp, the regular season would start at home for once, and the attitude would be better all around. "I'm highly confident we'll make the playoffs," he said, after we'd talked for half an hour on the final day of the meetings.

I didn't hear the rumors until the weekend, when Milt Northrup, a Buffalo writer, called me on Cape Cod. "I realize this sounds crazy," he would say, "but we've heard that Levin and John Y. Brown [the Braves' owner] are going to swap franchises. John Y. would own the Celtics, and Levin would move the Braves to San Diego. And there'd be a major trade, too. Marvin Barnes, Tiny Archibald, and Billy Knight would go to Boston for Kermit Washington, Freeman Williams, Kevin Kunnert and Sidney Wicks. It was in the works all last week."

Damn, I thought. Maybe that's what Auerbach was trying to tip me to early in the week. We'd been talking about his future—the contract he had with Levin ran out on August 1, and there had been feelers from CBS and talk of an offer from the Knicks.

"Hey," Auerbach had muttered when we were done, "here's something that might make a good story for you. Irv and John Y. Brown just went out for a walk together."

I had suspected they were hashing out a deal for Wicks—we had heard one had been discussed during the season. But it might have been merely an informal tête-à-tête. Brown wanted to move the franchise—Dallas, Florida, Louisville, Minneapolis, San Diego had all been mentioned. Levin was the chairman of the Board of Governors. It was only logical they'd be conferring.

When the rumors found print, Auerbach had denied them outright. Craziest thing I ever heard. But they were true. All of them. And Auerbach, who had taken the heat for Levin ("They're booing the wrong guy," he would insist), had been the last to know.

The oily bastard, I thought. Spare no effort and expense, and all the while Levin's reaching for the parachute and letting Auerbach be the fall guy. For the first time, I felt sorry for Auerbach. I never dreamed I'd ever have to think that.

The transaction was approved by the Governors with only one dissenting vote (Los Angeles, we guessed, worried about its TV market), and the trade went through. And Auerbach watched a whole year's worth of trading and drafting go down the chute. Before long, he was taking the shuttle to New York and talking to the Knicks.

No, Red, I thought. Not the goddamn Knicks. Not Gulf & Western and the play money and the crazy salaries, not after thirty years of standing for something totally opposite.

It must have hurt him desperately, I thought, having the tradition sold out from under him like a used car by an owner who didn't even have the courtesy (or the guts) to tell him.

Ever since Walter Brown had died, it had been Auerbach who had held the thing together, as the franchise passed through seven owners during the next ten years, from brewing companies to real estate tycoons to fast-buck hustlers who thought they could rub up against the mystique and come away sanctified.

It had been Auerbach who shelled out $9,000 so his Celtics could board a plane after one owner, Trans-National Communications, had taken the gate receipts and ignored the bills. It had been Auerbach who had to swallow his pride and draft Clarence Glover instead of Curtis Rowe in 1971, because the club had no money to sign Rowe. It had been Auerbach who'd had to sustain everything with his growl and his reputation and his shrewdness, who'd had to sit at the press conferences, year after year, and say that the new owner was totally committed to maintaining, etc. etc.

Now, there would be another press conference for John Y. Brown, who had folded his ABA franchise in Louisville for money, who had watched a solid franchise in Buffalo decay from his insane contracts and ruinous trades—and then moved out because there had been no support.

Anywhere Brown had ever been, there was no professional basketball when he left. He had bought out Colonel Sanders and sold his Kentucky Fried Chicken to Heublein, and who gave a damn if Sanders couldn't recognize his product anymore, all the special herbs and spices and the secret recipe sacrificed for profits?

Don't you understand, one of Brown's employees had told me. The man is a genius. He's just bought the Boston Celtics for nothing. I know, I replied. That's what frightens me. What if he wants to buy the Lakers tomorrow?

It frightened Auerbach, too. He had heard the same whispers as everybody else, that Brown had a reputation for dreaming up a deal a thousand miles away and making it without consulting his general manager.

Hell, if they wouldn't tell him that his franchise was being traded, why would they tell Auerbach that they were trading one of his starters?

So Auerbach went to Manhattan in early July, and the Knicks made the offer. We're reorganizing, and you'll be the president. Four-year contract, at the highest salary ever offered to an NBA executive. Auerbach returned to Boston, his mind made up. He was leaving.

I felt hollow inside when I heard that. The team I knew had vanished. Havlicek, Bing, and DiGregorio had retired. White was saying he'd demand a trade if Auerbach left. Washington and Wicks were headed West, to a city that had let two professional teams starve. Kevin Stacom and Tom Boswell were playing out their options, Stacom signing with Indiana, Boswell with Denver. Charlie Scott, Fred Saunders, Steve Kuberski and Jim Ard had been gone long before the season ended.

There would be strangers in the dressing room in the fall, a new face in virtually every cubicle. And there would be strangers in the front office if Auerbach left. Wouldn't Brown bring in his own people, from publicity man to vice presidents to secretaries? I would be an alien in a building I had known since I was seven.

The whole city felt that way. Auerbach would walk along a

downtown street, the shoulders hunched, the cigar preceding him, and a truck window would roll down. "Ayy, Red," a raspy voice would holler. "Stay." Elderly women would come up to him in Chinese restaurants. The shuttle pilot would stick his head out as Auerbach was boarding. Don't go, they told him.

Then his phone rang one day and it was Havlicek. If you're not here, the Captain said, they're not retiring my number.

"It was all so goddamn flattering," Auerbach would tell me. "And then my wife, Dot, she came up with a great quote. You started here, she told me. Why do you want an intermediate stop before you quit?"

So Auerbach went back to Manhattan for a final talk, as the New York writers maintained a vigil outside the team offices. I was waiting for him when he unlocked the door down at Causeway Street the next morning.

"Staying?" I asked him. He smiled sweetly. "Press conference this afternoon," he said. No further comment needed. He was in the office, wasn't he?

He had had a talk with Brown, Auerbach would tell me, and they had agreed that it would be a partnership. Auerbach didn't want to be jolted awake at 7:00 A.M. by a radio report that Dave Cowens had just been shipped to Kansas City for a mess of pottage. "I was afraid maybe I'd pick up the paper one day and find out I was traded," Auerbach said.

So they announced the multi-year contract, as Auerbach grinned and waved the cigar and let the anecdotes flow for the cameras and notepads. The people had gotten to him, he would say. It was "unbelievable in the history of sports" that there would be that much fuss over a general manager changing jobs. There had been stories in the *International Herald-Tribune,* in the Hong Kong papers, in London: AUERBACH LEAVING CELTICS?

At the *Globe,* we had had a whole special issue planned for his departure. "The Auerbach Legacy." We were going to run a cartoon in the sports section on Sunday, showing Auerbach trudging off to Manhattan with The Flags over his shoulder, the cigar smoke rising on all sides. WALKING TALL, the caption would read, and the stark irony was going to make you reach for the whisky jigger with one hand and dial Levin's Palm Springs number with the other.

And I was going to do a column, going very heavily with the Irish wake symbolism. "Arnold, We Hardly Knew Ye" and all that.

Instead, I stopped by his office to kibitz. Sit down, he muttered. You make me nervous standing up. "It was the tradition, wasn't it?" I said. "That and the idea of the Knicks."

He nodded, the lips pursed. "I can't flatter myself and say it was going to crumble when I left," he said, "but I'd be lying if I said it didn't enter my mind. And New York—working down there and living down there. That was what I was trying to envision. And I had a lot of misgivings. I thought about what it would be like to come back up to play the Celtics, to watch the ball game and look up at the flags. And I didn't know what my reaction would be."

Index